D1686018

Minority Languages in Europe

Minority Languages in Europe

Frameworks, Status, Prospects

Edited by

Gabrielle Hogan-Brun and Stefan Wolff

First published 2003 by
PALGRAVE MACMILLAN
Houndmills, Basingstoke, Hampshire RG21 6XS and
175 Fifth Avenue, New York, N.Y. 10010
Companies and representatives throughout the world

PALGRAVE MACMILLAN is the global academic imprint of the Palgrave
Macmillan division of St. Martin's Press, LLC and of Palgrave Macmillan Ltd.
Macmillan® is a registered trademark in the United States, United
Kingdom and other countries. Palgrave is a registered trademark in the
European Union and other countries.

ISBN 1–4039–0396–4 hardback

This book is printed on paper suitable for recycling and made from fully
managed and sustained forest sources.

A catalogue record for this book is available from the British Library.

Library of Congress Cataloging-in-Publication Data
    Minority languages in Europe: frameworks, status, prospects/edited
by Gabrielle Hogan-Brun and Stefan Wolff.
        p. cm.
    Includes bibliographical references and index.
    ISBN 1–4039–0396–4 (cloth)
        1. Linguistic minorities – Europe. 2. Language policy – Europe.
    I. Hogan-Brun, Gabrielle, 1955– II. Wolff, Stefan, 1969–

P119.315.M5624 2003
408'.6'93094—dc21   2003051976

10 9 8 7 6 5 4 3 2 1
12 11 10 09 08 07 06 05 04 03

Printed and bound in Great Britain by
Antony Rowe Ltd, Chippenham and Eastbourne

Contents

v

List of Tables and Figures

Preface

All over Europe, political, social, economic and cultural changes affecting the nature and position of new and old language minorities are occurring at an accelerating pace. In the face of the dynamics created by the parallel and interrelated processes of European integration and globalisation, the expression of cultural identity and the insistence on linguistic distinctiveness challenge the trend towards global harmonisation and have the potential to increase the momentum of already existing trends leading to greater fragmentation. Hence the recognition and safeguarding of cultural and linguistic diversity have become crucial issues of social significance with linguistic, psychological, cultural, political, legal and economic implications.

This collection explores the complex dynamics surrounding minority languages from an interdisciplinary perspective. It examines the contribution to and effectiveness of existing legal frameworks with regard to policy formulation and implementation in various minority language settings. Case studies dealing with social, economic, political and cultural aspects of a selected range of minority language communities focus on disputed languages (Ulster-Scots, Serbian/Croatian), non-territorial languages (Romani, [British] sign language), minority languages in the contested terrains of post-communist nation- and state-building (Russian in the Baltic, German in Central and Eastern Europe) and native regional languages (Galician).

Extending the dimensions of minority related issues, a wider context of social, political and educational theories is also provided that discusses the implications for language policy and practice, including the key aspect of maintaining public support for such policies. An analysis of the impact of EU policy and discourse on individual movements within states, as well as on the overall orientation towards linguistic heterogeneity and cultural diversity in both East and West rounds off the remit of this collection.

In this way, a comprehensive picture emerges of the status of European minority languages against the background of existing political and legal frameworks to gauge future prospects of cultural and linguistic diversity within a unifying Europe.

GABRIELLE HOGAN-BRUN AND STEFAN WOLFF
Bristol and Bath
February 2003

Acknowledgements

We would like to thank the European Science Foundation for their funding of an Exploratory Research Workshop on Minority Languages in Europe, held at the University of Bath in June 2000, which provided the impetus to this collection. Our thanks also go to Peter Foulkes for reading and commenting on parts of the manuscript, and to Antony Alcock for his comprehensive and constructive feedback on the final version of our manuscript. We would also like to acknowledge the support and encouragement we received from our editor at Palgrave, Jill Lake.

Notes on Contributors

Karl Cordell is Principal Lecturer in Politics at the University of Plymouth. His primary research interests centre on the German minority in Poland in particular, and the politics of ethnicity in general. His main publications include *Ethnicity and Democratisation in the New Europe* (1998), *The Politics of Ethnicity in Central Europe* (2000) and *Poland and The European Union* (2000).

Dieter W. Halwachs is Assistant Professor at the Institute for Linguistics at the University of Graz, where his research focuses mainly on Roma communities in Europe. His numerous publications include several reports on the codification of Romani, various collections of Roma tales and a number of edited volumes on different aspects of Romani and Roma.

Kristin Henrard is Senior Lecturer at the University of Groningen where she teaches human rights, refugee law and constitutional law. Her main publications pertain to the areas of human rights and minority protection. She is managing editor of the Netherlands International Law Review, member of the international advisory board of the Global Review of Ethnopolitics and country specialist on South Africa for Amnesty International – Dutch Section.

Gabrielle Hogan-Brun is Research Fellow in Language Studies at the University of Bristol. She works in the area of language diversity and possible changes under European harmonisation, with a current research focus on the changing language dynamics in the Baltic Republics. Her publications include edited books on *National Varieties of German Outside Germany. A European Perspective* (2000) and *Language Debates in Latvia* (2004).

Máiréad Nic Craith is Professor at the Academy for Irish Cultural Heritages, University of Ulster. An anthropologist, she has authored and edited several books including *Plural Identities, Singular Narratives* (2002) and *Culture and Identity Politics in Northern Ireland* (2003). Her research interests include European integration and regional cultures and languages.

Stephen May is Foundation Professor and Chair of Language and Literacy Education in the School of Education and Research Professor in the Wilf Malcolm Institute of Educational Research. He has written widely on language and education, with a particular focus on addressing and accommodating cultural and linguistic diversity. His most recent publications include *Ethnonational Identities* (2002), *Language and Minority Rights* (2001), *Critical Multiculturalism: Rethinking Multicultural and Antiracist Education* (1999) and *Indigenous Community-based Education* (1999).

Carmen Millán-Varela is a Lecturer in Applied Linguistics at the Centre for English Language Studies, University of Birmingham. Her main research interests and areas of publication include the role of translation in processes of identity construction, the discourse on translation, translation policy and planning and translation in language teaching.

Camille O'Reilly is a Lecturer in Social Anthropology at Richmond, the American International University in London. She is the author of *The Irish Language in Northern Ireland: The Politics and Culture of Identity* (1999) and editor of the two-volume collection *Language, Ethnicity and the State* (2001), as well as of many articles on nationalism, the Irish language and Northern Ireland.

John Packer served as Senior Legal Advisor to the OSCE High Commissioner on National Minorities (HCNM) from September 1995 to February 2000, and as Director of the Office of the HCNM from March 2000 to November 2003. Mr. Packer is currently a Fellow at the Carr Center on Human Rights Policy at the Kennedy School of Government, Harvard University, and a Visiting Assistant Professor at the Fletcher School of Law and Diplomacy at Tufts University.

Vanessa Pupavac is Lecturer in Politics at the University of Nottingham. She has a background in law and area studies, and has previously worked for the International Criminal Tribunal for Former Yugoslavia and for the OSCE in Bosnia. Recent research has been examining the politics of recognition and international minority rights approaches.

Graham H. Turner is Senior Lecturer in Deaf Studies at the University of Central Lancashire in Preston, England. He has worked with the Deaf community in the United Kingdom since the 1980s as a researcher and lecturer in applied sign linguistics, exploring language planning and policy-making, translation and interpreting, education and employment from a social perspective.

Stefan Wolff is Reader in Politics at the University of Bath. His main research interests are in the area of minority rights and ethnic conflict. His publications include two monographs – *Disputed Territories* (2002) and *The German Question since 1919* (2003) as well as several edited and co-edited volumes, including *Managing and Settling Ethnic Conflicts* (2003), *Peace at Last: The Impact of the Good Friday Agreement on Northern Ireland* (2002) and *German Minorities in Europe* (2000).

Part I
Introduction

1
Minority Languages in Europe: An Introduction to the Current Debate

Gabrielle Hogan-Brun and Stefan Wolff

I

The use of the language of choice is an important human right as it is through language – a primary marker of identity – that we are able to identify ourselves, others, and to be identified by others, that we think, communicate and generally relate to the world around us. The violation of this right bears a potential for conflict as is only too evident in many ethnic conflicts in Europe, Africa and Asia, where language rights are often among the demands behind which ethnic groups rally when they challenge states for a recognition of their distinct identities. Acknowledging this potential for conflict has generated a long history of specific rights afforded to linguistically defined minority communities in Europe. The Peace Treaty of Westphalia, the Final Act of the Congress of Vienna and the League of Nations Minority Treaties during the inter-war period in the first half of the twentieth century all included provisions for specific group-based rights in key areas related to language use, such as cultural institutions, education and communication with public services. In the post-1945 period, the new international system took a turn away from group rights and focussed on individual human rights. The Charter of the United Nations, the Universal Declaration on Human Rights, the International Covenant on Civil and Political Rights (ICCPR) and the European Charter of Human Rights (see references) all refer to language as an important human right, but in their focus on the individual, they provide less protection for languages that are only used by small groups within larger states. In Europe, these shortcomings have been recognized, and the period since the end of the Cold War has seen a reorientation towards group rights, not to replace, but to complement individual human rights: the Copenhagen Document of the Conference on Security and Cooperation in Europe, the Framework Convention for the Protection of National Minorities and the European Charter for Regional or Minority Languages (ECRML) (see references) are all evidence of that trend. Although it explicitly excludes the languages of immigrant communities, the latter is particularly important in that it is the first legally binding document for the protection of minority languages and clearly states the areas in which states have an obligation to take action on behalf of speakers of minority languages. These include education, communication with authorities, public services, media, culture, economic and social life and transfrontier exchanges. What is significant about these and other similar documents, regardless of whether they are of a legally binding nature, is that they set standards and define practice, and that they give expression to a norm according to which it is no longer acceptable to suppress minority languages actively or simply by neglect. Yet, the existence of such norms and standards does not automatically mean that they are immediately embraced by every national government and incorporated into national law and policy. On the contrary, politicians frequently proclaim their support for the protection and support of minorities in general, but may not recognize the need or applicability of a particular issue to their own country. For example, France, upon signing the ECRML deposited a lengthy declaration with the Council of Europe (COE), stating, amongst other things, that '[i]n so far as the aim of the Charter is not to recognize or protect minorities but to promote the European language heritage, and as the use of the term "groups" of speakers does not grant collective rights to speakers of regional or minority languages, the French Government interprets this instrument in a manner compatible with the Preamble to the Constitution, which ensures the equality of all citizens before the law and recognizes only the French people, composed of all citizens, without distinction as to origin, race or religion.' In other words, France does not recognize the existence of minority languages in its territory. Likewise, Croatia declared that 'the provisions of Article 7, paragraph 5, of the Charter shall not apply', that is the country does not extend the provisions made for regional languages to non-territorial languages, which primarily affects Romani.[1] With regard to the *Framework Convention on the Protection of National Minorities*, it was the inability (and unwillingness) of the contracting parties to reach a consensus on the definition of 'national minority' that subsequently gave signatory states a wide margin for interpretation, that is to deliberately exclude certain groups from the relevant provisions. Estonia, for example, noted in its signature document in 1997 that it defined a national minority as 'those citizens of Estonia who reside on the territory of Estonia; maintain longstanding, firm and lasting ties with Estonia ...', thereby circumventing the tricky issue of its large non-citizen Russian-speaking population.[2]

Interpretations and adaptations to specific national circumstances to one side, another and equally important question that also concerns states that incorporate international norms and standards in full into their national legislation is whether adequate language rights alone are enough to create conditions in which language minorities can express, preserve and develop their distinct identities. In the light of recent experience, the obvious answer to this question is that what is needed is 'language rights plus', and the 'plus' has to be an important component of any discussion about how to translate policy into practice both in the narrower context of language rights and in the wider one of human and minority rights. There are three main reasons for this. First, language policy alone that aims to modify the linguistic environment at a societal level is unlikely to be sufficient to give ethnic minorities the opportunity to preserve their identity, or in some cases even their language. Second, misunderstanding the role of language policy can easily lead to frustrations and tensions, exacerbating already volatile situations. A low economic and social status of a minority language can make it unattractive to learn and to retain through the generations, especially when it is seen as an impediment for upward social mobility. Furthermore, without opportunities to participate in public life as members of a particular language minority, the right to use one's mother tongue can become meaningless, and the language may degrade to a (dys-)functional variety usable only in limited, private contexts. Research on the economics of language and ethnicity has highlighted the relationship between language and labour, which goes some way to explain current developments in language planning (Grin and Villaincourt 1999).

However, and this relates to possible misjudgements of the role that language rights can play in a situation of more generally tense inter-ethnic relations, history has shown that more liberal language policies have not always been an appropriate mechanism to resolve the far more complex conflict situations involving ethnic minorities – it can be 'too little, too late' for an aggrieved minority to have its demands for language rights accommodated, but too much for a majority that feels threatened by such an assertion of identity on the part of a minority. The escalation of the conflict between ethnic Albanians and ethnic Macedonians in the Republic of Macedonia in 2000 is evidence of this dilemma, as is the situation in the Romanian province of Transylvania. In both cases, language minorities (Albanians in Macedonia, Hungarians in Romania) demanded the creation of a university that taught its courses in their native tongue. Rejection of this demand quickly led to an escalation of tensions; in the case of Macedonia it even led to a short civil war like violent conflict. Both situations were eventually resolved, but not without initial escalations of inter-ethnic tensions.

Language rights and language policy, therefore, are two important aspects within a wider framework of minority protection, and only if this framework is right, will it be possible to put the conditions in place in which language minorities can preserve their language as part of their identity, if they so wish. That is, members of minorities should be able to make a choice, individually and collectively, about how important a component their language is for their identity. Thus, while the protection of a minority language may not be the most important criterion for the preservation of a minority identity, its forced absence will leave a void in this identity with consequences not just for the individual, but also for society as a whole.

II

Over the past few years, the European Union (EU) has become an important forum for language minorities to articulate their demands. Whilst in the past their position had been marginalized in most European states, the EU's commitment to linguistic pluralism has had a beneficial effect for many (autochthonous) minority communities.

Despite such improvements in some European states, the relationship between democracy and language policies aimed at accommodating linguistic diversity in multilingual countries remains complex. The uniqueness of each minority situation requires that language planning be conducted jointly by government institutions, minority representatives and a wide range of other formal and informal stakeholders, including civil society and pressure groups. It is important to bear in mind that decisions affecting the policy domains of status and corpus planning, language standardization and management of language use can be made according to a wide variety of considerations, including ideology, identity, image or human and minority rights concerns, as well as a variety of economic factors. Against the background of such realities, an analysis of language policy always needs to focus on who formulates and implements specific policies and in whose interest they are. In other words, language policy is not made in a vacuum of normative aspirations, but in a concrete context in which different actors with often diverse interest and opportunity structures interact.

III

Taking these complex realities as a given and as its starting point, the aim of this collection is to examine how language policy has developed in different, and often changing, social, legal and political frameworks in Europe. Our aim is to be both descriptive and prescriptive; that is, in the chapters that follow our contributors analyse what is, assess the shortcomings of legislation and policy, and, where appropriate, make recommendations as to how language policy and/or the context in which it happens needs to be improved in order to accommodate and support linguistic and cultural diversity in different countries in which language minorities exist and articulate their demands. Throughout the volume, we use the term 'minority languages' to describe numerically inferior groups of people who speak a language different from that of the majority of a given country (i.e. the state or official language), are in a non-dominant political position, and, to some extent, seek to preserve their distinct linguistic identity (often as part of a wider ethno-cultural identity). We base this term on factual criteria, that is, a minority language in one state (such as Russian in Estonia) may constitute a majority language in another country (i.e. Russia). Minority languages may also include speakers of globally not widely used languages as is the case for instance with speakers of Welsh in Wales.

The first set of contributions focuses on different social, political and legal structures that determine the context in which language policy is formulated and implemented. Camille O'Reilly opens the discussion with an analysis of the significance that language has in the context of identity politics, reminding us to avoid oversimplification when dealing with the links between language and culture and arguing that even when language is 'just symbolic' it can play a key role in understanding the dynamics of conflict. The symbolic importance, which Gaelic still is found to have in Ireland, shows that language can figure as a highly salient feature of cultural differences and that it can become an important symbol of ethnic identity. Similarly, the Deaf community, who does not define itself on audiological criteria as do hearing people, are progressively expressing their (self-constructed) identity. Their drive for empowerment and increasing recognition of the right to self-ownership has led to a re-definition of identity on their part. Romani too has helped shape the identity of the Roma population but has not been an instrumental factor in creating political consensus amongst its speakers. The fragmentation of former Yugoslavia on the other hand exemplifies how ethnic boundaries and cultural differences may lie dormant for decades only to be reactivated as proof that it has become impossible for two groups to coexist. There had been peace between Serbs and Croats since 1945, and Serbo-Croat was considered to be one language. The main cultural differences were that they practise different variants of Christianity and that they use different scripts (the Orthodox Serbs follow the Cyrillic alphabet, while the Catholic Croats use the Latin script). But as the national borders between these new states solidified, their languages and other aspects of culture became more distinctive too on the basis of identity politics and policies of segregation. The symbolic aspect of ethnicity had hence been pivotal in the process of social exclusion/inclusion as attachment and loyalty to new nations were being created.

With reference to the disputed status of Ulster Scots in Northern Ireland, Mairéad Nic Craith then explores the political relevance of the ECRML for the non-official languages of Europe. The main aims of this 1992 Charter are the protection of regional and minority languages and the promotion of a series of concrete measures to help a language survive. These measures involve domains such as education, public services, media, administration, legal authority and the law, cultural facilities and activities, economic and social activities and trans-frontier exchanges. The Charter's impact is restricted in the sense that there is no common judicial framework to control its application in the member states which have ratified all parts of it. In her view the Charter, whose role is confined to autochthonous languages, has the potential to serve as a catalyst for the re-definition of some dialects as languages, as in the case of Ulster Scots, which was subsequently included in the Charter, along with Scots in Scotland. In this context, the revival of minority languages and their revitalization as community languages can be perceived as a political strategy within a new framework, in which nation-states no longer function as the main point of reference for their definition.

John Packer provides insights into the role played by the High Commissioner on National Minorities (HCNM) of the Organisation for Security and Co-operation in Europe (OSCE) in trying to secure conditions conducive to the preservation and free use of minority languages and for the equality of persons belonging to linguistic minorities. Established in 1992 as an instrument of 'conflict prevention at the earliest possible stage', the HCNM has played a crucial role in reducing inter-ethnic tensions in potentially explosive situations in a number of Central and Eastern European countries. The main instrument in that has been the issuing of recommendations, which can be either country-specific or relate to more general matters in facilitating peaceful inter-ethnic relations. In the context of our volume, the Oslo Recommendations on the Linguistic Rights of National Minorities of February 1998 are particularly valuable, as they have contributed to the earlier mentioned process of setting international standards and norms on the protection and promotion of minority languages.[3]

Taking an international law perspective, Kristin Henrard examines language rights as part of a comprehensive and adequate system of minority protection. Her assessment of individual human and minority rights standards reveals that, while both are important for the language rights of population groups in multinational societies, a qualified recognition of the right to self-determination for minorities is essential to improve the integration, but not (forced) assimilation, of language minorities into the social, economic and political structures of the countries in which they live.

As the second set of contributions shows, such a qualified recognition of the right to self-determination can manifest itself in many different ways – from basic non-discrimination provisions in constitutions to complex federal and autonomy regimes. Trends within Western Europe generally point in the latter direction. For example, Belgium, Italy and the United Kingdom all have systems of territorial organization in place which give far-reaching powers to different, and often ethnically or otherwise distinct parts of the population, allowing them to manage a wide range of issues, including areas that are of particular importance to the protection, expression and development of minority languages, such as education and culture. A similar situation exists in Spain, where, apart from Castilian, three other major languages are spoken – Catalan, Basque and Galician. While they share equal status with Castilian as official languages in the relevant autonomous areas, Spain nevertheless presents itself officially as a monolingual state with Castilian as the only official state language. The changed status of Spain's 'other' languages since devolution in 1978 has resulted in standardization and modernization processes to adapt these languages to an expanded set of social functions (Bastardas 1995: 21–2). It is in this context that Carmen Millán-Varela examines the ambiguous role of translation activities which she identifies as crucial tools in the (re-)construction and development of national languages and literatures. Her analysis leads her to call for better planning in translation activities in order to increase social domains in which they can be used, to create and consolidate registers and to contribute to the normalization of a (minority) language.

With few exceptions, such as some of the successor states of the Soviet Union, the territorial accommodation of minority rights is not the dominant trend in how states in Central and Eastern Europe deal with actual or potential ethnic conflict. Since 1989 the region has been rife with nationalist tension, often, but not exclusively linked to language issues. With the establishment of new states, language differences have been used in the creation of *abstand* (distance) and *ausbau* (elaboration) languages in the struggle for an unambiguous national identity. The importance of a language as a core component of national identity and the consequent need of corpus planning is the topic of the contribution by Vanessa Pupavac. She illustrates how language debates in the post-Yugoslav states are not linguistically but politically motivated to legitimize political claims. Following the fragmentation of the Yugoslav federation, the demise of a shared Serbo-Croat language and its multiplication into four separate languages – Bosnian, Croatian, Serbian and Montenegrin – has been intimately bound up with the state of majority–minority relations in this part of Southeastern Europe. In Croatia, for example, a situation has thus been created in which the insistence on minority rights for the country's Serb population (whose members have been singled out as members of an aggressor nation) is inappropriate to address current local needs.

The rationale of language legislation in newly independent states cannot but be closely linked to the goals of nation-state building. In the Baltic Republics, where independence has been achieved for a second time in the twentieth century, multinational polities had evolved as a result of Soviet internal migration policies. Consequently, language policy has been high on national and international agendas, and with the advancement of democratization, the management of language diversity has emerged as a principal issue. In her contribution, Gabrielle Hogan-Brun examines evolving language dynamics in the Baltic Republics since the restoration of independence in 1990. Conflicts over language and citizenship issues persist, particularly in Latvia and Estonia, where Russian-speaking language minorities form large parts of the resident population. Whilst Western monitoring has had an impact on existing policies, it is argued that legal advice needs to continually take account of local re-adjustments to past injustices.

In a comparative analysis of legislative and policy frameworks in Hungary, Poland and Romania, Karl Cordell and Stefan Wolff examine the situation of German language minorities in these three countries. Having lived in their homelands for hundreds of years, the twentieth century marked a sharp turn away from the previous, relatively peaceful coexistence with other ethnic minorities and majorities. German warfare and occupation policy in two world wars coupled with anti-German discrimination on the part of the three states in the interwar and Cold War periods meant that relations between ethnic Germans and other minority and majority communities deteriorated to such an extent that assimilation (Hungary) or emigration (Romania and Poland) seemed the only realistic ways for members of German language minorities to cope with their predicament. Analyzing developments in minority policy in all three countries, the authors conclude that the many positive changes that occurred here after the fall of communism, for the most part, came too late to revitalize and consolidate functioning community structures that would have been necessary to secure the long-term survival of German language minorities, in the sense of German remaining, or being restored, as a fully functional minority language.

Apart from the study of specific, often territorially concentrated *national* language minorities (i.e. communities who have a kin-state, in which their mother tongue is the official language), another and equally important dimension in the analysis of the situation of language minorities in Europe is the protection of non-territorial communities. The Roma, Europe's largest and fastest growing ethnic minority – estimated to have between six and 12 million members – share a common history and language. A scattered community, they are politically, economically and culturally marginalized and ethnically stigmatized. Originated in the Indian subcontinent, most of them are settled in Eastern Europe, where they are still seen as second-class citizens. Along with respect for minority rights in general, their treatment has been a central issue in the process of EU enlargement. In his analysis, Dieter Halwachs points out that, whilst the Romani language generally enjoys a low prestige and the relationship with the contact languages has never been one between equals, its internal and external status have recently improved. As a result, moderate official attention has been attributed to Romani as a European minority language, and it has been granted official minority status in Austria.

In contrast to the widespread interest that ethnic language minorities have received over the past decade in East and West, national and international policies have to date only made a limited impact on the recognition and development of sign languages. An estimated 320,000 Deaf Europeans use sign languages, a visual–spatial, natural set of languages which has developed independently of spoken tongues. Many Deaf people are bilingual, using sign language for conversation whilst being fully literate in a majority language. There is no written form, which may in the past have distracted from a move towards official recognition of its status when compared to other minority languages with a literary tradition. The linguistic rights and needs of the Deaf communities are arguably also a minority rights issue, as these are groups with a claim to a distinct cultural identity. On 19 November 1988, the European Parliament resolved that member states should grant their indigenous sign languages equivalent status to that of the national spoken languages. By 1998, Denmark, Finland, Sweden and Portugal had afforded some degree of official acknowledgement to their indigenous sign languages, and this process is under way in the Netherlands. The British Deaf community has sought recognition under the ECRML, with limited progress so far (Woll 2001). In his chapter, Graham H. Turner pinpoints the Deaf community's primary requirement of enactment policies that give due recognition to the ongoing significance of British Sign Language within the signing community. Highlighting their claims to the status of a cultural and ethnic group, he traces how the Deaf have fought to cast off their identification as disabled, and introduces arguments that have been put forward for treating sign languages like any other minority language within the EU. In his view, democratic institutions should provide mechanisms for effective recognition and representation of distinct voices and perspectives, allowing for the self-organization of group members that could lead to collective empowerment.

In the concluding chapter of this volume, Stephen May examines the links between nationalism, language and democracy in Europe. Focussing on legitimation and institutionalization, he argues that an effective challenge of the idea of cultural and linguistic homogeneity can only be mounted when the origins and developments of today's dominant languages and language ideologies are properly understood. Legitimation and institutionalization, among other things, May contends, have enabled some languages to become official, national, state languages, whereas others, deprived of legitimation and institutionalization, have become marginalized, minority languages often struggling for their very survival in the face of the greater national functionality of majority languages and the greater global appeal of English. These difficulties notwithstanding, May also points to several positive developments and new opportunities for minority languages to share in a similar degree of legitimation and institutionalization that has been afforded to national languages, which have arisen in the context of both higher levels of supranational integration in the EU as well as through the parallel and closely related processes of devolution. As May points out with reference to the case of Catalan, increasing the levels of self-governance for minorities, gives them enhanced opportunities for the legitimation and institutionalization of their mother tongue. However, the very processes that historically led to the dominance of today's national languages are often perceived as discriminatory by speakers of majority languages when applied to minority languages.

This implies a fundamental point that is relevant to all the contributions in this volume: perceptions of individual speakers of both minority and majority languages as to the status of their own and other languages play a crucial role in determining the prospects of the future of minority languages. While majority languages hardly need to worry about the status their language has in society, speakers of minority languages are often in a completely different, far less advantageous position, having to make difficult choices between functionality and social mobility, on the one side, and preserving the cultural heritage of their community, on the other. However, the debate among academics and policy makers has since long moved beyond this stark choice. Linguistic rights of national minorities (but not yet those of immigrant communities, with which we are not concerned in this volume) have become key elements in a much broader set of legal and policy tools to enable speakers of minority languages to be recognized and treated as equal members of societies. From this perspective, it is also important to acknowledge that the maintenance of language diversity is a task for society as a whole, not just for a handful of minority language speakers and activists. To make a contribution to this effort is one of the tasks that the editors and contributors hope to achieve with this volume.

Notes

1. For the full text of these and further reservations and declarations, see http://conventions.coe.int/Treaty/EN/DeclareList.asp?NT=148 and CM=1 and DF=10/02/03.
2. For the full text of this and further reservations and declarations, see http://conventions.coe.int/Treaty/EN/DeclareList.asp?NT=157 and CM=1 and DF=10/02/03.
3. For an overview of all country-specific and general recommendations of the HCNM, see http://www.osce.org/hcnm/documents/recommendations/.

References

Official documents

Charter of the United Nations, http://www.un.org/aboutun/charter/index.html
Document of the Copenhagen Meeting of the Conference on the Human Dimension of the CSCE, http://www.osce.org/docs/english/1990–1999/hd/cope90e.htm
European Charter for Regional or Minority Languages, http://conventions.coe.int/Treaty/EN/WhatYouWant.asp?NT=148 and CM=1 and DF=10/02/03
European Convention on Human Rights, http://www.un.org/aboutun/charter/index.html
Framework Convention for the Protection of National Minorities, http://conventions.coe.int/Treaty/EN/WhatYouWant.asp?NT=157 and CM=1 and DF=10/02/03
International Covenant on Civil and Political Rights, http://www.unhchr.ch/html/menu3/b/a_ccpr.htm
The Oslo Recommendations Regarding the Linguistic Rights of National Minorities, http://www.osce.org/hcnm/documents/recommendations/oslo/index.php3
Universal Declaration of Human Rights, http://www.un.org/Overview/rights.html

Secondary sources

Bastardas, A., 1995, Language Management and Language Behaviour Change: Policies and Social Persistence, *Catalan Review*, 9(2): 15–38.
Grin, F. and F. Villaincourt, 1999, *The Cost-Effectiveness Evaluation of Minority Language Policies. Case Studies On Wales, Ireland And The Basque Country*. Flensburg, European Centre for Minority Issues (ECMI), Monograph #2.
Woll, B., 2001, The Unheard Languages of Europe. Policy into Practice for Lesser used Languages in Europe. A paper presented at the British Council conference 'Policy into Practice for Lesser used Languages in Europe.' Hilton Hotel, Cardiff, 30 September–5 October 2001.

2
When a Language is 'Just Symbolic': Reconsidering the Significance of Language to the Politics of Identity

Camille C. O'Reilly

Introduction

When I was carrying out research on the Irish language revival in Northern Ireland in the 1990s, a common criticism of the revival movement was that the Irish language was peripheral and unimportant. No one really spoke the language any more, people would say – at best it was 'just symbolic', at worst it was a dead language with no relevance to an understanding of the conflict. My interest in the revival continued in spite of such comments, and throughout the decade of the nineties I witnessed the language movement grow and take on a small but significant role in the political process. Moreover, I have argued elsewhere that an investigation of the Irish language movement has provided a unique opportunity to better understand the nuance and complexity of the political situation in the North (O'Reilly 1996, 1999).

It is true that Irish has not been a language of everyday communication in what is now Northern Ireland for many generations. With the exception of a few fluent Irish speakers who learned the language in adulthood and even fewer of their offspring who grew up speaking it (being in an unusual position as native speakers of 'learned' Irish), the language has been very much on the margins of both public and private life. Much the same could be said of the Republic of Ireland, although there are still small communities of native Irish speakers and fluent Irish-as-a-second language speakers. Whatever the difficulties and traumas experienced by those who made the decision to switch to English in the past, the great majority of Irish people today have comfortably adapted to English and have made the language their own.

Nevertheless, there continues to be a complex and ambiguous relationship between Irish identity and the Irish language, as evidenced by surveys commissioned in the Republic of Ireland since the 1970s. All three of the surveys carried out to date indicate a fairly consistent association between the language and Irish ethnic identity, although this does *not* correlate with actual language use nor with optimism about its future (see O'Reilly 1999, chapter 8; 2001c: 80–3; O'Riagáin 1997, chapter 6). Whatever the eventual fate of Irish as a living language, it continues to influence Irish identity in both Northern Ireland and the Republic, regardless of whether people embrace the language or consciously reject it. The powerful historic connection between the Irish language and Irish nationalism makes it a potent element in today's politics of culture and identity, in spite of its assumed 'symbolic' status.

Fishman (1999) has discussed the mismatch often found between attitudes and actual functionality of a language. Extensive use of a language does not necessarily mean a positive attitude towards it, and likewise positive feelings about a language do not necessarily translate into a desire to know or use it. Languages obviously have a functional aspect – we use them to communicate with each other, on topics ranging from the mundane to the sublime. Having a language – or languages – is part of the human condition and, as the medium through which we apprehend our culture and environment, our feelings and ideas about them can be deep, passionate and above all complex.

From an anthropological perspective, meanings – how people interpret things and events – are central to an understanding of culture and society. This is as true of language as it is of any other aspect of culture. It is not just about formulating 'objective' opinions on the viability of a language or compiling statistics on language use, although the latter can of course be very useful. The aim is to understand how different actors interpret the significance of their language, its relationship to their sense of individual self and collective identity, how they think outsiders perceive it and so on. And because identity is so often in the eye of the beholder, as Jenkins (1996) points out, it is also important to understand the meanings of these things for those in society who are not members of a particular ethnic group. For example, in the case of Northern Ireland, there is a significant discrepancy in the way the Irish language is perceived by Catholics (who consider the language part of their cultural heritage even if they do not speak it) and Protestants (who tend not to see the language as part of their heritage), highlighting the potentially dangerous degree of misinterpretation and misunderstanding that occurs on a regular basis between the two communities in matters of culture and politics. Even where a society is not as strongly divided as in Northern Ireland, language and identity issues need to be considered from a diversity of perspectives to provide a complete understanding.

So what does it mean to say that a language is 'just symbolic'? Symbolism pervades human behaviour, to the extent that one anthropologist suggests symbols are 'the visible features of invisible aspects of social organization' (Hendry 1999: 83). The meaning of a symbol is shared by members of the same group, but not necessarily by outsiders who may ascribe completely different meanings to the same symbol. In fact, a great deal of symbolic meaning is not consciously noticed on a day to day basis, and may even be considered 'natural' by cultural insiders. While symbols are by definition shared, part of the efficacy of symbols is their malleability (Cohen 1986). While retaining a common form, individuals can read somewhat different meanings into them depending on their own personal experience or social position. Meaning can also vary according to context – for example, an American flag flying on a flagpole in front of the White House symbolises something quite different from one in the hands of protesters outside the same building. This multivocality of symbols is part of their power. These properties are as true of the symbolic aspect of language as of any other symbol. Language is also unique because it is both a complex system of symbols and a symbol in and of itself.

When people told me that the Irish language was 'just symbolic', they meant in part that it had no necessary communicative function, since everyone could also speak English. There was also a clear implication that being 'just symbolic' made it less important than other languages (including English) that are 'more' than merely symbolic, being 'useful' or simply 'better'. Yet symbolism is an element of all languages, minority or otherwise. As Fishman (1991) points out, a language can come to symbolise the group with which it is associated in a powerful way, both for members of the group and outsiders. So just how important is language to ethnic identity, symbolic or otherwise? And how much attention should we pay to language as a part of the politics of identity?

Language, culture, ethnicity

Understanding the relationship between language, culture and ethnicity, both in general terms and in specific cases, is a key part of understanding and improving the position of minority languages and their speakers. Unfortunately academic and popular concepts are often conflated, and it is all too easy to lapse into popular notions of ethnicity where language is seen as essentially synonymous with culture and even the ethnic group itself. This sort of discourse is common among minority language advocates, and sometimes slips into language planning and academic works as well. To cite just one such example from a recent collection of essays on European minority languages:

> No text on cultural policy leaves out the fundamental principle of respect for cultural diversity. And diversity of cultures by implication means diversity of languages. Whoever rejects a language, denies a culture and vice versa. (Extra and Gorter 2001: ix).

Essentialised notions about the relationship between language, culture and ethnicity can be hard to avoid.

Fishman (1991) has tackled the difficulty of this relationship by highlighting that language and ethnocultural identity are linked in three ways: indexically, in a part–whole relationship, and symbolically. The indexical link has to do with the way a language is best able to name the artefacts and express the values and worldviews of a particular culture, at least when the link between a language and culture is still intact. This is not to suggest that no other language could do the same job in the long term,[1] however in the short term the language that is historically and intimately associated with a particular culture is best suited to it. The part–whole link refers to the way in which so many aspects of a culture are verbally constituted – prayers, laws and proverbs, songs, history and myths. They are communicated, conceptualised and lived through language. More than this, the socialisation of children, interpersonal relations and even the ethical principles that underlie everyday life come to be associated with the language and can be seen as inseparable from it. Finally, symbolically languages come to represent or stand for the ethnic/national groups that speak them, both in the perception of the group themselves and that of outsiders. The future of a language becomes tied to the fate of the people who speak it. A language does not rise or fall according to its linguistic merits, with stronger or 'better' languages replacing lesser ones. Rather, the symbolic and communicative status of a language becomes inexorably linked to the social and political fortunes of its speakers (Fishman 1991: 20–4).

Fishman's outline of the links between language and ethnic identity shows just how powerful the relationship between language, culture and ethnicity can be, and suggests how the three can easily be conflated in both popular thinking and academic analysis. The symbolic link in particular can lead group members and non-members alike to closely associate a language with group identity to the point of directly equating the two. The connection between language, ethnicity and culture can seem so 'natural' that it passes without comment unless challenged. Speakers of dominant or state languages tend to take the connection for granted. Speakers of non-state or minority languages, however, are usually less able to do so and may feel the need to forcefully assert the 'naturalness' of the connection between their language and identity, putting it forward as a key reason why their language must be supported or revived.

The orthodoxy of the language/culture/(ethnic) identity link is widely accepted, and to a certain extent has an empirical basis. Yet collectivities can share common cultural traits but speak different languages and have different ethnic identities. For example, we can speak of 'European culture' in certain contexts, referring to common cultural heritage or shared values without seeing as problematic the diversity of languages spoken in Europe. Likewise, many countries share a language but are culturally distinct, as with Spanish in Latin American countries or English in the United States and Britain. Using the example of the United States again, it is also clear that a country can have a population with a shared language and widely shared civic culture, yet be made up of many distinct ethnic groups. Language is not always a core value of ethnicity, yet we often equate the two.

This tendency is particularly strong in cases where a minority language is associated with an active nationalist movement. Taken to its extreme, people sometimes assert that the loss of a minority language would entail a total loss of ethnic identity, and some may advocate political separatism to protect linguistic and cultural 'purity'. The modernist conception of the nation-state, where one state means one language and one culture, is pervasive and has had a powerful influence on our thinking in relation to minority languages. Language has come to symbolise or represent some of the fundamental principles of modernity. While in some senses we appear to be experiencing a shift away from the modernist emphasis on homogeneity, assimilation and unitary identities towards an increasingly postmodern focus on difference, heterogeneity and hybrid identities (Grillo 1998; O'Reilly 2001a: 14), at the same time a belief in the essential link between language and nation, nation and state seems to be as strong – and as troublesome – as ever.

The way that the terms 'culture' and 'ethnicity' are used can also be problematic. A certain amount of slippage between them is probably inevitable (O'Reilly 2001a, 2001b), but although often used interchangeably they are not synonyms. Ethnic identification tends to be a narrower form of classification. For example, two different ethnic groups can use a limited number of traits to highlight their distinctiveness, in spite of a great deal of shared culture between them. As Roosens (1995) points out, cultural identity may or may not be congruent with ethnic identity. Schöpflin suggests that any subjectively identifiable group might be said to have a common culture, while ethnicity is a conscious awareness of that culture (1995: 42). The problem with this formulation is that it leaves out the reality of unequal power relations. Both 'culture' and 'ethnicity' can have subtle political inflections, suggesting dominance or deviance. Dominant groups have cultures. Minority groups have ethnicities. When the nation and the state are conflated the culture of the majority becomes civic culture of the state (May 2001), while the culture of the minority becomes divisive (Schmid 2001) and 'ethnicised'. To have an ethnicity rather than a culture is to be wrong-footed from the start, signalling divergence from the 'norm' of state culture. Add language to the equation and 'ethnic' languages and their speakers become less important and of lower status than state languages and their speakers and a potential threat to the state.

The association between language, culture and ethnic identity takes many forms in the real world, a complexity that is smoothed over by the circular logic of nationalism with its tendency to promote a simple language/nation/state equation (O'Reilly 2001a: 8–9). Language can play a greater or lesser role in the relationship, with the current condition and status of a language and its speakers stemming from the specific social, cultural and political history of the language and people. When ideology is set aside and each case considered in detail, the nuances of the relationship between language and identity is revealed – including the possibility that a language may have lost its saliency in relation to identity, or is considered to be less important than other factors by the group with which it is historically associated. Efforts to support a language must consider the views and interpretations of its speakers (or potential speakers) in order to succeed. It is unfortunate that language enthusiasts can sometimes fail to understand fully the needs and day to day lives of minority language speakers (see e.g. McDonald 1989; Timm 2001).

The survival or decline of minority languages has to do with how the linguistic homeland became integrated into a central state. If we really want to alter the fortunes of minority languages and their speakers the traditional organisation of nation-states may need to be radically rethought because, according to May, it is this 'more than anything else, which most threatens the ongoing survival of minority languages' (2001: 15–16). A common assumption of opponents of minority rights is that granting recognition to minority languages will lead to increasing fragmentation, disunity and ultimately conflict. This view is not supported by the evidence in most cases.[2] In fact May argues convincingly that 'ethnic and national conflicts are most often precipitated when nation-states *ignore* demands for greater cultural and linguistic democracy' (2001: 17).

Conflict over language has become a part of or a proxy for all kinds of political struggle, from break-up of the former Yugoslavia, to the nationalist revival of the Irish language in Northern Ireland, to the issue of immigration in the United States. Writing about the United States, Schmid argues that 'bilingual education and the usage of non-English languages in the public realm has become a substitute for tensions over demographic and cultural change, increased immigration from third world countries, new linguistic based entitlements, and changing attitudes toward racial and ethnic assimilation'

(Schmid 2001: 4). Wherever it is not possible – or not politically correct – to debate openly in terms of 'race', nationalism or ethnicity, language can be used as a shorthand for cultural and identity politics (O'Reilly 1999).

The relevance of language to identity, and consequently to the politics of identity, cannot be taken as given. May argues that 'the language we speak is crucial to our identity *to the degree to which we define ourselves by it*' (May 2001: 135). This can change over time under the influence of powerful economic, cultural and political forces, including the activities of nationalist movements. Its relevance may vary at a particular point in time amongst different sections of a group as well, say between elites and the general population (see e.g. Woolhiser 2001) or between urban and rural populations. Perhaps most importantly, it is dangerous to attempt to make judgements about the significance of a language from an 'objective' outside perspective. The way a language is subjectively experienced may not tally with expectations, and it can be easy to over- or underestimate its importance. To avoid the potentially destructive consequences of such a mistake and to enhance both equality and stability, it is necessary to have a detailed and intimate understanding of each situation as well as a grasp of the wider contexts of identity politics.

Language and the politics of identity

Wherever there is political agitation or controversy over language, other political issues will also be at stake. Increasingly over the last few decades, these political issues have taken the form of a politics of identity, very often centred on ethnicity (O'Reilly 2003). Not all ethnic revival movements are associated with language or language revival. Nevertheless, struggles for civil and human rights are very often tied to issues of language, as are debates over nationalism and national identity. The relative centrality of language to an ethnic or nationalist movement is sometimes taken as the mark of a 'genuine' popular movement, but even when fairly marginal language can be crucial to understanding the essence of a conflict or potential conflict. It might be fair to ask to what extent do other political issues follow in the wake of a language movement, or to what extent does language become an issue in other types of political movement, becoming a symbol or shorthand for wider, more complex issues? Language is a valuable political currency, and can enter into the political equation in a number of ways. In this section I will outline a number of examples to give a feel for the diversity of ways that language figures in the politics of identity.

Since the ethnic revival began in the 1960s and 1970s, things 'ethnic' have become imbued with an air of trendiness in certain circles – from clothing and music to language and lifestyle. Throughout the seventies, eighties and nineties minority language issues became attached to a host of left-wing political issues, alongside the development of 'solidarity' links between ethnic and nationalist movements in different parts of Europe. In a partial inversion of modernist value judgements, 'ethnic' and 'traditional' became positive traits in at least some contexts. 'Celtic' languages and culture in particular became popular with those interested in alternative politics and lifestyles, sometimes accompanied by a new age Celtic mysticism.

Championing minority linguistic rights can be an attractive cause, particularly for the disaffected who may feel alienated from their own cultural background. In an effort to find their roots or escape from what they see as the negative aspects of life in the modern world, some activists have gone so far as to learn a minority language and adopt what they perceive to be the associated lifestyle. McDonald (1989) noted this trend in Brittany with humour and an occasional hint of disdain, particularly regarding Breton activists' lack of understanding when it came to actual native Breton speakers. I noticed a similar element of trendiness in the more youthful wing of the Irish revival movement in the Republic of Ireland during the 1990s, though it was rather less prominent than that described by McDonald and associated with youth culture rather than a hippie lifestyle. It is interesting that in her book on the Gaelic revival in Scotland, Macdonald (1997) comments on the fact that hippie incomers did *not* become involved in the Gaelic linguistic and cultural revival and did not attempt to appropriate a Gaelic identity. Apparently the Presbyterian lifestyle associated with the revival movement in that area was not attractive to them, clashing as it did with their more liberal values (Macdonald 1997: 140–3). Although there are exceptions, the connection between alternative or left-wing politics and minority language movements continues to be strong in many European countries.

Language has also become a proxy for more sensitive political issues, such as race and immigration in the United States. The importance of English as a unifying force in a country of immigrants has perhaps made Americans particularly sensitive to its status, regardless of its undeniably secure position of dominance at home[3] and its rising hegemony worldwide. Schmid (2001) argues that loyalty, American national identity and the English language became linked from the end of the nineteenth century. Nativist movements have sprung up periodically since then, most recently in the guise of 'English Only' initiatives against bilingual education and the use of non-English languages in the public realm. She argues convincingly that these issues are in fact a substitute for tensions over demographic and cultural change, increased immigration from 'third world' countries, and changing attitudes over race and assimilation (Schmid 2001: 4). Language has become a new idiom of race and cultural conflict, with anti-bilingual education campaigns in reality being aimed primarily at Hispanics[4] and controversy over the use of Ebonics[5] in the classroom frequently having racist overtones.

In former Yugoslavia language issues have been both a reflection of inter-ethnic tensions and a catalyst for deepening inter-ethnic animosities (Greenberg 2001). Since the break-up of the Yugoslav Federation in 1991, the Serbo-Croatian language has been split along ethnic lines. While ordinary people may have joked about the absurdity of the situation (Greenberg 2001: 17), during the 1980s the language issue indicated the extent of simmering ethnic division in the years before the country's collapse. Opposing nationalist camps used language symbolically as a tool to foment division and conflict, and eventually language planning became a key element in the emergence and re-imagining of separate Bosnian, Croatian, Serbian and Montenegrin identities and states. Elites and policy makers are using dialectal differences to carve out at least three separate successor languages, Bosnian, Croatian and Serbian, to go with the new successor states established in the 1990s. It is as if proving each language to be different confirms the right to separatism and sovereignty no matter what the costs. The power of language as the most essential symbol of ethnic nationhood has been invoked for political ends through language planning. Greenberg argues that the fate of Serbo-Croatian as a language relies ultimately on the direction of ethnic and nationalist politics in the new states. If nationalist extremists prevail, increasingly prescriptive norms may mean the development of three separate languages rather than a single language with three different ethnic names (Greenberg 2001: 38–9).

Language issues and activism can be used as tools of legitimation in many contexts, as well as shorthand for wider political issues where language is not the central concern. Both have been aspects of the politics of identity in Northern Ireland, where the increasing importance of the Irish language in nationalist[6] politics has recently been mirrored by the development of an Ulster-Scots movement. Over the last few decades a broad support for the Irish language has grown among nationalists, along with a general feeling that it is an important aspect of Irish identity.[7] Political developments of the mid-1990s brought official acceptance for public expressions of Irishness that had hitherto been restricted. Evidence of this change included nationalist political marches being allowed into Belfast city centre for the first time in the history of the state, and the gradual improvement in provision of funding for Irish-medium schools and cultural activities. Because there was already a small but fairly healthy grass roots revival movement, the Irish language became a key part of this politico-cultural struggle (O'Reilly 2003). For many nationalists, the status of the language has come to be seen as a sort of litmus test for parity of esteem for Catholics in the North, symbolising complex issues of identity and sovereignty. Although clearly not the core problem, the rather peripheral role of the Irish language, coupled with its historical associations with Irish nationalist and cultural identity, has made it ideal for this purpose. While the violence of the conflict was still intense, support for the Irish language was also a way for some nationalists to express their sense of Irishness and desire for political change without necessarily supporting the violence of republican paramilitaries.

Because of the importance attributed to it as an ethnic signifier and the legitimacy that this incurs, the promotion of a minority language can be seen as a means to a political end. The dominant popular model of an ethnically distinct group includes a fairly standardised set of cultural criteria, of which one of the most important elements is language. As the militarised conflict in Northern Ireland is replaced by a largely symbolic and cultural one, indeed language has become part of the new battlefield. Ulster-Scots[8] has recently been taken up by a section of the unionist population to achieve their own cultural and political ends, using similar means to those of the nationalist-dominated Irish language movement (McCoy and O'Reilly 2003). Some critics have argued that the promotion of Ulster-Scots as a language in its own right is an attempt by unionists to compete with the level of perceived authenticity enjoyed by the Irish language revival movement. Regardless of the controversial status of Ulster-Scots – there is no agreement on whether it is a language or a dialect, or even whether anyone actually speaks it – rigorous campaigning has kept the issue in the public arena. Throughout the 1990s a government funded body called the Cultural Traditions Group supported projects related to Ulster-Scots, alongside its support for the Irish language and other cultural initiatives. In 1993 Ulster-Scots was recognised as a variety of the Scots language by the European Bureau of Lesser-Used Languages, and later was also recognised by the British Government when it signed the European Charter for Lesser-Used Languages in 2000. As part of the new political structures that were established in the wake of the Good Friday Agreement of 1998, a Linguistic Diversity Unit was formed within a branch of the Northern Ireland Office to deal with both Ulster-Scots and the Irish language (and in theory at least, other ethnic minority languages).

In spite of the level of official support, there are limits to the extent to which Ulster-Scots can become the symbolic language of unionism. The movement itself is very small, and has frequently been associated with the more extreme wing of unionism in spite of the efforts of organisations such as the Ulster-Scots Language Society to promote itself as non-sectarian and non-political. The areas in which Ulster-Scots is traditionally spoken are limited and do not include Belfast, the capital city of Northern Ireland. Thus many unionists cannot associate Ulster-Scots with their personal histories or their localised identities. In addition, the emphasis on Presbyterianism that characterises much of the Ulster-Scots movement alienates many Protestants of different denominations and those who identify with an increasingly secular dominant culture. Finally, many unionists see themselves as part of a modern British state. Ulster-Scots and its accompanying rural-based traditions may appear too parochial to have widespread appeal (McCoy and O'Reilly 2003). In spite of its failure to date to gain widespread acceptance within the Protestant community, the rise of the Ulster-Scots movement has changed the shape of the politics of identity in Northern Ireland by raising the stakes in the battle for a new cultural and political order.

When people debate whether or not minority languages ought to be supported and granted official recognition, one of the most common arguments against this is the fear of fuelling separatism and division. The case of Quebec is frequently cited as an example of how calls for separatism, far from being quelled by increased protection for French, seemed to be strengthened. While campaigns to protect the French language have been very successful, strong laws designed to protect the French-speaking population have done little to alleviate anxiety about being a small enclave in an overwhelmingly English-speaking continent. The complex situation in Quebec raises the question of to what extent, and under what conditions, can the protection and support of a minority language lead to political separatism? Québécois identity shifted from a primarily Catholic and rural identification to a chiefly territorial and linguistic one after the changes of the 'quiet revolution' of the 1950s and 1960s brought about the modernisation of the region. An increasing focus on language as the core of Québécois identity led to legislation in the 1970s actively promoting French, and also facilitated the rise of the nationalist Parti Québécois. During the 1980s and 1990s the question of Quebec's relationship to the rest of Canada became increasingly fraught, culminating in a 1995 referendum on sovereignty that was lost by just 1.6 per cent of the vote (May 2001: 230). Support for secession seems to have receded since then, and in practice the major focus of Québécois nationalism has been cultural, particularly in relation to language.

While this may seem like a fairly straightforward case where the granting of language rights encouraged a separatist movement, it is not quite as simple as it might at first appear in such a brief précis. A deeper discussion of the case is not possible here,[9] but what the Quebec case shows is the complex interplay between economic development and modernisation, nationalist cultural production, and changing ideas about individual and group rights over the last few decades. As the region modernised, language become the key feature of ethnic identification. The strong ideological connection between language, ethnic identity and nationalism, coupled with an increased focus on civil and human rights across the globe from the 1960s, created fertile ground for ethnic and nationalist mobilisation.

However, a context of cultural and linguistic pluralism has been actively fostered in Canada at the same time as the use of the French language within Quebec has been institutionalised and promoted. Without legal intervention in support of French, economic and political developments in the region and in Canada as a whole may well have led to linguistic decline, ethnic division and potentially even greater political instability than has occurred to date. There is no doubt that language issues can indeed be politically explosive, but they can be handled in such a way as to mitigate negative consequences. Quebec may well be an example of how to protect minority language rights while largely avoiding the worst of potential outcomes.

A cursory examination of the last decade or so throws up countless examples of the diverse and complex relationship between language and ethnicity and the symbolic use of language in the politics of identity. In some of the Soviet successor states the languages of titular majorities have had their status changed from minority language to state-supported majority language in a short time. This has not always been achieved in a manner sensitive to the rights of those who do not speak the new state languages. For example, in Latvia state support for Latvian has been used punitively against speakers of Russian, formerly dominant but now a minority language within the country (Dobson 2001), while in Ukraine Russian speaking Jews find themselves in the awkward position of a minority ethnic group that speaks the language of the former oppressive state majority (Golbert 2001). Occasionally we find a seemingly 'classic' and straightforward case where language is a central part of ethno-nationalist mobilisation, such as the cases of Catalan and Basque. But here the differing political outcomes highlight once again the importance of context. An accommodation has been found for the Catalan language and identity within the Spanish state (DiGiacomo 1985, 2001; Woolard 1989), while violence rumbles on in the Basque country (Heiberg 1989; Urla 1988, 1993). Some states have launched well-intentioned attempts to recognise minority rights, but even these can have unintended consequences. For example, attempts to institutionalise minority Bulgarian representation in Romania has led to a situation where language is being used to underline and deepen internal divisions between two groups seeking to justify their position as the 'authentic' representatives of the Bulgarian community in the country (Guentcheva 2001). And so on, as language in its symbolic aspect is called upon to play a part in ethnic and identity politics in a variety of ways across the continent and around the world.

Conclusion

The role of language in ethnic identity is always symbolic in part and no less significant for this, even where the communicative status of a language is in question. When language is said to have symbolic significance, there is often an implied sense of 'merely' symbolic. The suggestion that the symbolic aspect of the relationship between language, ethnicity and culture is somehow secondary or of lesser significance can lead to an underestimation of the importance of language in real life situations. The successful management of conflict and potential conflict requires not only a broad theoretical understanding of language and ethnicity, but also a sensitive and nuanced understanding of how these relationships play out in the complexities of actual situations. If we want to go beyond the management of conflict – and surely this must be the goal – such an understanding can help us to create multicultural democracies where individual and group rights are balanced and respected, and the rich diversity of languages and cultures in Europe is allowed to flourish.

Is a politics of identity the best way forward for minority languages and their speakers? Drawing on the powerful ideologies of ethnonationalism, identity, and civil and human rights, it is perhaps easier to follow the established pattern in order to achieve political goals. There is little doubt that identity politics can move people in a way that other forms of social or political movement cannot. It seems that for the foreseeable future this will continue to be the dominant political idiom. Tempered by a context of multiculturalism and respect for the rights of all concerned, including an emphasis on the obligations of citizenship as well as the rights it confers, the potent cocktail of language, ethnicity and nationalism can be used to further the aims of democracy and equality, as well as undermine them.

May (2001) argues convincingly that the disavowal of cultural, linguistic and political expression of minority ethnicities is the cause of many problems and conflicts in the modern world. Minority language rights are essential to the maintenance and extension of democracy. While some in both Europe and the United States still cling to the traditional nationalist model of the nation-state believing it to be the most stable, it clearly does not fit changing circumstances, is highly likely to promote the conditions for conflict, and goes against the very ideals of rights and democracy they claim to hold dear. There are clear dangers involved in balancing the rights of minorities and majorities, and in handling the potentially volatile mix of language and ethnicity in the idiom of identity politics. Nevertheless, there is even greater danger in ignoring it.

Notes

1. As the Irish case seems to illustrate.
2. For example, May (2001) and Schmid (2001) both make detailed arguments against this point of view.
3. More than 97% of Americans speak English well, according to a source quoted in Schmid (2001: 178).
4. Since the 1970s the majority of immigrants to the United States have been from Spanish-speaking countries.
5. Also known by linguists as African American Vernacular English.
6. In Northern Ireland a nationalist is someone who generally supports the political goal of a united Ireland. A unionist is someone who supports the continued status of Northern Ireland as a part of the United Kingdom. The apparently religious labels Catholic and Protestant are in fact more commonly intended as ethno-political terms – Catholics are usually nationalists and have an Irish identity, while Protestants are usually unionist and have a British identity. However, these are generalisations that gloss over a more complex reality.
7. For a more detailed account of the Irish language and Irish identity in Northern Ireland see Maguire (1991) and O'Reilly (1999).
8. Ulster-Scots is a speech variety closely related to Scots, which is descended from the Northumbrian dialect of Old English. Scots was influenced by the Old Norse of Viking invaders, as well as French, Dutch and Scots Gaelic. Scots speakers came to Ireland during the Plantation of Ulster (1610–25) and in migrations over the remainder of the seventeenth century. Although they settled primarily in counties Antrim, Down, Derry and Donegal in the northern part of the province of Ulster, the English accent of much of Ulster came to sound similar to that found in Scotland.
9. See Handler (1988), May (2001) chapter 6, Schmid (2001) chapters 6 and 8.

References

Cohen, A., 1986, *Symbolising Boundaries: Identity and Diversity in British Cultures*, Manchester: Manchester University Press.

DiGiacomo, S., 2001, ' "Catalan is Everyone's Thing": Normalizing a Nation', in *Language, Ethnicity and the State, Volume One: Minority Languages in the European Union*, ed. C. O'Reilly. Houndmills, Basingstoke: Palgrave Macmillan.

Dobson, J., 2001, 'Ethnic Discrimination in Latvia', in *Language, Ethnicity and the State, Volume Two: Minority Languages in Eastern Europe Post-1989*, ed. C. O'Reilly. Houndmills, Basingstoke: Palgrave Macmillan.

Extra, G. and D. Gorter, 2001, 'Comparative Perspectives on Regional and Immigrant Minority Languages in Multicultural Europe', in *The Other Languages of Europe: Demographic, Sociolinguistic and Educational Perspectives*, (eds) G. Extra and D. Gorter. Clevedon, England: Multilingual Matters.

Fishman, J. A., 1991, *Reversing Language Shift: Theoretical and Empirical Foundations of Assistance to Threatened Languages*. Clevedon, England: Multilingual Matters.

Fishman, J. A., 1999, *Handbook of Language and Ethnic Identity*, Oxford: Oxford University Press.

Golbert, R., 2001, 'Language, Nation and State-building in Ukraine: The Jewish Response', in *Language, Ethnicity and the State, Volume Two: Minority Languages in Eastern Europe Post-1989*, ed. C. O'Reilly. Houndmills, Basingstoke: Palgrave Macmillan.

Greenberg, R. D., 2001, 'Language, Nationalism and the Yugoslav Successor States', in *Language, Ethnicity and the State, Volume Two: Minority Languages in Eastern Europe Post-1989*, ed. C. O'Reilly. Houndmills, Basingstoke: Palgrave Macmillan.

Grillo, R., 1998, *Pluralism and the Politics of Difference: State, Culture and Ethnicity in Comparative Perspective*, Oxford: Clarendon Press.

Guentcheva, R., 2001, 'Debating Language: The Bulgarian Communities in Romania after 1989', in *Language, Ethnicity and the State, Volume Two: Minority Languages in Eastern Europe Post-1989*, ed. C. O'Reilly. Houndmills, Basingstoke: Palgrave Macmillan.

Handler, R., 1988, *Nationalism and the Politics of Culture in Quebec*, Madison, Wisconsin: University of Wisconsin Press.

Heiberg, M., 1989, *The Making of the Basque Nation*, Cambridge: Cambridge University Press.

Hendry, J., 1999, *An Introduction to Social Anthropology: Other People's Worlds*, Houndmills, Basingstoke: Palgrave Macmillan.

Jenkins, R., 1996, *Social Identity*, London: Routledge.

Macdonald, S., 1997, *Reimagining Culture: Histories, Identities and the Gaelic Renaissance*, Oxford: Berg.

McCoy, G. and C. O'Reilly, 2003, 'Essentializing Ulster? The Ulster-Scots Language Movement', in *Language and Tradition in Ireland: Continuities and Displacements*, ed. M. Tymoczko and C. Ireland. University of Massachusetts Press.

McDonald, M., 1989, *'We are not French!' Language, Culture and Identity in Brittany*, London: Routledge.

Maguire, G., 1991, *Our Own Language: An Irish Initiative*, Clevedon, England: Multilingual Matters.

May, S., 2001, *Language and Minority Rights: Ethnicity, Nationalism and the Politics of Language*, Harlow, England: Longman.

O'Reilly, C., 1996, 'The Irish Language – Litmus Test for Equality? Competing Discourses on Identity, Parity of Esteem and the Peace Process', Irish *Journal of Sociology*, 6, 154–78.

O'Reilly, C., 1999, *The Irish Language in Northern Ireland: The Politics of Culture and Identity*, Houndmills, Basingstoke: Palgrave Macmillan.

O'Reilly, C., 2001a, 'Introduction', in *Language, Ethnicity and the State, Volume One: Minority Languages in the European Union*, ed. C. O'Reilly. Houndmills, Basingstoke: Palgrave Macmillan.

O'Reilly, C., 2001b, 'Introduction', in *Language, Ethnicity and the State, Volume Two: Minority Languages in Eastern Europe Post-1989*, ed. C. O'Reilly. Houndmills, Basingstoke: Palgrave Macmillan.

O'Reilly, C., 2001c, 'Irish Language, Irish Identity: Northern Ireland and the Republic of Ireland in the European Union', in *Language, Ethnicity and the State, Volume One: Minority Languages in the European Union*, ed. C. O'Reilly. Houndmills, Basingstoke: Palgrave Macmillan.

O'Reilly, C., 2003, 'The Politics of Culture in Northern Ireland', in *Peace at Last? The Impact of the Good Friday Agreement on Northern Ireland*, (eds) J. Neuheiser and S. Wolff. With a Foreword by Lord Alderdice, Speaker of the Northern Ireland Assembly, New York and Oxford: Berghahn.

Ó Riagáin, P., 1997, *Language Policy and Social Reproduction: Ireland 1893–1993*, Oxford: Oxford University Press.

Roosens, E., 1995, 'Ethnicity as a Creation: Some Theoretical Reflections', in *Nationalism, Ethnicity and Cultural Identity in Europe* (eds) K. von Benda-Beckman and M. Verkuyten. Utrecht, The Netherlands: ERCOMER.

Schmid, C. L., 2001, *The Politics of Language: Conflict, Identity, and Cultural Pluralism in Comparative Perspective*, Oxford: Oxford University Press.

Schöpflin, G., 1995, 'Nationalism and Ethnicity in Europe, East and West', in *Nationalism and Nationalities in the New Europe*, ed. C. A. Kupchan. Ithaca, New York: Cornell University Press.

Timm, L., 2001, 'Ethnic Identity and Minority Language Survival in Brittany', in *Language, Ethnicity and the State, Volume One: Minority Languages in the European Union*, ed. C. O'Reilly. Houndmills, Basingstoke: Palgrave Macmillan.

Urla, J., 1988, 'Ethnic Protest and Social Planning: A Look at Basque Language Revival', *Cultural Anthropology*, 3, 379–94.

Urla, J., 1993, 'Cultural Politics in an Age of Statistics: Numbers, Nations and the Making of Basque Identity', *American Ethnologist*, 20, 818–43.

Woolard, K. A., 1989, *Double Talk: Bilingualism and the Politics of Ethnicity in Catalonia*, Stanford, California: Stanford University Press.

Woolhiser, C., 2001, 'Language Ideology and Language Conflict in Post-Soviet Belarus', in *Language, Ethnicity and the State, Volume Two: Minority Languages in Eastern Europe Post-1989*, ed. C. O'Reilly. Houndmills, Basingstoke: Palgrave Macmillan.

Part II
Legal and Policy Frameworks

3
Devising an Adequate System of Minority Protection in the Area of Language Rights

Kristin Henrard

Introduction

Since tensions involving language, language use and language rights are often a source of problems in multinational states, it seems appropriate to focus on language rights against the background of a theory regarding an adequate system of minority protection.

First of all, the concept of minority is briefly touched upon, including its potential relevance for multinational societies. Subsequently, the link between an adequate system of minority protection on the one hand and conflict prevention and/or resolution in multinational societies on the other hand is clarified. Prior to the assessment of the respective contribution of individual human rights and the current minority rights standards to the protection of language rights, the two basic principles of minority protection are highlighted. The assessment reveals that both individual human rights and the current minority rights standards are important for the protection of language rights of population groups in a multinational society, while the latter take up the *acquis* of the former and further the right to identity of minorities. Nevertheless, the degree of protection at the level of these two categories of rights remains in many ways deficient. Therefore, a qualified recognition of a right to internal self determination for minorities might very well heighten that protection in a way that improves integration without forcing the assimilation of the population groups concerned.

Defining the concept 'minority'

When focusing on minority protection, it seems in any event important to clarify first of all (to some extent) the meaning of the concept 'minority'. Although up until now there is no generally accepted definition (Schulte-Tenckhoff and Ansbach 1995: 17), a review of various definitions proposed does reveal that there are certain elements that recur, some of which are objective, others subjective. These elements thus seem to be essential components of a definition of the concept minority.[1]

Among the objective elements, the one on specifying ethnic, religious and linguistic characteristics, which differ from the rest of the population of the state, is the most compelling (Capotorti 1991: 12). Second, a numerical minority position is required, more specifically the population group concerned should be less numerous than the rest of the population of the state. Arguably suppressed majorities should be distinguished from minorities, the former having rights beyond those of minorities like the right to rule themselves (Capotorti 1991: 12, 96).

Although several authoritative definitions do include a nationality requirement (Deschênes 1986: 262–4), recently this requirement has had to face mounting criticism (Shaw 1992: 26). It is indeed all too easy for states to manipulate their nationality legislation so as to exclude certain population groups that would otherwise qualify as minorities (Thornberry 1993: 28–30). Furthermore this requirement is problematic in the case of population groups without fixed abode, such as the Roma and also when the borders of existing states change due to secessions or associations (Gilbert 1992: 72). Consequently, the trend at international law seems to be to dispense with the nationality requirement.[2]

The final objective requirement is the one of non-dominance, excluding dominant minority groups from the definition of minority. Obviously such dominant minorities would not need minority needs (Ramaga 1992: 104), while dominated majorities need much more than minority rights, more specifically self-determination and the right to rule themselves (Thornberry 1991: 9).

On the subjective side, the population groups concerned should have the wish to hold on to their separate identity, in community with the other members of the group (ibid.: 165). Although population groups that chose to assimilate should clearly not be considered minorities, this subjective requirement should not be too demanding. Indeed, many reasons can explain a silence on the part of a population group, including suppression by the authorities (Ramaga 1992: 115). It can therefore be argued that the mere continued existence of a population group should be sufficient in itself.

On the basis of the preceding analysis, the following working definition of the concept minority can be put forward, namely:

> A population group with ethnic, religious and linguistic characteristics which differs from the rest of the population is non-dominant, is numerically smaller than the rest of the population and has the wish to hold on to its separate identity.

Since the reference to 'the rest of the population of the state' does not need to be a monolithic bloc, but can consist of several population groups, the concept minority can also be applied in a multinational state without a clear majority population. In that case, all the distinctive population groups in the state are minorities in so far as they are non-dominant and have the wish to hold on to their separate identity (even implicitly) (Capotorti 1991: 96).

The link between minority protection and conflict prevention/resolution

An adequate system of minority protection in multinational states actually amounts to the most appropriate accommodation of population diversity of these societies. This in turn requires a neat balancing process so that all population groups consider themselves to be reasonably accommodated. This can be achieved when policy makers acknowledge the interrelation between individual human rights, minority rights and the right to self-determination.

Whereas I have set out this overall argument at length elsewhere (Henrard 2000: 56–321), the emphasis here is on language rights and the appropriate accommodation of linguistic population diversity in a multinational state.

Considering the link between an appropriate system of minority protection and the accommodation of population diversity in multinational settings, minority protection measures tend to contribute to the prevention of ethnic conflict and can also be used as mechanisms of conflict resolution.

The two basic principles of minority protection

A comprehensive system of minority protection consists of a conglomerate of rules and mechanisms enabling an effective integration of the relevant population groups, while allowing them to retain their separate characteristics. Such a system is based on two pillars or basic principles, namely the prohibition of discrimination on the one hand and measures designed to protect and promote the separate identity of the minority groups on the other hand (Capotorti 1991: 40).

The first pillar deals with rules that are expressions and further elaborations of the prohibition of discrimination. Such rules guarantee formal equality and are at the same time conducive to achievement of substantive equality. They are, consequently, considered to be a necessary prerequisite for the second pillar and its rules, which are actively geared towards realising substantive equality. Substantive or real equality can indeed require differential treatment for people in different circumstances. For (members of) minorities these rules would be focused on devising appropriate means to retain and promote their distinctive characteristics (Benoit-Rohmer 1996: 16).

Although 'special' measures for minorities are not entirely uncontroversial,[3] it is currently rather widely accepted that each system of minority protection should follow this double approach.[4] It is furthermore important to emphasise that both pillars, the non-discrimination principle in all its manifestations and the measures of minority protection, can be considered to be implementations of the equality principle. Both aspects of minority protection are indeed closely connected and intertwined because of their focus on equality (Rodley 1995: 50–1).

Specific concerns of minorities regarding language use

The point of departure regarding 'languages', according to social linguistic theory, is that the linguistic value of languages and their relative political strength and importance are different matters. Whereas all languages are linguistically equivalent, the speakers of

the different languages are not equal in terms of political power relations. These relations are manifested in national policies regarding
the official languages of a country.

The need to have one specific *lingua franca* for purposes of administrative efficiency plays in any event an important role. This perception could indeed result in the *de facto* preponderance in a state's
public life of a language, which is not the mother tongue of the dominant population group(s) (De Varennes 1997: 167). For example,
currently English has the status of *lingua franca* in South Africa while
it is only the mother tongue of about 15 per cent of the population.
It can be argued that the pressure emanating from a linguistically
dominant group is considerable and that this would oblige states to
take positive measures to protect the other linguistic groups so as to
abide by the requirements of substantive equality (Blair 1994: 7–9).

Typical demands of linguistic minorities concern the institutional
foundations of cultural reproduction and more specifically the use of
minority languages in the (public) media, the public education system and communications with public authorities and courts (Tabory
1980: 212–14). The issue of names in the minority language and the
language of street names and other topographical indications are also
quite emotionally charged, and often constitute sensitive topics for
both minorities and states, as the latter are rather reluctant to make
concessions in this regard (Benoit-Rohmer 1996: 46; De Varennes
1997: 152).

The status of official language is neither the only possible way of
granting minority languages some kind of official recognition, nor a
panacea for all the demands of linguistic minorities, since 'official
language status does not signal that the use of such a language in a
state is provided by law, ... the exact scope of a right to use an official
language can always be subjected to various limitations and considerations' (De Varennes 1997: 166). This statement applies *inter alia* to
states where many of the languages spoken are given official status
due to political considerations; South Africa is a case in point.[5]

The demands of linguistic minorities should be evaluated against
the principle of substantive equality for this would demonstrably
require a differential approach to linguistic regulation depending on
the circumstances. Language is undeniably a necessary component of
almost every service provided by public authorities. Consequently,
members of linguistic minorities are systematically put in an unequal

and disadvantaged position regarding the enjoyment of public services when these are exclusively provided in the dominant language (De Varennes 1997: 1, 53; De Witte 1992: 58).

Considering the preceding argument that certain minority language rights are required by the principle of substantive equality on the one hand and the concern of states regarding 'exaggerated' demands on public funds on the other hand, a possible solution to the dilemma could be found in the application of a sliding-scale approach in view of its proportionality considerations (Blair 1994: 11; De Varennes 1997: 169, 173). As is also reflected in the Oslo Recommendations, the proportionality principle is indeed generally accepted as being crucial in the matter.

In general, the determination of language rights for (members of) minorities can be compared to the search of a just *equilibrium* between national unity on the one hand and the accommodation of linguistic diversity on the other. Although the goal to have a *lingua franca* is in itself legitimate, that process should not be allowed to wipe out linguistic differences (De Varennes 1997: 86–7).

Relevant factors for decisions concerning the regulation of language use in the public sphere include: demographic importance in combination with territorial concentration of the linguistic groups, the limited human and financial resources of the state, the level and type of government services or advantages (as this determines the degree of the disadvantage concomitant to a certain language preference by the state for those speaking a different mother tongue) and the desirability of a common national language for the state (Blair 1992: 11; De Varennes 1997: 87, 89, 93, 95, 99). Still, it is advisable to be cautious regarding the factor of financial capacity of states, 'since "affordability" will often be a matter of interpretation, that is, of political will and priorities' (Blair 1992: 11).

Protection of language rights through individual human rights?

Concerning individual human rights, I will focus my analysis on the European Convention on Human Rights (ECHR) considering it as one of the most successful and far-reaching systems for the protection of human rights. The few articles of the ECHR and the several additional protocols, which do include explicit provisions on language and language rights, concern procedural and police related matters (articles 5 and 6). Articles 5, § 2 and 6, § 3(a) and (e), dealing respectively with the right to be informed of the reason for one's arrest and of the nature and cause of one's accusation and with the right to an interpreter in court, refer only to a language understandable for the person concerned. Consequently, these articles do not enshrine any right to be informed of these matters in the mother tongue, let alone the language of choice.[6]

Article 14 does imply a prohibition of discrimination on language grounds but the Court (as the Commission) has seldom concluded to its violation in this respect. The Commission has nevertheless explicitly acknowledged that the only more or less specific protection by the Convention of members of minorities would be provided by the prohibition of discrimination in article 14.

The requirements of articles 5 and 6 do not go beyond what is strictly necessary for the right of defence and the concomitant requirement of procedural fairness and equality of arms. Consequently, the language provisions at issue do not correspond to all the demands and desires of linguistic minorities. For example, someone who understands the language of the court has no right to use his/her mother tongue or language of choice in court proceedings and this also applies to members of linguistic minorities.[7]

The jurisprudence of the Court and the Commission has furthermore underlined that article 14 cannot be used in combination with these articles to obtain recognition of such a right. The linguistic prescriptions of articles 5 and 6 are considered as '*leges speciales*' of article 14 in that the former would determine the limit of the requirements of the non-discrimination principle regarding language rights in procedural and police related matters.[8]

The two articles with explicit linguistic provisions have induced the Court and the Commission to develop a steady line of jurisprudence that, *a contrario*, the Convention would not guarantee a right to use a certain language in dealings with the authorities. This is the case for the right to education (see next), the freedom of thought, conscience and religion and the freedom of expression (De Varennes 1997: 73).

The Court has furthermore explicitly stated that article 3 of the first additional protocol to the ECHR (election rights) does not have a linguistic component. Article 3 does not guarantee an absolute right either so it was held acceptable that certain requirements were imposed, like the requirement that elected persons would take their oath in a certain language[9] or the obligation to register a political party in a certain language.[10] The Commission clarified explicitly in *Fryske nasjonale partij and others v Netherlands* that articles 9 and 10 do not guarantee linguistic freedom as such. In particular, these articles would not guarantee the right to use the language of one's choice in administrative matters.

This line of jurisprudence clarifies and emphasises that the other articles of the Convention cannot be relied upon to ensure certain language rights. According to the Commission no right to linguistic and cultural identity can be inferred from articles 9 and 10.[11] Furthermore, the Commission underlined in *X v Austria* that the Convention does not include a right for linguistic minorities and that consequently the protection of their members is limited to non-discrimination on the ground of association with a national minority. The case concerned a linguistic census in Austria in which a member of the Slovene minority was not able to express her association to a minority because her mother tongue was German. According to the applicant, this situation would amount to a degrading treatment prohibited by article 3, but the Commission dismissed the application since the situation complained of would 'fall outside the scope of the provisions of the Convention and in particular article 3'.

The preceding overview of the jurisprudence of the Court and the Commission regarding language rights (with special attention to cases concerning members of linguistic minorities) reveals that the degree to which the ECHR accommodates the wishes and needs of (members of) linguistic minorities is minimal. The protection is indeed explicitly limited to the implications of the non-discrimination principle, which is only one of the pillars of a full-blown system of minority protection. As the following analysis will demonstrate, the same is true regarding the right to education.

The right to education and especially the way in which it is conceptualised is very important for (members of) minorities. Education has not only an obvious qualification function but also an important socialisation function, which involves the passing on of certain values, a certain culture and so on[12] to the next generation. Several aspects of education have the potential to contribute to the protection and promotion of the separate identity of minorities. One of the most important of these aspects is the choice of the language(s) of instruction.

Although article 2 of the first additional protocol to the ECHR does not contain explicit stances on this issue, the jurisprudence of the Court and the Commission provide quite a number of clarifications.

The well-known *Belgian Linguistics case* was until recently the case most in point regarding the possible linguistic aspects of the right to education and is consequently highly relevant for linguistic minorities. The case concerns French-speaking persons living in the Dutch linguistic region who contested the Belgian regulation regarding language in education, which is based on the division of the country into four linguistic regions. The regulation specifies that public education in the linguistic region of the applicants can only be given in Dutch. The diplomas of schools in that region which would provide education in another language would not be officially recognised.[13]

The Court underlines first of all that the first sentence of article 2 of the first additional protocol ('(n)o person shall be denied the right to education') does not give any indication about the language in which education should be provided for in order to comply with the requirements of the right to education. The Court postulates nevertheless that the right to education would not mean anything if it would not imply the right to receive education in one of the official languages.

Furthermore, the duty on states to respect the right of parents to ensure such education and teaching in conformity with their own religious and philosophical convictions '[i]n the exercise of any functions which it assumes in relation to education', would not imply that the states have an obligation to accommodate the linguistic preferences of the parents (32). Although this attitude is supported by the *travaux préparatoires*, in *Campbell and Cosans v UK*, the Court adopted a more generous approach and indeed defined 'philosophical convictions' as 'such convictions as are worthy of respect in a democratic society [...] and are not incompatible with human dignity' (para. 50). In view of this definition, it would not be too far fetched to argue that 'the desire of parents, based on cultural and linguistic association with an ethnic group, to have their children educated in their mother tongue' should be accepted as such a conviction (Hillgruber and Jestaedt 1994: 26, n. 64).

The Court also holds that the Belgian regulation does, in general, not amount to a violation of article 14 in combination with article 2 of the first additional protocol.[14] The regulation on language in education and the concomitant differential treatment have indeed, according to the Court, an objective and reasonable justification. The challenged distinction is 'in accordance with the law' and also has a legitimate aim namely 'having all school institutions that are dependent on the State and are located in a uni-lingual region provide their instruction in the primary language of that region' (44). Finally, the Court deems the means used to reach this legitimate aim not disproportionate (ibid.).

The Commission, however, took a more critical stance concerning the Belgian government's position and contended that the Belgian regulation has as its goal 'to prevent the spread, if not the maintenance even, in one region, of the language and culture of the other region' and also 'to assimilate minorities against their will into the language of their surroundings'.[15] It should be emphasised that measures of forced assimilation of (members of) minorities are, however, prohibited by international law (see infra).

Importantly, the Court seems to be moving away from its rigid stance with respect to the protection of mother tongue education in its *Cyprus v Turkey* judgement of 10 May 2001. In that case, the Court notes that 'children of Greek-Cypriot parents in North Cyprus wishing to pursue a secondary education through the medium of the Greek language are obliged to transfer to schools in the south, this facility being unavailable in the Turkish Republic of Northern Cyprus (TRNC) ever since the decision of the Turkish-Cypriot authorities to abolish it' (para. 277). Although the Court at first seems to repeat its stance that the provision on the right to education 'does not specify the language in which education must be conducted in order that the right to education be respected' (ibid.), it does conclude that 'the failure of the TRNC authorities to make continuing provision for [Greek-language schooling] at the secondary-school level must be considered in effect to be a denial of the substance of the right at issue' (para. 278). Indeed, the Court argues that because the children had already received their primary schooling through the Greek medium of instruction, '[t]he authorities must no doubt be aware that it is the wish of Greek-Cypriot parents that the schooling of their children be completed through the medium of the Greek language' (ibid.). Consequently, it seems that because the authorities assumed responsibility for the provision of Greek-language primary schooling, they have the obligation to do the same for the secondary school level.

Even though this reasoning does not rely explicitly on the importance of mother tongue education for the cognitive development of the students and related substantive equality considerations, and although it does not read into the article on the right to education a right to mother tongue education, it clearly attaches more weight to the parents' convictions about the benefits of a certain medium of instruction and should thus be welcomed. It is to be hoped that in subsequent jurisprudence of the ECHR will further elaborate and enhance the protection of mother tongue education for minorities.

Interim conclusion

Despite the positive development in the jurisprudence of the ECHR pertaining to mother tongue education, it can still be argued that individual human rights accommodate only to a very limited extent language rights adopted to the special situation of minorities. Consequently, it is interesting to investigate to what extent the current minority rights standards contribute to a protection of language rights.

Protection of language rights through current minority rights?

Article 27 of the International Covenant on Civil and Political Rights (ICCPR)

The international law provision on minority rights par excellence, article 27 ICCPR, is very vague in that the only explicit language right it contains reads as follows:

> In those States in which Ethnic, Religious or Linguistic Minorities exist, persons belonging to such minorities shall not be denied the right – in community with the other members of their group ... to use their own language.

Issues of relevance for minorities concerning languages, like language use in courts, in education, in communication with public authorities and so on are not explicitly dealt with either. The Human Rights Committee (HRC), the supervisory body to the ICCPR, in its *General Comment on article 27* (para. 5.3) only distinguishes the implications of article 27 from other articles of the Covenant, without giving an indication of the contribution of article 27 to linguistic minority rights. Consequently, article 27 ICCPR does not seem to provide much extra protection related to the individual human rights provisions regarding language use.

The 1992 UN Declaration on Minorities

The 1992 UN Declaration on the Rights of Persons belonging to National or Ethnic, Religious and Linguistic Minorities is the first international instrument exclusively devoted to the protection of minority rights. It contains a further specification of article 27 ICCPR, while not being burdened by the restrictions inherent in this article (Spiliopoulou-Akermark 1997: 181).

The explicit provisions on language and education (article 4), and the encouragement of states to adopt appropriate legislative and other measures to protect the linguistic identity of minorities and to encourage the conditions for the promotion of that identity (article 1) undoubtedly constitute improvements vis-à-vis the individual human rights regarding language (Packer 1996: 157). However, it should be acknowledged that nothing is said about the crucial issue of communication between members of minorities and public authorities.

Although the Declaration contains some more elaborated standards in comparison to article 27, these are still rather vague and furthermore formulated in such a cautious way that states can easily argue that they comply (Benoit-Rohmer 1998: 23). The use of formulations like 'wherever possible', 'when appropriate', 'adequate opportunities' inevitably concede a wide margin of appreciation to states.

The UNESCO Convention on the Elimination of Discrimination in Education

The UNESCO Convention on the Elimination of Discrimination in Education also takes up specific concerns of linguistic minorities (Symonides 1995: 201) while going beyond the *acquis* of the individual human right to education, but again not in a sufficiently satisfactory way.

Article 2(b) states, for example, that the establishment or maintenance of separate educational institutions because of linguistic reasons does not amount to discrimination in education as prohibited by the Convention (Thornberry 1991: 289). This provision implies merely that states CAN allow separate educational institutions in certain circumstances but does not oblige them.

In article 1(5)(c) the contracting states do agree to allow members of national minorities to establish and maintain – in certain circumstances – and under certain conditions, their own educational institutions. However, this right of members of national minorities contains numerous restrictions, which hedge rather heavily in the recognition of the right, so that in practice they enable the state to frustrate the operation of the clauses referred to (Thornberry 1991: 290).

The 1990 Copenhagen Document of the OSCE

At the European level certain documents of the Organisation for Security and Co-operation in Europe (OSCE) and of the Council of Europe (COE) should be discussed in this respect.

Paragraph 34 of the 1990 Copenhagen Document of the OSCE is undoubtedly important as it addresses two linguistic issues of special relevance for linguistic minorities, namely language in education and language use in communication with public authorities. However, this provision is a prime example of a provision with many escape clauses (Hannum 1991: 1442), leaving a huge margin of discretion to states.

The COE Framework Convention for the Protection of National Minorities

At the level of the COE, two documents should be considered: the Framework Convention for the Protection of National Minorities and the European Charter for Regional or Minority Languages (ECRML).

The COE's Framework Convention for the Protection of National Minorities clearly demonstrates in what way individual human rights and minority rights are interrelated for an adequate protection of human rights in general and also more specifically for linguistic rights. Indeed, several articles of the Framework Convention take up individual human rights of the ECHR, which are of special relevance for minorities (articles 7, 8 and 12), while adding at times extra requirements because they are essential for the purpose of safeguarding the specific fundamental right for minorities (article 9). The Convention also enshrines several minority rights, but each time suitably circumscribed.

The Framework Convention is undoubtedly very important for minority protection purposes since it is the first international treaty with a multilateral, general protection regime for minorities (Benoit-Rohmer 1998: 145). Nevertheless, it consists of vague programme declarations and includes several escape clauses, thus granting states a wide margin of appreciation (Benoit-Rohmer 1994: 50).

Article 10 guarantees the right to use the minority language but its second paragraph, concerning the right to use this language in communication with the public authorities is very heavily qualified (Benoit-Rohmer 1998: 139). Not only is the right contingent on finding a high geographical concentration of members of the linguistic minority required but it is also weakened by discretionary phrases like 'where such a request corresponds to a real need' and 'as far as possible'.[16] The effective application of this provision can thus be seriously questioned (Benoit-Rohmer 1998: 139).

Article 14 regarding the right to learn the minority language and being taught or receiving instruction in a minority language, is equally cautiously formulated.

Moreover, the states appear not to have an obligation to take positive measures regarding the right to learn the minority language. Particularly the right to instruction in a minority language is very tentatively phrased in that states are not obliged but merely encouraged to provide this service (Benoit-Rohmer 1994: 48–9). Together with the requirement of territorial concentration, article 14, para. 2 also contains vague conditions like 'as far as possible' and 'within the framework of their education system'.

The European Charter for Regional or Minority Languages of the Council of Europe

Finally, the ECRML of the COE should be analysed. First of all, certain typical features of the Charter should be highlighted. It is first and foremost remarkable that the Charter does not grant any rights to speakers of certain minority languages or to certain linguistic groups but is focused on the languages themselves and thus on a recognition, protection and promotion of multi-lingualism.[17] Second, certain general principles in article 7 aside, the contracting states can under certain minimum requirements choose their obligations *à la carte*.[18] For each subject matter the Charter contains several alternative state obligations ranging from very weak to rather strong ones. Each state can even determine for itself to what languages spoken in its territory the Charter will apply (article 2), thus taking the state discretion very far (Benoit-Rohmer 1998: 146).

The states ratifying the Charter then commit themselves (to a greater or lesser extent) to protect and promote the use of regional or minority languages in the domains of education (article 8), judicial authorities (article 9), administrative authorities and public services (article 10), access to media (article 11) and also in the domains of cultural, economic and social activities (articles 12 and 13).

It should in any event be pointed out that the Charter clearly aims in article 7 para. 2 at substantive equality since it underlines that 'positive measures aimed at bringing about greater equality between the users of regional or minority languages and the rest of the population are not to be considered as discriminatory against the majority' (Blair 1994: 58).

The actual contribution of the Charter to minority protection is of course modulated and balanced in view of its high flexibility as regards the content of state obligations. The Explanatory Report on the Charter reveals however that the states may not choose arbitrarily between these options but have to do so 'according to the situation of each language'. Arguably this would tend to entail that 'the larger the number of speakers of a certain language and the more homogenous the regional population, the stronger the option which should be adopted' (Blair 1994: 59–60).

Interim conclusion

The preceding analysis has revealed that minority rights undoubtedly contribute to minority protection in that they take up the essence and achievements of the individual human rights, while tailoring the ones of special relevance for minorities further to the specific position of minorities and the ensuing needs. In this way, minority rights in general and also those specifically dealing with language rights give further shape to the right to identity of minorities and interrelate with the category of individual human rights for the elaboration of an adequate system of minority protection. However, in several respects the current standards on minority rights are deficient and disappointing, which is mainly due to the extensive use of escape clauses and the weak formulations, leaving too much discretion to states.

Additional benefit of a qualified recognition of a right to internal self-determination for minorities

In this respect, a qualified recognition of a right to internal self-determination for minorities could further improve the accommodation of the population diversity in a state, could enhance the integration without assimilation of the distinctive minorities and could thus contribute to conflict prevention and/or conflict resolution. Here it should be pointed out that arguments, based on fundamental principles of international law concerning territorial integrity of states, do not have any force regarding forms of internal self-determination for population groups within existing states. Indeed, internal self-determination – unlike external self-determination – does not have any impact on territorial integrity of existing states as it is merely concerned with internal state structures and institutions.

There is ongoing controversy about the exact meaning of the concept 'people', especially as it concerns the right to external self-determination. There is arguably a tendency, however, to recognise a certain right to internal self-determination for minorities. The findings of the Arbitration Commission for Yugoslavia established by EU in 1991, more specifically in its second opinion of 11 January 1992 regarding the situation of the Serbian minorities in Croatia and Bosnia, confirms this. Although that minority would not have the right to secede and join Serbia, the Commission's reasoning reveals that the right to self-determination is not non-existent for the population group concerned. The Commission underscores that self-determination is not exclusively a principle of state creation but would be a fundamental and basic principle of state and more specifically designed to protect the separate (also linguistic) identities of the various population groups in a state by a certain status (Musgrave 1997: 170–1).

When looking at the actual practice, there have been several instances where states have granted certain forms of internal self-determination to their minorities, like forms of territorial autonomy, decentralisation, federalism or also personal autonomy (education as self-determined by a specific ethnic group). In so far as the concomitant measures of self-government include areas of linguistic policy, this obviously has potential to further the accommodation of linguistic population diversity in the states concerned.

Conclusion

The protection of language rights and hence the accommodation of linguistic population diversity is very meagre indeed at the level of individual human rights. While linguistic minority rights do enhance the level of this protection in a way which gives more body to the right to identity of the various linguistic groups in states, their actual contribution remains minimal and disappointing. The granting of a certain level of internal self-determination to the linguistic population groups concerned has significant potential to enhance the accommodation of linguistic population diversity.

Notes

1. For an explicit enumeration of the so-called 'essential components' of a definition of the concept 'minority' see *inter alia* Deschênes 1986: 289. For further elaboration of the concept 'minority' see Henrard 2000: chapter 1.
2. Human Rights Committee, General Comment 23, Article 27 (UN Doc. HRI\GEN\1\Rev.1 at 38), § 5.2; Human Rights Committee, General Comment 15, The Position of Aliens under the Covenant (UN Doc. HRI\GEN\1\Rev.1), § 7.
3. Cf. the book edited by Raikka which is constructed around the critical question 'Do We Need Minority Rights?', in J. Raikka (ed.), *Do we Need Minority Rights? Conceptual Issues*, The Hague, Martinus Nijhoff, 1996.
4. PCIJ, Advisory Opinion regarding Minority Schools in Albania, 6 April 1935, PCIJ Reports, Series A/\b No 64, 1935, 17; UN Sub-Commission on the Prevention of Discrimination and the Protection of Minorities, Report of its First Session, UN doc. E/CN.4/52/52, section V.
5. Section 6 of the 1996 Constitution of South Africa recognises 11 official languages: Afrikaans, English and nine of the indigenous African languages.
6. See *inter alia* Bideault v France, Eur. Comm. H. R., Application No 11261/84, 6 October 1986, *D.R. 48*, 234; K. v France, Eur. Comm. H. R., Application No 10210/82, 7 December 1983, *D.R. 35*, 207.
7. See *inter alia* Isop v Austria, Eur. Comm. H. R., Application No 808/60, 8 March 1962, *YB. Eur. Conv. 5*, 108; Kamasinski v Austria, Eur. Ct. H. R., 19 December 1989, *Series A no 168*. For an analogous decision of the Human Rights Committee in terms of article 14 ICCPR, see Dominique Guesdon v France, Communication No 219/1986, § 10.2.

8. Bideault v France, Eur. Comm. H. R., 232 (refusal to hear witnesses in a criminal case in the Breton Language).
9. Mathieu-Mohin and Clerfayet v Belgium, Eur. Ct. H. R., 2 March 1987, *Series A no 113*, § 52, 57.
10. Fryske Nasjonale Partij and Others v Netherlands, Eur. Comm. H. R., Application No 11100/84, 12 December 1985, 242.
11. Inhabitants of Alsemberg and Beersel v Belgium, Eur. Comm. H. R., Application No 1474/62, 26 July 1963, *YB. Eur. Conv. 6*, 342, 344.
12. See also Campbell and Cosans v UK, Eur. Ct. H. R., 25 February 1982, *Series A no 48*, § 33.
13. For an overview and explanation of the legal and constitutional regulations which were then in force, see Belgian Linguistics Case, Eur. Ct. H. R., 23 July 1968, *Series A no 6*, 6–19.
14. For an aspect of the Belgian regulation which is held to amount to a violation of the prohibition of discrimination, see Belgian Linguistics Case, Eur. Ct. H. R., 70.
15. Belgian Linguistics Case, Eur. Comm. H. R., *Series A no 6*, 48. For more criticisms on the judgement in the Belgian Linguistics Case, see Hillgruber and Jestaedt 1994: 28–31.
16. Explanatory Memorandum on the Framework Convention for the Protection of National Minorities, *H.R.L.J.* 1995, § 65.
17. The Definitions of article 1 clarify that the field of application of the Charter is limited to indigenous languages and thus excludes the languages of immigrants. Cf. Blair 1994: 57.
18. For a strong criticism as regards this flexible approach of the European Charter in that it leaves so much choice to the states, see De Varennes 1997: 156.

References

Benoit-Rohmer, F., 1996, *The Minority Question in Europe: Towards a Coherent System of Protection of National Minorities*, Strasbourg: International Institute for Democracy.

Benoit-Rohmer, 1998, 'Le Conseil de l' Europe et les Minorités Nationales', in *Minority Policy in Central and Eastern Europe: The Link between Domestic Policy, Foreign Policy and European Integration* (eds) K. Malfliet and R. Laenen. Leuven: KULeuven, 128–48.

Blair, P., 1994, *The Protection of Regional or Minority Languages in Europe*, Fribourg: Institut du Féderalisme.

Capotorti, F., 1991, *Study on the Rights of Persons belonging to Ethnic, Religious and Linguistic Minorities*, New York: United Nations.

Deschênes, J., 'Qu'est-ce qu' une Minorité?', *Les Cahiers de Droit* (1986), 255–91.

De Varennes, F., 1997, *Language, Minorities and Human Rights*, The Hague: Kluwer.

De Witte, B., 1992, 'Les Principes de l'Egalité et la Pluralité Linguistique', in *Les Minorités en Europe: Droits Linguistiques et Droits de l'Homme*, ed. H. Giordan. Paris: Kime, 55–62.

Gilbert, G., 1992, 'The Legal Protection accorded to Minority Groups in Europe', *Netherlands Yearbook of International Law*, 67–104.

Hannum, H., 1991, 'Contemporary Developments in the International Protection of the Rights of Minorities', *Notre Dame Law Review*, 1431–48.

Henrard, K., 2001, *Devising an Adequate System of Minority Protection: Individual Human Rights, Minority Rights and the Right to Self-determination*, The Hague: Kluwer.

Hillgruber, J. and Jestaedt, 1994, *The European Convention on Human Rights and the Protection of National Minorities*. Köln: Verlag Wissenschaft und Politik.

Musgrave, T. D., 1997, *Self-Determination and National Minorities*, Oxford: Clarendon Press.

Packer, J., 1996, 'On the Content of Minority Rights', in *Do we need Minority Rights: Conceptual Issues*, ed. J. Raikka. The Hague: Martinus Nijhoff, 121–78.

Ramaga, P. V., 1992, 'Relativity of the Minority Concept', *Human Rights Quarterly*, 104–19.

Rodley, N. S., 1995, 'Conceptual Problems in the Protection of Minorities: International Legal Developments', *Human Rights Quarterly*, 48–71.

Shaw, M. N., 1992, 'The Definition of Minorities in International Law', in *The Protection of Minorities and Human Rights* (eds) Y. Dinstein and M. Tabory. Dodrecht: Martinus Nijhoff, 1–31.

Schulte-Tenckhoff, I. and Ansbach, T., 1995, 'Les Minorités en Droit International', in *Le Droit et les Minorités* (eds) A. Fenet and G. Koubi. Brussels: Bruylant, 15–81.

Spiliopoulou-Akermark, 1997, *Justifications of Minority Protection in International Law*. London: Kluwer.

Symonides, J., 1995, 'The Legal Nature of Commitments Related to the Question of Minorities', in *New Forms of Discrimination*, ed. L. A. Sicilianos. Paris: A. Pedone, 197–216.

Tabory, M., 1980, 'Language Rights as Human Rights', *Israel Yearbook on Human Rights*, 167–223.

Thornberry, P., 1991, *International Law and the Rights of Minorities*, Oxford: Clarendon Press.

Thornberry, P., 1993, 'The UN Declaration on the Rights of Persons belonging to National or Ethnic, Religious and Linguistic Minorities: Background, Analysis and Observations', in *UN Declaration on Minorities* (eds) A. Phillips and A. Rosas. Turku: Institute for Human Rights, 101–38.

1998, The Oslo Recommendations regarding the Linguistic Rights of National Minorities and Explanatory Note, The Hague: Foundation of Inter-Ethnic Relations.

4

Facilitating or Generating Linguistic Diversity: The European Charter for Regional or Minority Languages

M. Nic Craith

Relevance

The European Charter for Regional or Minority Languages (ECRML) was drawn up by the Council of Europe (CoE), which is an entirely separate body from the European Union (EU). The CoE was established in 1949 in the aftermath of Second World War and its 44 member states (including the 15 EU members) are committed to principles of democracy and human rights. Some CoE states have applied for membership of the EU. For members such as Hungary, Malta or Iceland or those currently establishing themselves, such as the new Slav states of Central and Eastern Europe, participation in the CoE is especially significant as it offers international affirmation of their status and is evidence of their wish to be viewed as countries with liberal credentials (Mundy 1997: 70–1).

The origins of the ECRML can be traced to a public debate in 1984 on regional and minority languages at the Palais de l'Europe in Strasbourg. At that time the Standing Conference of Local and Regional Authorities of Europe established a Committee of Experts to draft a charter for Europe's regional and minority languages. Four years later the ECRML was adopted by the Standing Conference and was favourably received by the Parliamentary Assembly of the Council of Europe. In June 1992 the Minister's Deputies of the CoE gave the Charter the legal form of a Convention. This decision was not unanimous; Cyprus, France, Turkey and the United Kingdom abstained from the vote while Greece voted against it. The Charter required ratification by five member states of the CoE and officially came into force in March 1998.

Essentially there are two levels of adherence to the Charter. A signature commits a member state to principles of respect for regional languages as set out in the initial sections of the ECRML. Ratification of the Charter is a more intense undertaking, as it formally requires states to adopt certain measures for the promotion of designated languages in sectors such as education, justice, public service and the media. States signing the Charter are not obliged to immediately extend its terms of reference to all regional or minority languages within their boundaries. Instead they identify those to which it will apply initially and are free to extend the number of nominated languages at a later stage. To date 29 member states of the CoE have volunteered to sign this covenant. Table 4.1 shows the states that have confined themselves at the time of writing, to a signature of the Charter. Table 4.2 outlines those who have undertaken the greater commitment of ratification.

Analytical framework

In the context of international Charters, the ECRML is very unusual as it is the sole Charter designed specifically for languages rather than

Table 4.1   Member states of the CoE that have signed the ECRML

State	Date of signature
Azerbaijan	21 December 2001
Czech Republic	9 November 2000
France	7 May 1999
Iceland	7 May 1999
Italy	27 June 2000
Luxembourg	5 November 1992
Malta	5 November 1992
Moldova	11 July 2002
Romania	17 July 1995
Russia	10 May 2001
FYR of Macedonia	25 July 1996
Ukraine	2 May 1996

Table 4.2 Member states of the CoE that have signed and ratified the ECRML

State	Date of signature	Date of ratification	Date of entry into force
Armenia	11 May 2001	25 January 2002	1 May 2002
Austria	5 November 1992	28 June 2001	1 October 2001
Croatia	5 November 1997	5 November 1997	1 March 1998
Cyprus	12 November 1992	26 August 2002	1 December 2002
Denmark	5 November 1992	8 September 2000	1 January 2001
Finland	5 November 1992	9 November 1994	1 March 1998
Germany	5 November 1992	16 September 1998	1 January 1999
Hungary	5 November 1992	26 April 1995	1 March 1998
Liechtenstein	5 November 1992	18 November 1997	1 March 1998
Netherlands	5 November 1992	2 May 1996	1 March 1998
Norway	5 November 1992	10 November 1993	1 March 1998
Slovakia	20 February 2001	5 September 2001	1 January 2002
Slovenia	3 July 1997	4 October 2000	1 January 2001
Spain	5 November 1992	9 April 2001	1 August 2001
Sweden	9 February 2000	9 February 2000	1 June 2000
Switzerland	8 October 1993	23 December 1997	1 April 1998
United Kingdom	2 March 2000	27 March 2001	1 July 2001

individuals or groups (Ó Riagáin 2000: 68). In the past many covenants and agreements applied to the protection of minority groups. More recently, some international charters have placed special emphasis on individual rather than collective identities, but the ECRML does not refer to persons speaking languages or to minority language groups. Instead it is concerned with languages and is quite specific in its delineation of regional or minority languages. It pertains to languages that are spoken traditionally within a specific region of a nation-state by citizens of that state who form a minority group. It is only concerned with languages that are different from the official language(s) of a state.

Although the European Charter was quite specific in its intentions, it failed to define its terms of reference in any real sense and much of its terminology would benefit from further exploration. In the first instance the Charter claims to be 'European' but in this context one could ask where is 'Europe' or who is 'European'? The Charter refers solely to autochthonous languages and offers no protection to speakers of non-indigenous tongues in the territories of Europe. This implies, for example, that speakers of Cantonese in Northern Ireland or of Turkish in Germany or of Arabic in France cannot realistically expect protection from this international covenant.

Essentially this Charter excludes the languages of migrants and non-ethnic Europeans from its terms of reference, which ignores the real extent of linguistic and cultural diversity within the territories of Europe. There is much more to Europe than its ethnic Europeans. Africans began to settle there when they had completed their service for the Roman legions. Spain's culture has been strongly influenced by Moorish colonizers. Millions of non-Europeans contributed to the rebuilding of the continental economy after the two world wars in the twentieth century. Since then further millions have taken up the rights to settle in Europe (Mundy 1997). Yet the languages of these peoples are not included within the terms of reference of the ECRML. Instead it is aimed at languages spoken by nationals of a state in a particular territory and implies an essential link between culture, space and place. Unless a culture and an ethnic group can be identified with a specific region, they are rarely tolerated for any length of time, especially if the host nationality is itself under threat or seeking to extend itself. 'Europe's new ethnic minorities – Asian, African and Caribbean – are discovering the accuracy of this assertion' (Mundy 1997: 32)

This raises the question whether societies are required to accommodate and recognize all cultural differences and languages. It is generally accepted that it is not necessary to give parity of esteem to all groups that are different and issues of recognition appear to rest in the categorization of some cultural groups as more entitled to recognition than others. A typology of minorities has been constructed by several sociologists (cf. Eriksen 1993; Kymlicka 1995; Fenton 1999; May 2001). Such typologies usually prioritize proto-national and indigenous minorities in a state, which is the same strategy as that of the ECRML. Unlike national minorities, immigrant groups have not consistently demanded self-governing status within nation-states. While many seek political affirmation of their cultural significance, they do not necessarily aspire to self-determination. This is a factor, which can change over time, particularly in instances where such groups settle together and acquire self-governing power (Kymlicka 1995). For example, white settlers in Australia, Canada, the United States and New Zealand have clearly sought and acquired self-governing power, despite their original minority status.

Although the Charter was aimed at minority languages, it did not define the term 'minority'. This concept is complex (e.g. Packer 1996, 1999), and many international organizations have failed to clearly define it. This may be due to variations in understandings of the term not just from West to East, but also from region to region. Usually the concept is understood in a negative sense – as a collection of people who are culturally different from and numerically inferior to the majority, yet many of us are familiar with situations where very large numbers were considered a 'minority'. In the apartheid era in South Africa the ethnic population constituted the greater number, but was denied access to privileges and power. The principal characteristic of a minority is a lack of access to power, which has frequently (but not always) been denied on the basis of numerical and sometimes alleged 'cultural inferiority' (Minority Rights Group 1997).

The concept 'minority' can refer to shared characteristics within a group who have identified themselves as different or separate from the majority. In the case of languages, a minority language could be defined as that of 'a group of people who freely associate for an established purpose where their shared desire differs from that expressed by the majority rule' (Packer 1993: 45). The minority speaks a different language and has a relationship, which stimulates them to act together for a common cause. In these circumstances it is the limited number of speakers and/or their lack of access to power that generates the concept of 'minority language', but language minority would be a more accurate representation of the concept.

The Charter also failed to define the notion of 'language'. While 'language' may appear to be an obvious concept, which hardly requires any definition, this is far from accurate. It may well be the case that language is a political rather than a linguistic construct, which depends on the status of its speakers rather than the language itself. For example, Dutch is somewhat similar to Low German. Yet only the former is internationally recognized as an independent language reflecting the development of the Netherlands as a separate nation-state.

If the notion of 'language' is a political or cultural construct, this applies even more strongly to the concept of 'minority language'. In recent decades, anthropologists and sociolinguists have endeavoured to arrive at an alternative, more acceptable terminology for the non-official, non-national languages of Europe. Terms such as 'lesser-used', 'marginalized', 'minorized' and 'less widely-taught, less widely-used' languages have been used but they all imply some qualification of the concept of 'language'.

The difference between languages, minority languages and dialects is important politically as dialects are perceived to be 'more emotional than rational. They are viewed as detrimental to educational and professional success' (Broadbridge 2000: 59). In any social context there is greater prestige attached to languages than to dialects but very often there is little to distinguish between them. From a descriptive linguistic perspective, Piedmontese constitutes a language and is quite distinct from both French and Italian. Moreover, it has a long historical tradition of writing and grammatical study. Yet Tuscan rather than Piedmontese became the standard language of Italy, and the latter was relegated to the status of dialect (Billig 1995).

As in the case of other cultural concepts, groups frequently endeavour to confer legitimacy on their own speech form as a language rather than a dialect. This ideology is exemplified in the work of Boelens (1990: 8–9) who writes that 'Frisian is a language because this is what the Frisians want'. He further argues that 'if the Frisians neglect their language it will become a dialect. It is absolutely necessary that the Frisian language keeps up with the times and continues to develop, because otherwise it will be pushed aside by other stronger languages'. Similarly McClure (1997: 24) argues that speakers of Scots must not wait until they have 'proved' it to be a language. Instead they must persuade the Scottish people that Scots is a 'highly distinctive and expressive tongue, which is also the vehicle for a literature of great antiquity, merit and durability'.

Affirmations regarding the status of language or dialect do not necessarily refer to the grammatical structure and vocabulary of a speech form. Instead they are concerned with the symbolic status of the concept. When defining their tongue as a language rather than a dialect, speakers are conferring legitimacy not only on their medium of communication, but also on their own social role. This self-affirmed legitimacy is hardly satisfactory and speakers of such languages usually seek affirmation of their language at another level.

Data

The implementation of the Charter in several regions has provided this affirmation and boosted the status of many language minorities. This applies, for example, to Sater Frisian, which is spoken in the villages of Ramsloh, Scharrel and Strücklingen in the community of the Saterland in Cloppenburg, Germany. Several factors generated an increase in the numbers of Frisian speakers here. Of particular note was the inclusion of Frisian by the local authorities within the terms of reference of the ECRML. Speakers of Sater Frisian exceed 2,000 and their number is on the increase. Similarly, Scots speakers in Scotland have a new-found confidence as a result of the inclusion of their speech form by the British Government within the terms of reference of the Charter.

In some instances, minority languages have benefited inadvertently from the mere signature of the Charter. When France signed the ECRML in May 1999, it was assumed that six or seven regional languages such as Alsatian, Basque, Breton, Catalan, Corsican, Flemish and Occitan would benefit. This enthusiasm was subsequently undermined when France's Constitutional Council made it clear that it had no intention of actually ratifying the Charter. Several factors compounded the situation.

A report by Bernard Cerquiglini (1999) identified the '75 languages of France'. His list included non-indigenous languages such as

Arabic, which has developed its own French characteristics and Berber, which does not receive official protection in any county. Moreover Cerquiglini's report included disputed languages such as Gallo and Picard, which are more usually regarded as dialects of French. This was a highly controversial assertion as to claim the same status for Picard as for Breton or Catalan could be compared to asserting that Yorkshire English should have the same status as Welsh or Cornish. Such an argument could have significant financial repercussions for speakers of official regional languages as state funds could be diverted to contested languages. Cerquiglini concluded that all 75 languages – whether autochthonous, non-indigenous or contested came under the remit of the Charter (Judge and Judge 2000).

From the perspective of the French Government, the report was convenient as it provided an argument against the adoption of the Charter at that point in time. In the first instance, how could the Government justify meeting the terms of the Charter for some of the 75 languages and not others? Moreover, it was unethical to offer privileges to indigenous languages such as Breton or Catalan while failing to safeguard non-indigenous, and particularly non-European language groups within French boundaries, such as Arabic.

Further factors hindered the ratification of the Charter in France. The Council believed that the recognition of languages other than French in specific territories was contrary to the principles of the unity of the French people and the indivisibility of the Republic. This issue generated widespread debate concerning the potential threat of the Charter to the French Republic; reopening the question of centralization against regionalism: a replay of the Girondins against the Jacobins during the 1789 Revolution. Some expressed fears of the Charter as a political tool, which could destabilize the country and serve as the catalyst for movements for regional autonomy. Regional languages are frequently associated with nationalism or separatism. This applies to the examples of Irish in Northern Ireland or the Basque language in Spain (Kockel 1999).

In the case of France, the issue of equality was also raised. Those in favour of ratification of the Charter argued that regional differences should be recognized and individuals should be permitted to operate publicly in their mother tongue, even if that were not French. Those against the Charter argued that differences of language or race were a matter of private concern. If every individual had the right to speak French in public, then all were treated equally. These different interpretations of the notion of equality are prime examples of what Charles Taylor (1994) terms the politics of difference and universalism. In the former instance, equality is achieved when group differences are recognized. For the latter, equality implied uniformity and homogeneity.

At the time of writing, France is officially a monolingual country and has failed to ratify the Charter. Yet proponents of the ECRML feel that its signature has benefited language minorities in the country as the debate that surrounded this act gave these language groups a high profile in French public life. 'French is seen in a far less prescriptive manner than previously, and the minority languages are now seen as enriching and part of the national heritage – and therefore worthy of support' (Judge and Judge 2000: 127). Furthermore, tongues which were previously regarded as dialects of French such as Franc-Conntois and Lorrain, have now received some affirmation as languages in their own right. In this sense the Charter could be regarded as more than a facilitator of languages. It is also a catalyst for the re-definition of some dialects as language. Ulster-Scots in Northern Ireland is another case in point.

The case of Ulster-Scots

In the late 1970s and early 1980s, there was little public awareness of the speech form known as Ullans or Ulster-Scots. Adams (1977) referred to it simply as a variety of English spoken in particular regions of Ulster. Ian Adamson (1991: 78) classified Ullans as a version of English at this time stating that 'there are many parts of Ulster, therefore, where people are still bilingual in two varieties of the English language. They use Ulster Lallans while speaking among themselves and the approximation of the regional standard of Ulster English, in talking to strangers'. Native speakers usually refer to this speech form as 'Scotch' and it has also been termed 'Ullans' by some writers.

Speakers of Ulster-Scots are unionist rather than nationalist in perspective and are highly committed to maintaining Northern Ireland's relationship with the British monarchy. Its supporters tend to be ethnic rather than civic in approach and are generally found within the cultural wing of loyalism or the ethnic branch of unionism. These individuals live along the Antrim coastline and in residential regions congruent with what the Ulster Defence Association call 'the retainable homeland'; the territory that they define as theirs. It is also associated with some border regions in the northern county of Donegal in the Republic of Ireland. This speech form has strong symbolic import for those who speak it on a daily basis, but many non-speakers react with incredulity to its legitimacy as a distinct language.

Since the early nineties the people of Northern Ireland have become increasingly aware of the Ullans phenomenon and the construction of an Ulster-Scots ethnolinguistic identity. Several milestones occurred in the process (Montgomery 1999). In 1992 the Ulster-Scots Language Society was established with the specific intention of promoting the study, application and use of Ulster-Scots. The society's journal was inaugurated in the following year. *Ullans: The Magazine for Ulster-Scots* provides an outlet for the publication of literary and linguistic items. Essentially this constituted the reinvention of an Ulster-Scots print community and several novels in Ulster-Scots have since been issued (e.g. Robinson 1997, 1998).

In the past two decades Ulster-Scots has generated considerable debate in Northern Ireland. Much of the controversy relates to the question of whether Ulster-Scots is a language or a dialect. 'There are three options when it comes to Ulster Scots. Ulster Scots is language. Ulster Scots is a dialect. Ulster-Scots is nonsense. The option you choose has more to do with your politics than with your capacity for linguistic analysis' (Langan 2002: 39). Essentially the debate is political rather than linguistic and focuses on whether Ulster-Scots has independent status or is merely a dialect which is not suited to complex literary expressions.

As already noted with the examples of Frisian and Scots, a debate on the status of language occurs in other regions. For some speakers of Alsace, Alsatian is simply a variety of German and Alsatian speakers are a German-speaking minority in France. Although the relationship of Alsatian and Alemannic in general, to High German, is a matter of descriptive linguistics rather than perception, some perceive Alsatian to be a language in its own right and deny any kinship with High German. From this perspective, the Alsatian-speaking people are simply an Alsatian-speaking minority and not a German-speaking one (Broadbridge 2000: 48).

The lack of official statistics for Ulster-Scots and the ongoing dissension regarding its linguistic status make it difficult to justify as an official language in Northern Ireland. Many linguists believe that the syntax and vocabulary of Ulster-Scots are hardly sufficiently distinctive to justify conferring the status of a language on its current usage (cf. Görlach 2000; Kirk 2000; Nic Craith 2001). Many civic unionists appear ambivalent or even embarrassed in their response to the concept of an Ulster-Scots language. O'Connor (2002: 232) regards the financial and administrative support for Ulster-Scots in the 1998 Good Friday Agreement as laughable. 'Many Protestants, including some senior Unionists, are embarrassed by official approval for a recent invention which is supposed to be a vital part of their identity.' Langan (2002) has compared the position of Ulster-Scots to African American Vernacular English. African Americans who are disappointed with the 'false promises of equality through assimilation, are re-asserting African American "difference" through the promotion of African American Vernacular English'. As with Ulster-Scots, some African Americans such as the Rev. Jesse Jackson have called it 'garbage' while others celebrate it as an emblem of difference.

The disputed status of Ulster-Scots is a problematic issue, which is recognized by its speakers who complain that this speech form is frequently treated as socially stigmatized. They argue that the perception of Ulster-Scots as simply bad English undermines the self-confidence and self-esteem of individuals and groups who speak the language. Whether Ulster-Scots is a dialect or a language remains a controversial issue and the debate is hardly surprising, as speakers of English understand spoken Ullans easily. Although mutual intelligibility should not serve as a criterion in the language or dialect debate, the layman frequently uses it as such. Ulster-Scots speech does not appear significantly different from English and this lessens its effectiveness as a vehicle of exclusion.

When the British Government initially opted to sign the ECRML, it did not nominate Ulster-Scots for inclusion within the terms of reference of the document. Subsequently the Government commissioned research to help it decide how to treat this speech form. In consequence it affirmed that Ulster-Scots would be included within the ambit of the Charter. This recognized Ulster-Scots as the Scots language in Ulster and placed it on a par with Scots in Scotland. Speakers of Ulster-Scots have interpreted this inclusion as national affirmation of the status of language for Ulster-Scots. It represents considerable improvement from the Good Friday Agreement of 1998, which noted the importance of Ulster-Scots as an element of Northern Ireland's linguistic diversity but failed to acknowledge it specifically as a language.

There has been a strong reaction against this government recognition of Ulster-Scots as a language. Some commentators query the status of the ECRML and its associated body, the European Bureau for Lesser-Used Languages. Others remark that inclusion within the terms of reference of the Charter merely implies that Ulster-Scots is a dialect of Scots rather than English. Yet supporters of this speech form perceive the process as affirmation of their language. In this context the Charter may be generating 'new' languages and is possibly being used for a purpose beyond its original intentions. This has also applied in the case of France where disputed languages such as Gallo were given limited affirmation of the status of language rather than dialect.

Language and identity

Closely related to the affirmation of a language is the legitimization of the associated identity. 'Investment has been made in Ulster-Scots by some unionists for the return of a distinctive cultural identity' (McCall 2002: 205). Linguistic communities such as the Catalonians frequently think in terms of their 'own' language (Conversi 1990: 59). In Northern Ireland, the expression 'our own language' is often used in relation to Irish (Maguire 1991). Language is invoked as a medium through which individuals become aware of their own personalities and bear the impression of their own peculiar circumstances (Kedourie 1933: 56). To belong is to be with a people who understand your codes and 'speak your language' (Ignatieff 1994: 7).

For this reason the defence of a community language can become extremely emotive. Language can be as important, if not more important than territory or history for the generation of a sense of belonging. 'One can, of course, be understood in languages and in countries other than one's own; one can find belonging even in exile. But the nationalist claim is that full belonging, the warm sensation that people understand not merely what you say but what you mean, can only come when you are among your own people in your native land' (Ignatieff 1994: 7).

In the case of Northern Ireland, Ulster-Scots is promoted as primarily (and in some quarters exclusively) the language of those whose ancestors hailed from Scotland in the early seventeenth century. (A more contentious theory of ethnogenesis traces its origins in Ulster to a pre-Celtic tribe called the Cruthin.) The official recognition of the language through the ECRML is used to promote an Ulster-Scots identity. In this case the legitimization of the language has served to justify the existence of a new 'minority' in need of protection.

Several initiatives have reinforced the concept of an Ulster-Scots identity in Northern Ireland. In 1995 an Ulster-Scots Heritage Council was established. Essentially this is an umbrella organization for five cultural and historic groups. An academic conference sponsored by the Cultural Traditions Group was held at the Queen's University in Belfast. This event explored varieties of Scottishness in Northern Ireland (Erskine and Lucy 1997). In May 1999, Belfast celebrated its first Ulster-Scots festival. The promotional leaflet explained that the festival was intended to give participants an insight into the cultural traditions of the Ulster-Scots. Cultural festivals have become increasingly common throughout Northern Ireland and an annual Autumn festival in Derry/Londonderry incorporates a strong Ulster-Scots dimension.

But the revival of Ullans has also generated tensions within the Ulster-Scots community, between those who focus on the language issue and those who wish to develop an Ulster-Scots cultural space. Some proponents of Ulster-Scots view these tensions in terms of a class divide. Whereas intellectuals and academics focus on the recognition of Ulster-Scots as a language, those from a working-class background are more interested in emphasizing the social aspects of Ulster-Scots identity with a particular focus on culture, music and dance.

An interesting aspect of the Ulster-Scots phenomenon is the relationship it affirms between language, community and boundary. In this instance the quest for legitimate status for a disputed language is generating a community boundary but the speakers of Ulster-Scots are not seeking to establish a new imagined community and do not avail of a discourse of de-colonization. Instead they speak of cultural capital. While they are different, they are decidedly British. The use of Ulster-Scots affirms their imagined community with speakers of Scots in Scotland although the linguistic relationship between Scots and Ulster-Scots is as yet undefined. Some proponents of Ulster-Scots are operating from a defensive position and are culturally asserting the legitimacy of the British claim to Northern Ireland. Their appeal in this instance is to the wider imagined community of the United Kingdom.

In the case of Ulster-Scots, a speech form is being used to construct an appreciation of a distinct tradition with a strong sense of difference. This has applied to many other minority languages. Franco regarded Basque culture and especially the Basque language as such a strong maker of difference that it had to be suppressed. For this reason Franco's regime operated a vigorous campaign of cultural repression. The populace was forbidden to speak in Basque or to greet one another in the language. Basque names, publications and the teaching of the language were forbidden during the era of Franco's dictatorship (Heiberg 1989: 90). Similarly the Breton language is regarded as a signifier of difference in Brittany. The use of the language defines 'insiders' and 'outsiders'. In this instance as in many others the revival of the minority language and the revitalization of the language community is perceived as a political rather than a linguistic strategy (McDonald 1989).

McCall (2002) has compared proponents of the Ulster-Scots movement with their European counterparts in their approach to generating community consciousness. The Ulster-Scots movement has a plethora of Northern Ireland, Ulster and Loyalist flags. It has also appropriated national symbols such as Cúchulainn and developed a mythical history of the Cruthin (cf. Nic Craith 2002). The Europe Day and the traditional celebration of Ulster-Scots Burns night with a supper of haggis, tatties and neaps constitute 'contrasting contemporary social gatherings where ingested cosmopolitanism and ingested ethnicity, enjoyment and a "feel-good" factor make people more amenable to a European consciousness and an Ulster-Scots consciousness respectively' (McCall 2002: 208).

Conclusion

European initiatives designed simply to facilitate linguistic diversity in Europe have acquired a new potential. For many regions the ECRML is an opportunity to legitimate new languages that have previously been ignored by the nation-state. These regions are frequently differentiated by language from the host nation of which they are a part and their participation in the nation-state is frequently a result of conquest rather than integration. The cultural identity which persists defines them as different and marks out a distinctive territory. Suddenly the nation-state is no longer the inevitable structure within which they have to operate.

Inclusion within the terms of reference of the ECRML is perceived as an endorsement of linguistic status from the CoE – although national committees have a significant role in the process of affirmation. Changing forces in the process of legitimization for languages reflect a shift of definitional factors in other spheres and a new mechanism for the affirmation of linguistic status has been identified. In consequence nation-states may be compelled to concede legitimacy to tongues they may prefer to view as dialects. In this context, the ECRML is serving as a catalyst for 'new' languages, although this role is still confined to autochthonous, rather than non-indigenous languages in Europe.

References

Adams, G. B., 1977, 'The Dialects of Ulster' in *The English Language in Ireland*, ed. D. Ó Muirithe. Dublin and Cork: Mercier Press, 56–70.

Adamson, I., 1991, *The Identity of Ulster: The Land, The Language and the People*. Bangor: Pretani Press.

Billig, M., 1995, *Banal Nationalism*. London: Sage.

Boelens, K., 1990, *The Frisian Language*. Leeuwarden: Provincial Government of Friesland.

Broadbridge, J., 2000, 'The Ethnolinguistic Vitality of Alsatian-speakers in Southern Alsace' in *German Minorities in Europe: Ethnic Identity and Cultural Belonging*, ed. S. Wolff. Oxford and New York: Berghahn, 47–62.

Cerquiglini, B., 1999, *Les Langues de la France: Rapport au Ministre de l'Education Nationale, de la Recherche et de la Technologie, et à la Ministre de la Culture et de la Communication*. Paris: l'Institut National de la Langue Française.

Conversi, D., 1990, 'Language or Race?' *Ethnic and Racial Studies*, 13(1), 50–70.

Eriksen, T., 1993, *Ethnicity and Nationalism: Anthropological Perspectives*. London: Pluto.

Erskine, J. and Lucy, G., 1997, *Cultural Traditions in Northern Ireland: Varieties of Scottishness*. Belfast: Institute of Irish Studies.

Fenton, S., 1999, *Ethnicity: Racism, Class, Culture*. Basingstoke: Macmillan.

Görlach, M., 2000, 'Ulster Scots: A Language?' in *Language and Politics: Northern Ireland, the Republic of Ireland, and Scotland* (eds) J. Kirk and D. Ó Baoill. Belfast: Queen's University Press, 13–31.

Heiberg, M., 1989, *The Making of the Basque Nation*. Cambridge: Cambridge University Press.

Ignatieff, M., 1994, *Blood and Belonging: Journeys into the New Nationalism*. London: Vintage.

Judge, A. and Judge, S., 2000, 'Linguistic Policies in France and Contemporary Issues: The Signing of the Charter for Regional or Minority Languages', *International Journal of Francophone Studies*, 3(2): 106–27.

Kedourie, E., 1933, *Nationalism*. Oxford: University Press.

Kirk, J., 2000, 'Two Ullans Texts' in *Language and Politics: Northern Ireland, the Republic of Ireland, and Scotland* (eds) J. Kirk and D. Ó Baoill. Belfast: Queen's University Press, 33–44.

Kockel, U., 1999, *Borderline Cases: The Ethnic Frontiers of European Integration*. Liverpool: University Press.

Kymlicka, W., 1995, *Multicultural Citizenship*. Oxford: Oxford University Press.

Langan, A., 2002, 'Heim Swate Heim': The Future of Ulster Scots is Dependent on Power, not Language', *Magill*, July: 39.

Maguire, G., 1991, *Our Own Language: An Irish Initiative*. Clevedon, Philadelphia, Adelaide: Multilingual Matters.

May, S., 2001, *Language and Minority Rights: Ethnicity, Nationalism and the Politics of Language*. Essex: Pearson Education Ltd.

McCall, C., 2002, 'Political Transformation and the Reinvention of the Ulster-Scots Identity and Culture', *Identities: Global Studies in Culture and Power*, 9, 197–218.

McClure, D., 1997, *Why Scots Matters*. Edinburgh: The Saltire Society.

McDonald, M., 1989, *'We are not French!' Language, Culture and Identity in Brittany*. London and New York: Routledge.

Minority Rights Group, 1997, *World Directory of Minorities*. London: Minority Rights Group.

Montgomery, M., 1999, 'The Position of Ulster Scots', *Ulster Folklife*, 45, 86–107.

Mundy, S., 1997, *Making it Home: Europe and the Politics of Culture*. Amsterdam: European Cultural Foundation.

Nic Craith, M., 2001, 'Politicised Linguistic Consciousness: The Case of Ulster Scots', *Nations and Nationalism*, 7(1), 21–37.

Nic Craith, M., 2002, *Plural Identities: Singular Narratives: The Case of Northern Ireland*. New York, Oxford: Berghahn.

O'Connor, F., 2002, *Breaking the Bonds: Making Peace in Northern Ireland*. Edinburgh and London: Mainstream Publishing.

Ó Riagáin, D., 2000, 'Language Rights as Human Rights in Europe and in Northern Ireland' in *Language and Politics: Northern Ireland, the Republic of Ireland, and Scotland* (eds) J. Kirk and D. Ó Baoill. Belfast: Queen's University Press, 65–73.

Packer, J., 1993, 'On the Definition of Minorities' in *The Protection of Ethnic and Linguistic Minorities in Europe* (eds) J. Packer and K. Myntti. Åbo: Institute for Human Rights, Åbo Akademi University, 23–65.

Packer, J., 1996, 'On the Content of Minority Rights' in *Do We Need Minority Rights?*, ed. J. Räikkä. Amsterdam: Kluwer Law International, 121–78.

Packer, J., 1999, 'Problems in Defining Minorities' in *Minority and Group Rights in the New Millennium* (eds) D. Fottrell and B. Bowring. Amsterdam, Kluwer Law International, 223–74.

Robinson, P., 1997, *Esther, Queen o tha Ulidian Pechts*. Belfast: Ullans Press.
Robinson, P., 1998, *Wake the Tribe O'Dan*. Belfast: Ullans Press.
Taylor, C., 1994, 'The Politics of Recognition', in *Multiculturalism: Examining the Politics of Recognition*, ed. C. Taylor. Princeton: Princeton University Press, 25–73.

5
The Practitioner's Perspective: Minority Languages and Linguistic Minorities in the Work of the OSCE High Commissioner on National Minorities

*John Packer**

Introduction

Since the end of the Cold War, especially in Central and Eastern Europe following the collapse of the Communist bloc, Europe has experienced the revival of nationalism. Typically, language has been one of the primary markers of ethnicity and a (or the) defining characteristic of the nation. As a consequence, language and language policy have been key areas in which contested ethnic identities have sought to assert or re-assert their status: official and/or state languages have been (re)established, their knowledge made a requirement for the conferral of citizenship rights and for access to public services, and education and public administration have been reformed in large part along linguistic lines. These developments have often had significant consequences for persons belonging to linguistic minorities (Wilson 2002; Bíró and Kovács 2001).

It is, therefore, not surprising that language and its regulation has become a topic of international relations and law as it constitutes a driving force behind many ethnic disputes and conflicts between majorities and minorities across Europe – from the Baltic to the Balkans, from Central Europe to the Caucasus and beyond. These conflicts, and their root causes, have been a major security concern for the international community, which in turn has tried to play an active role in addressing their sources, especially through the development and application of standards and through mediation. In this respect, the High Commissioner on National Minorities (HCNM) of the Organisation for Security and Cooperation in Europe (OSCE) has played a particular role. By analysing the work of the HCNM in relation to minority languages[1] and linguistic minorities,[2] this chapter seeks to complement other contributions by providing insights into the real experiences and practicalities of an external actor's involvement in trying to secure conditions conducive to the preservation and free use of minority languages and for the equality of persons belonging to linguistic minorities. Given the nature of the institution of the HCNM, the specific experience through the first 10 years of work has been gained predominantly in the countries of Central and Eastern Europe, but is nonetheless valuable for policy- and law-makers throughout the OSCE and beyond.

The OSCE and the HCNM: a brief overview of origins, procedures and mandates

It is important to understand the role and work of the HCNM in the context of the OSCE as essentially a *security* organisation. Possessing no military assets (unlike NATO), the OSCE may be characterized as 'soft' insofar as it is largely diplomatic in nature. Originating in the Conference on Security and Cooperation in Europe (CSCE) as a Cold War inter-governmental diplomatic conference aimed at finding some common ground between the then two opposing defence alliances (NATO and Warsaw Pact) and their main super-power protagonists (the United States and the USSR), the OSCE is a fully pan-European and North Atlantic organisation enjoying the participation of all European states together with Canada and the United states. The initial conference of 35 participating states was held in Geneva and Helsinki in the period 1972–75 concluding with a summit of Heads of State and Government in Helsinki where the Final Act of Helsinki[3] was signed on 1 August 1975 (Bloed 1993, 1997; Ghebali 1996; Bothe et al. 1997; Cohen 1999).

Forming the basis of an ongoing conference which survived the Cold War were and remain two principal OSCE theses: 'comprehensive security' and 'cooperative security'. Having divided the broad areas of their interest into three 'baskets' concerning (1) security questions (meaning mainly military matters); (2) economic cooperation and environmental concerns and (3) 'human contacts, information and human rights' (later known as 'the human dimension'), the participating states agreed to the *Final Act* on the basis of consensus (underlining each state's strict sovereign equality). The essence of the two theses and the resultant accord is, first, that there is an intimate interrelation and dependency among the three baskets/dimensions such that there is no security in the absence of attention to each and all of the three areas of concern. Closely connected to the first thesis is the second, that is, that there is no security for any one participating state in the absence of security for all, and so each and all are committed to cooperate in the mutual interest of their own security.

Despite an ongoing series of meetings between 1975 and 1989, only when the Cold War neared its end was it possible to make substantial progress on the Human Dimension. This occurred in the course of three meetings on the human dimension held in Paris (1989), Copenhagen (1990) and Moscow (1991). At the Copenhagen meeting in June 1990, agreement was reached on a much expanded catalogue of human rights standards, including notably a long list of standards concerning persons belonging to minorities which, until then, was by far the most substantial and progressive text in this field ever adopted at the multilateral level (Buergenthal 1990). Soon thereafter in November 1990 the participating states felt confident enough to hold their second summit of Heads of State and Government at which they signed the Charter of Paris for a New Europe, thereby committing themselves to base their societies on the twin principles of (1) democratic legitimacy of authority and (2) market economy. In that same period and soon thereafter, the Communist regimes of Central and Eastern Europe collapsed and the Soviet Union itself dissolved.

The euphoria of 1990 was also followed by the shock of the bloody collapse and dissolution of the former Yugoslavia. It soon became clear that a declared commitment (however sincere) to democracy and the free market did not mean an easy transition, nor did it ensure peace and security. In response, the OSCE decided at its second Helsinki Summit in July 1992 to establish the HCNM, giving him the mandate to 'provide "early warning" and, as appropriate, "early action" at the earliest possible stage in regard to tensions involving national minority issues which have not yet developed beyond an early warning stage, but, in the judgement of the High

Commissioner, have the potential to develop into a conflict in the CSCE area, affecting peace, stability or relations between participating states'. It is notable that the HCNM was created as an instrument of the *security* basket, that is, not as a mechanism of the human dimension, with a view to preventing possible armed conflict. Importantly, the mandate limits the HCNM's possible involvements: he is only to address situations which have the propensity to erupt into international armed conflict or cause instability affecting relations between states; he is not to consider violations of C/OSCE commitments with regard to an individual person; and he is precluded from considering national minority issues in situations involving 'organised acts of terrorism'.

Through more than 10 years of work, the HCNM has developed a specific approach interpreting the mandate in a proactive manner as befits the aim and tasks of conflict prevention (Kemp 2001; Holt 2003). Fundamentally, the HCNM pursues a problem-solving approach in addressing the root causes of disputes and tensions which threaten to worsen. By means of quiet diplomacy, mainly conducted through confidential meetings at the highest levels of government and with community leaders, the HCNM is able to ascertain true positions and act without the glare of media attention to persuade parties to come to understandings and find arrangements which diminish, if not resolve, their disputes.

Minority languages, linguistic minorities and the HCNM

Issues relating to the use of language have been a principal focus, if not the dominant concern, of the work of the HCNM. This may be due to the fact that Europe is in large measure composed of essentially linguistically defined nations around which modern states were formed. Indeed, the nation-building – or, more accurately, nation-state-building – projects of the last part of the twentieth Century reasserted the geopolitical significance of language. In parallel to this development was the dissolution of old regimes (notably the Soviet Union and the former Yugoslavia) in which one language had dominated, to be replaced within independent states by (often very) different national languages. This language inversion almost overnight altered drastically the social, economic and political relations among linguistic groups. Since no social order is neutral in terms of language in contexts of different linguistic groups living together, the effect of such a sudden language inversion was to advantage substantially some and equally to disadvantage substantially others. Typically, the majority's language was designated the 'state' or 'official language' prescribed by law for (often exclusive) use in public affairs and sometimes important domains beyond. In these historical circumstances, disputes arose and tensions grew – sometimes with the considerable express interest of neighbouring 'kin-states'.[4]

Evidently language has mattered in terms of internal and external peace and stability. Experience shows that disputes over language issues are real, often intense and sometimes violent. This appears to follow from the fundamental nature and important functions of language. There are at least two fundamental aspects to language: (1) the primordial, which largely defines the identity of many (national) groups; and (2) the instrumental, which is required to organize modern society. In both cases, language has a tremendous mobilizing capacity which has been activated by numerous politicians – with and without scruples. As such, there has emerged a clear need to address and resolve generally and early the underlying issues.

In fulfillment of his mandate, the HCNM has addressed issues of minority languages and linguistic minorities in a number of situations and ways. So far, little has been written about the HCNM either in general or in relation to specific issues. Nonetheless, the fact is that the HCNM has addressed issues relating to minority languages and linguistic minorities in a consistent manner since he first took up his mandate in 1993 (Packer 1999b, 2001; Holt and Packer 2001; Zaagman 1999). Rather than recounting all those instances, which would exceed the aim and nature of this book, it should suffice to summarize the work the HCNM has been doing through the tools he has developed and the issues he has addressed.

Certainly, the primordial issue of (linguistic) identity has been often at the root of disputes, that is, the equal right of each person to determine, maintain and develop his or her (linguistic) identity free from prescription or coercion. This strikes at the heart of human dignity. It concerns self-esteem. It raises questions relating to the status and use of language, the status and use of names, symbolism; and so on. It also relates to interests in citizenship, political participation, employment, education, culture and other primary fields of life – interests which people typically do not surrender easily. It is certainly the case for persons whose mother tongue is not the main or official language of the state; in the European Union (EU) alone an estimated 40–50 million citizens speak a language other than the main official language of the state of which they are citizens.

No less common have been the disputes revolving around the instrumental function of language as minorities (and sometimes majorities) have faced linguistic barriers – or sometimes sought to erect them. This strikes at equality. It concerns the distribution of goods within the state and material well-being. It raises some of the same questions as indicated earlier, but also relates to interests in public services, social services, commerce and trade.

Importantly, the HCNM has analysed, evaluated and acted in various situations always on the basis of reference to existing international standards, to which he has also made a significant contribution (see Henrard, this volume). The HCNM bases himself on these existing international standards and then works within their parameters to encourage policy developments contributing to conflict prevention through a range of specifically developed tools.

The Tools of the HCNM

The mandate of the HCNM does not prescribe the tools by which he is to work, although it does set out some of the parameters and entitlements as required for quiet diplomacy such as access to persons including governmental officials at the highest level. From this, it would appear the mandate foresaw dialogue as the principle tool of the HCNM. But to advance the effectiveness of such dialogue, the first HCNM developed a number of additional tools. These include: (1) public pronouncements; (2) formal recommendations in specific situations; (3) general recommendations; (4) public research reporting and (5) projects. In all cases language issues have featured prominently.

Public pronouncements

By invitation and his own initiative, the HCNM has given numerous speeches through which he has projected a general orientation to liberal accommodations of the linguistic plurality existing in any state. This has often been expressed as a strong preference for (indeed a duty of) integration as opposed to assimilation. The essence of the message is the view that linguistic pluralism should be treated as a material asset, a source of cultural richness and a central feature of European identity, rather than as a costly liability, a cultural dilution and threat. In policy terms, this message means to find the effective balance between preserving everyone's linguistic identity and ensuring the functionality of the state for reasons of the common good. Practically, this implies a policy of support for bilingualism at least for minorities. As the HCNM has showed, this is not only conceptually possible, it is also practically attainable without great intellectual effort or material cost. Indeed, numerous existing examples show that it is relatively easy to design and not so costly, but often a good investment in economic terms.

Formal recommendations in specific situations

Aside from the views he shares and advice he offers in the course of the confidential oral dialogues he conducts in various situations, the HCNM has established the practice of exchanging formally with Governments letters of specific recommendations in concrete situations.[5] Typically, these written exchanges eventually become public following some period for subsequent direct follow-up contacts, for domestic steps to be taken, and not before circulation and consideration behind the closed doors of the OSCE Permanent Council which meets in Vienna each week. This tool has become a principal element of the HCNM's method and is now an established practice having never been contested by a participating state. It is also to be noted that these formal written exchanges are only one part of the HCNM's dialogue which normally follows considerable direct personal contacts in the form of visits, telephone conversations and other types of communication. Moreover, there are other written exchanges which may include specific recommendations but are not intended to be made public.

The great majority of the HCNM's recommendations have had some relation to language. For example, the HCNM has addressed letters to the Romanian Government concerning educational matters including access to tertiary education in the mother tongue of large minorities and the language of instruction of certain subjects in schools. Educational matters were also addressed in exchanges with the Slovak Government, specifically regarding efforts by a Slovak nationalist party to interfere with the right and opportunity of speakers of minority languages (in particular Hungarians) to receive instruction in their mother tongue, and the desire of ethnic Hungarians to have their children attending Hungarian-language schools receive their school certificates also in the Hungarian language, that is, to receive at least bilingual certificates (as was the practice) rather than unilingual Slovak-language certificates (insofar as Slovak is the only state language). Other issues raised with the Slovak Government included: the use of minority languages in official communications with state bodies, agencies and services; the extent of cultural subsidies available to minorities (including for minority language publications and productions); and the general regulation of language use in the state (i.e. the effects of, and relationship between, regulation of the Slovak language as the only state language and protection of minority languages). The HCNM has also had numerous exchanges with the Estonian and Latvian Governments focused on concerns about especially their Laws on Citizenship and naturalization procedures in relation to the persistent problem of the huge number of stateless persons in these countries, specifically easing language requirements and enhancing opportunities to learn the state languages. One seemingly minor issue which gained major importance was the focus of an appeal by the HCNM to the President of Estonia (and later to the Government of Latvia): the HCNM addressed the issue of linguistic requirements to stand for elected office which evidently impeded the accessibility of persons belonging to linguistic minorities and limited the choice of the electorate. In this connection, it may be noted that a different, but related, issue regarding elections was raised with the Slovak Government which sought to fix electoral representation along ethnic lines which, in fact, reflected a linguistic nationalism whereby ethnicity was largely to be indicated by language. Many more examples could be given.

While the arguments made in the exchanges of letters are to be evaluated on their own merits, some further comments are warranted. First, it is apparent from the tone of the letters that the exchanges have been typically diplomatic – assistance-orientated on the part of the HCNM and generally cooperative on the part of the Governments. A notable exception on the part of a Government was the rather curt responses from the Slovak Minister for Foreign Affairs under the Meciar Government expressing limited interest in or patience for a serious dialogue and, moreover, its basic disregard for international standards or the concerns of minorities. Previous to the current Government coming to power, there was a similar experience with Turkey. Indeed, the marked difference in tone and depth between the responses from the Meciar Government and its successor under Prime Minister Mikulas Dzurinda (who succeeded Meciar in October 1998) is palpable. It was further reflected in immediate positive steps taken by the Dzurinda Government (which includes an ethnic Hungarian coalition party). In the exchange with the President of Estonia mentioned earlier, the Estonian President responded to the HCNM in a polite but in effect dismissive tone as the President had already acted contrary to the HCNM's specific recommendation.

The HCNM's exchanges of letters also reveal his attention to practical concerns such as financing, his specifically preventive action (e.g. to stop adoption of damaging legislation), his attention to political timing (e.g. the possible effect of a parliamentary programme on elections), and his effort to promote the further applicability of international law (e.g. his encouragement of Slovakia to accede to the *European Charter for Regional or Minority Languages* and Latvia to ratify the *Framework Convention for the Protection of National Minorities*).

Overall, the HCNM's exchanges of letters must be read in the wider context of then ongoing dialogues (sometimes expressly mentioned in the letters) and the importance of events (usually ongoing and evolving). Notwithstanding the availability of not always accurate press reports, the full stories have yet to be told, including the sometimes important interests and actions of third and fourth parties. In sum, however, the HCNM's exchanges of letters clearly indicate his practical, problem-solving, assistance-orientated approach as he raises issues and makes specific recommendations argued with precision and clarity. The exchanges also highlight the critical function of law (whether 'hard' or 'soft law') as the HCNM applies the standards voluntarily accepted by the state in question and sometimes interprets them in an effort to find solutions for specific issues.

General recommendations

Aside from the HCNM's recommendations regarding specific issues in the particular situations of individual states, the HCNM has tried to fill the need for guidelines accessible to policy- and law-makers vis-à-vis recurrent issues especially in the field of use of language. In this connection, the HCNM invited a group of internationally recognized independent experts to elaborate a set of general recommendations, for use in all OSCE participating states and beyond, which resulted in the *Oslo Recommendations Regarding the Linguistic Rights of National Minorities* published in February 1998. The HCNM's initiative drew on the previous positive experience he had with another group of independent experts which resulted in *The Hague Recommendations Regarding the Education Rights of National Minorities*. Since the story of the elaboration of the Oslo Recommendations, together with some analysis, appears elsewhere (Packer and Siemienski 1999), only a few comments are warranted here. In particular, it is to be observed that the current era of transitional democracies and economies features societies and governments adopting new regimes where key notions, such as the distinction between the 'private sphere' and the 'public sphere' (as addressed in Recommendation 12 of the Oslo Recommendations), raise complex and difficult issues such as the legitimacy of purported public interests and, to the extent these may be established, their restriction proportionate to the aim sought. Indeed, these issues are still in the process of being fully worked out in the 'old' democracies. They are of added importance in situations of inter-ethnic tension amid fragile democratic institutions (including still weak judiciaries) such that regional peace and stability require resolution of these issues on an urgent basis.

There are intense specific disputes over the role of linguistic proficiency requirements affecting access to employment, or language requirements in the media (both public and private), not to mention the highly problematical question of the actual supervision and implementation of such requirements (i.e. to what extent and by what means may such requirements be imposed, and with what implications for, *inter alia*, the freedom of expression and the right to privacy?). Such issues test the meaning and limits of 'freedom' and challenge policy- and law-makers to find accommodations which respect both legitimate public interests and prerogatives on the one hand and the protection of human rights, including minority rights, on the other hand. Certainly, it is clear that the majority may not claim everything is 'public' which simply coincides with majoritarian interests or identity. The Oslo Recommendations aim, therefore, to assist states in finding appropriate accommodations consistent with existing international standards. Fully endorsed by the HCNM and available in several languages, they have been circulated widely, have been the subject of seminars organized by the HCNM, have been discussed in the OSCE Permanent Council and at the 1999 OSCE Summit meeting in Istanbul, and have generally become a reference at least among OSCE participating states. There remains enormous scope to employ the Oslo Recommendations as a useful tool in various situations.

In addition to the Oslo Recommendations which address issues of language use in most domains (Eide 1999) except education (which is addressed in the already noted Hague Recommendations), two other sets of recommendations should be read and used in conjunction. These are the *Lund Recommendations on the Effective Participation of National Minorities in Public Life* and the *Guidelines to Assist National Minority Participation in the Electoral Process*. Participation of minorities in public life (in particular *vis-à-vis* matters which affect them especially), including in the electoral process, can and do bear upon language issues.

Public research reporting

Ó Riagáin and Nic Shuibhne (1997: 21–2) have observed that so far 'scholarly debate over human rights has been dominated by normative theorists' and that '[l]ess work has been done in the area of assessing the operation of language rights legislation in practice', in particular that there is '[v]ery little research address[ing] the feasibility of official status, or assess[ing] the optimum means of state intervention'. It was precisely because of the paucity of such research and available synthetic references that the HCNM undertook to survey the existing state practice in the OSCE area. While the results reflect only the official government responses (which reveal a considerable disparity in reporting and may well be challenged in terms of the veracity of certain claims and also effectiveness at the point of implementation), nonetheless the HCNM's survey is the first published compilation of at least what governments claim to be the case within their jurisdictions. The full texts of the replies are also publicly available, and form an Annex to the HCNM's report.

On the basis of this survey, and with reference only to the standards, the HCNM published a Report on the Linguistic Rights of

National Minorities in the OSCE Area as an analytical summary of the responses received from 51 of the 53 states surveyed.[6] With a questionnaire containing nine questions being sent out in mid-December 1996, responses were mainly received in the course of 1997 and 1998, indicating law and practices to the varying dates of submission. On request of the HCNM, analysis of the responses was made initially by Professor Steven Ratner of the University Texas School of Law (then working with the Office of the HCNM as Fulbright Senior Scholar in OSCE Studies) by grouping them not only according to the questions asked, but from the perspective of relevant international standards. In so doing, the HCNM intended both to indicate the range of existing practices and also to suggest which options or implied 'best' practices met or surpassed minimum international standards – and, by implication, which fell short. In this way, it was hoped that OSCE participating states would see that virtually all states in fact address (one way or another, and to varying degrees) the issues surveyed and could draw upon the range of practices in developing or reforming their own policy, law and practice to the benefit of their populations and regional peace and stability.

In the course of 1999, the HCNM conducted a second survey of state practice focusing on those countries with significant populations of Roma, Sinti, Travellers and Gypsies. A different approach was taken in this case, with visits made to a number of countries by an independent scholar, Prof. Diane Orentlicher of the American University in Washington D.C., who was then attached to the Office of the HCNM. On the basis of this policy-orientated research, the HCNM published in April 2000 a Report on the Situation of Roma and Sinti in the OSCE Area. While language was neither a principle subject of research nor features as a separate topic within the report, it is clear that language appears as a subtext throughout the report. Indeed, not only does it relate significantly to issues of identity and equality, but it raises particularly challenging questions in terms of language development and accommodation.

In both cases of the HCNM's published reports, a number of objectives were pursued. In particular, the reports sought to inform OSCE participating states of which practices (good and bad) exist, what solutions are possible, what standards apply and (by implication) how balance and progress can be achieved. This should result in fewer excuses from governments and, in the end, better policies, laws and practices.

Projects

Over the years the HCNM has increasingly turned to specific project activities to achieve forward movement in various situations. Very many of these have to do with issues of language. A few representative examples should suffice here. In the first place was the organization of both *ad hoc* and standing dialogues around minorities and their concerns. Thus, in several situations the HCNM has organized seminars of policy and lawmakers aimed at policy development and legislative reform. Dedicated institutions and bodies have also been established or encouraged, such as minority councils of offices in the ministries of education. In this last field, the HCNM has supported the teaching of the state language to students belonging to linguistic minorities, for example, in Moldova and the Former Yugoslav Republic of Macedonia (fYROM). The HCNM has also established or reformed minority higher language education in Macedonia and Romania. Currently, the HCNM is conducting research into social integration in Estonia and Latvia and developing a practitioners' manual for State Language Inspectors in Latvia. A study has also been commissioned of comparative law and practice relating to the use of minority languages in the broadcast media.

Issues addressed

While the roots of disputes and the particular historic circumstances may differ, the status of the mother tongue and the regulation of the use of language are particularly contentious elements that tend to polarize parties like no other. As indicated earlier, linguistic identity has both primordial and instrumental aspects. These have arisen in the work of the HCNM through a variety of issues which, in a non-exhaustive way, may be grouped as follows.

Integrating diversity

It is the task of the democratic state to provide the framework within which each individual can be free to maintain and develop his or her identity pursuant to a social contract which both legitimizes and sustains the state in that same task for the benefit of others. In doing so the state has a responsibility to ensure an even-handed (as opposed to a completely neutral 'hands-off') approach in responding to competing claims – including matters of ethnic, cultural and linguistic identity – with the aim of ensuring equal respect for all (Carens 2000). While no liberal democratic regime can ever be culturally or linguistically neutral – since every state has to make choices regarding, for example, the language(s) to use for government, the courts and in public education – cultural particularism should be kept strictly to a minimum. Thus, the overarching issue confronted by the HCNM has been the challenge of integrating diversity within the contemporary democratic state.

Since the creation of new states (or the restoration of their sovereignty) in post Cold War Europe has been accompanied in many areas by national and ethnic revivals, the OSCE has had to pay particular attention to problems of diversity, especially linguistic minorities. The objective promoted by the OSCE is one of 'integrating diversity', that is the simultaneous maintenance of different identities and the promotion of social integration. This implies a pluralist, multicultural model of societal organization based on the principle of non-discrimination (as opposed to an assimilationist or exclusivist approach). A common fear is that support for integration, as opposed to assimilation, within the state will in fact lead to its disintegration. The OSCE approach informs that the reverse is true. Specifically, the HCNM's experience is that: 'A minority that has the opportunity to fully develop its identity is more likely to remain loyal to the state than a minority who is denied its identity' (van der Stoel 2000).

Within the framework of integrating diversity, as informed by international standards, the state is entitled and indeed obliged to seek integration in accordance with the foundational principles of equality and non-discrimination (Eide 1999; also Henrard, this volume). This is a matter of balancing general and particular interests and wills. Distinctions and preferences must constitute a *proportionate balance* between the different interests in accordance with respect for the dignity of the individual and the protection of their rights – most relevantly the rights to freedom of expression and association. In order to determine whether such preferences (in this case, linguistic ones) are discriminatory, various factors must be taken into account, including a state's demographic, historical and cultural circumstances: what is reasonable in the context of one state may be completely unadaptable in another (de Varennes 1996).

Furthermore, states have an obligation (in accordance with paragraph 33 of the Copenhagen Document) to encourage conditions for the promotion of identity that goes beyond mere protection and requires special or 'positive' measures to ensure equal enjoyment and development of the rights of minorities in fact as well as under law. Crucial in this regard are the language and educational policies of the state concerned. Persons who have the official language of the state as their mother tongue (usually the numerical majority) are automatically advantaged over those who speak a minority language. The privilege of the state language must therefore be balanced by adequate compensatory measures aiding persons belonging to linguistic minorities. At the same time, the international instruments for the protection of minorities provide that the exercise of positive rights shall neither impinge on the rights of others (Dunbar 2001), nor shall they in any way compromise the territorial integrity of the state.

Accordingly, in practice, in OSCE states (Slovakia, Moldova, Latvia and Estonia, Georgia and Ukraine among others) where language regulation has been a source of tension, the HCNM stresses that, while he remains aware of and sensitive to the historical experiences of past repression, there is a need to balance efforts to preserve and promote the language of the majority with measures to ensure the maintenance and development of the languages of persons belonging to minorities. At the same time, the HCNM reminds minorities that as members of the larger society of the state, they also have interests and even certain obligations to learn and use the language(s) of the state.

Citizenship

While learning the state language promotes intra-state cohesion it also benefits linguistic minorities in terms of their integration into society and their access to public goods. Of course, this assumes that such minorities are fully 'inside' the state. This raises the issue of citizenship where knowledge of the state language is required in order to facilitate access to citizenship. While this may seem normal for any situation typical of naturalization, it has been abnormal in its effects especially in Estonia and Latvia where, upon restoration of their sovereignty after decades of Soviet occupation and Russification, large numbers of long-term residents found themselves non-citizens and subject to examinations in the (for them new) state language in order to acquire the citizenship. A similar fate has befallen groups of persons internally deported by Stalin who have returned to what are now newly independent states with state languages differing from their mother tongues. These effects of a language inversion within the state have created major problems of access to and equal enjoyment of citizenship. As a consequence, a number of other issues relating to the status and use of language(s) have arisen.

Status

The practice amongst OSCE participating states varies considerably in terms of the official recognition and legal protection of minority languages. Within the OSCE area a number of newly independent states or of restored sovereignty have elevated selected language(s) to enjoy official status over others – in some cases directly inverting the hierarchy imposed under the previous regime, and thereby signalling the dominance of those for whom the official language is the mother tongue. In the Baltic states and elsewhere, the objective of the titular communities or so-called 'state-forming nations' has been to enact the real and symbolic restoration of the language(s) spoken by the majority to primacy as the sole official languages of the state in a process of 'cultural recovery'. This has important implications for the use of language(s) in contact with public authorities.

While some states make no provision for languages other than the dominant state language, other states do make provision for minority languages to a greater or lesser degree in their Constitutions. For example, the Georgian Constitution provides for the additional official use of Abkhazian in the Abkhaz region. Similarly, Tajikistan has enshrined minority language rights for Tajik, Russian and Uzbek speakers in its Constitution. A number of Central European states follow the same approach. Other Constitutions (e.g. those of Uzbekistan and Ukraine) embody a wider, more liberal approach to language issues whereby the state guarantees to respect, protect and create the conditions for the free development of all minority languages.[7] Provisions for the official use of language(s) varies tremendously from state to state, but there is a clear tendency towards greater accommodation at least at local level. An interesting case is that of Kyrgyzstan which upon independence made Kyrgyz the only official language and then some years later, following difficulties caused by the language inversion, restored to official status the Russian language. In response to demands from other linguistic minorities (especially Uzbeks), there is currently discussion about accommodating other minority languages at least at local level. An opposite example might be the case of Azerbaijan which first made Azeri the only state language and has recently acted in effect to prohibit the use of other languages in a number of fields.

Effective implementation of law

De jure protection does not, however, guarantee equality in practice. Even where constitutional protection exists, failure to enact and implement language legislation can create uncertainty on the part of linguistic minorities as to the content and extent of the rights granted to them, leading to anxiety and creating tensions. Failure to adopt regulations for the swift implementation of existing laws can have a similar effect. In 1996, for example, the HCNM recommended that the implementation of the Romanian Law on Education be speeded up in order to address the uncertainty and fears of the Hungarian minority. Similarly, on the adoption of the State Language Law in Slovakia, the HCNM encouraged the rapid adoption of a law on minority languages as a counterbalance in order to avoid a legal vacuum on issues such as the use of minority languages in official communications. In addition, the need for promoting more *understanding* of relevant legislation regarding minority rights has also been an issue, for example, in Kazakhstan. This last element is crucial insofar as there frequently exists a considerable gap between widely held 'folk' beliefs about the rules of language – which can contribute to distrust and resentment between linguistic groups – and the reality in law (Kontra 1999).

Even where good laws exist at a national level, reluctance or inability to implement them at local public administration level can generate problems. In the FYROM, for example, there was a dispute at the Pedagogical Faculty of the principal university in Skopje in 1998 as the Dean refused to implement a special law ensuring instruction in the Albanian language with a view to training a sufficient number of Albanian-language instructors to fill posts in Albanian-language schools throughout the country. In another case, unnecessarily restrictive interpretation of language legislation in Estonia and Latvia has kept state authorities from communicating in languages minorities understand regarding the possibilities and procedures to apply for citizenship.

Names

Intimately linked to an individual's and group's identity is one's name, both the choice of name and its language of expression. In some countries, until recently the choice of name was restricted by law. This is still the case to some degree. More common have been problems of official registration, especially in the original language. While transliteration has always been possible, countries such as Slovakia and Latvia have required translations which have affected one's name per se officially and sometimes portended material effects such as obstacles to inheritance. Another problem has arisen for groups both in terms of registration of their own names and also those of topographical indications in places where they live or for points of historical significance. This has been the case, for example, in Crimea.

Political participation

Language restrictions have been an important barrier to effective participation in public affairs for linguistic minorities in a number of countries and ways. Aside from the issue of citizenship noted earlier, limits on language use have negatively affected minorities in the context of elections. For example, for a long time in Estonia and Latvia citizens seeking to stand for elected office had to demonstrate high proficiency in the state language. The same applies for candidates for president in Kazakhstan, Kyrgyzstan and Ukraine. In Estonia, as restrictive interpretation of the language legislation results in minorities having to ensure translation of all their public election advertisements into the state language and to bear the cost thereof. Perhaps most importantly, most states limit the use of minority languages within elected bodies such that minorities are sometimes disadvantaged in expressing themselves and advocating their interests. This has recently been again the subject of intense debate in FYROM, and is an ongoing subject in several countries. Finally, also in FYROM the issue of the use of language in the conduct of the official state census was a significant point of contention.

Commerce

For obvious reasons, this can be a major source of dispute. Almost all states have some form of linguistic requirement in specific fields relating to legitimate public interests such as health and safety, for example, requiring the labelling of products for consumer protection and the posting of signs for workplace and public safety. These are generally not contentious. By contrast, requirements for the use of the state language (either only or additionally) on commercial signs, notices, advertisements, trademarks, and so on are contested. Likewise, prescriptions (sometimes amounting to effective proscriptions) for the substantial use of the state language in private radio and television broadcasting result in unfair terms of trade and effectively reduce or deny access to minority language media.

Education

Undoubtedly, the most hotly contested issue relating to language is that of education, both as a subject of study and as the medium of instruction. This seems to be because of the critical role education plays in transmitting linguistic proficiency and identity between generations and also its function in preparing the next generation for both cultural reproduction and development. Thus, education is the key functional element in the primordial and instrumental aspects of language. On this basis, the HCNM was moved to initiate the elaboration of a first set of general recommendations that is *The Hague Recommendations regarding the Education Rights of National Minorities*. Understandably, a considerable amount of the HCNM's efforts through the years have been towards policy and legislative reform aimed at balancing legitimate interests and demands in the field of education. This has been true at all levels, from pre-school through tertiary. It has also stimulated the HCNM to engage in a variety of project activities.

Language development

An interesting issue which has arisen in a few situations relates to the technical development of languages in terms of vocabulary, script and standardization. For example, in Kazakhstan and Kyrgyzstan, the new state languages have suffered from a lack of vocabulary and proficient officials to ensure its effective use in all fields of governance.

In the case of the Roma and Sinti, the problem is that there exists no single standardized Romani language – indeed, there are at least four principal streams and numerous dialects which are mutually non-intelligible among different speakers. A similar situation applies for Kurdish. Moreover, some parts of these groups prefer not to identify themselves in terms of language and may not speak any version of the language(s) (often due to past assimilation). These cases raise a host of sensitive issues engaging the delicacy of science much less public policy. Vital in these regards is the full participation of the communities in the policy and programme development.

Conclusion

It is clear from the work of the HCNM that the protection of minority languages and linguistic minorities is a central objective for the OSCE. This constitutes a multifaceted challenge which implies a variety of responses. Through the preceding indicative account of the HCNM's work, I have tried to show the basis for OSCE concern and engagement, the innovative nature of the HCNM as an institution of conflict prevention and the place of language within these.

To a significant degree, the contemporary challenge is due to the lingering effect of the European notion of the 'nation-state' with its ideal of the pure cultural-*linguistic* 'nation' or, at least, the dominant linguistic majority (which is titular to the state, e.g. Germans in Germany or Hungarians in Hungary). This Romantic ideal is often at the root of linguistic disputes as persons belonging to linguistic minorities seek equality both in law and in fact. The substantial distance between public policy and law (reflecting the nation-state ideal), on the one hand, and the plurilingual reality of every state, on the other, demonstrates that most European states have yet to adapt their thinking and governance to either the socio-cultural reality of their populations or to the international standards to which they are committed.

The extreme *linguistic* nationalism, often underpinning policies and laws of inequality and outright prohibition (including sometimes punishments), still has considerable resonance among political leaders and voters in many parts of Europe (both among majority AND minority groups). Such nationalism inevitably leads to a separatist logic and objectives. Therefore, it is of critical importance that the understanding of the issues and relevant standards be significantly improved at popular and policy-making levels. If policy and law can be better devised and applied, the number of issues giving rise to tensions may be reduced and disputes might be resolved or even avoided altogether. To this end, there is a key role for international standards to be applied under the rule of law, and where conflicts may be inevitable (e.g. in the field of public administration) for the standards to be applied carefully. In this connection, it is worth recalling, as Ó Riagáin and Nic Shuibhne (1997: 18) put it, that 'both positive and negative elements (i.e. obligations of performance and forbearance) are essential prerequisites to effective enforcement of minority language rights'. But beyond this, it is no doubt essential for there to be enlightened leadership on all sides supporting good governance responding to legitimate interests and desires beyond what the minimum international standards may require. Only then can we all come to know and enjoy the cultural richness and comparative advantages brought by diversity understood as a public asset and value rather than as a liability and threat.

For his part, the HCNM has taken this approach in advising governments both in general terms and in specific situations. Especially in relation to legislation, the HCNM has had a significant and direct impact, notwithstanding the complexity of the problems he has had to confront and the political difficulties encountered in many cases. On the basis of this experience, it is apparent that the combined principles of comprehensive and cooperative security work to prevent conflict at least as pursued through the innovative institution of the HCNM. In this respect, it is evident that standards can and do matter – not only the minimum standards of international law, but also the more maximum-orientated standards of good governance which respond to legitimate demands within the democratic state (such as demands for higher education in the mother tongue). Drawing especially on the principle of non-discrimination, this implies considerable accommodation for all minority languages and linguistic minorities – and not just so-called historical ones.

Notes

*   The views expressed herein are those of the author alone, and are not necessarily shared by either the OSCE or the High Commissioner. The author wishes to thank his colleagues Ms Sally Holt and Matthew Draper for their assistance in preparation of this chapter.

1. This chapter was written while its author served as Director of the Office of the High Commissioner on National Minorities of the OSCE. The views expressed herein are those of the author alone, and are not necessarily shared by either the OSCE or the High Commissioner. The author wishes to thank his colleagues Ms. Sally Holt and Mr. Matthew Draper for their assistance in preparation of this chapter.
2. In contradistinction to the position of a language, the notion 'linguistic minorities' refers to the group of *persons* who speak a language (essentially as a mother tongue) other than that spoken by those in the majority within a specific jurisdiction. On the question of definition of minorities (including linguistic ones), see Packer (1993 and 1999a).
3. A full list of all official documents cited in this chapter is included in the bibliography.
4. The notion 'kin-state' has no legal significance, but is often used to indicate a state with a dominant and 'state-forming' ethno-linguistic community which shares ethno-linguistic characteristics with minorities in other (often neighbouring) states.
5. Usually, according to protocol, the exchanges are conducted with Ministers for Foreign Affairs. But, addressees may include other important personalities, such as Heads of Government and State, with sometimes copies being sent to other relevant Ministers (e.g. Ministers of Education) or addressed to them with copies being sent to the Minister for Foreign Affairs.
6. Questionnaires were addressed to all OSCE participating states except rump Yugoslavia (which was then considered either 'suspended' or 'non-recognised') and the Holy See. Responses were never received from Albania (which suffered significant domestic turmoil) and Belgium.
7. The Uzbek Constitution (in Article 4) prescribes that Uzbek is the state language, but at the same time obliges the state to 'ensure a respectful attitude towards the languages, customs and traditions of all nationalities and ethnic groups living on its territory, and create the conditions necessary for their development'. Similarly, Ukraine's Constitution (in accordance with a recommendation of the HCNM) guarantees the free development, use and protection of Russian and other languages of national minorities in Ukraine, as well as guaranteeing the right of citizens to receive instruction in the native tongue or to study the native language in state and communal educational establishments and through national cultural societies.

References

Official documents

Charter of Paris for a New Europe, http://www.osce.org/docs/english/1990–1999/summits/paris90e.htm

Document of the Copenhagen Meeting of the Conference on the Human Dimension of the CSCE, http://www.osce.org/docs/english/1990–1999/hd/cope90e.htm

Guidelines to Assist National Minority Participation in the Electoral Process, http://www.osce.org/odihr/documents/guidelines/

Helsinki Final Act, http://www.osce.org/docs/english/1990–1999/summits/helfa75e.htm

Report on the Linguistic Rights of Persons Belonging to National Minorities in the OSCE Area, http://www.osce.org/hcnm/documents/reports/linguistic_rights/linguistic_rights_en.pdf

The Hague Recommendations Regarding the Education Rights of National Minorities (with Explanatory Note and supplemented with scholarly articles: *International Journal on Minority and Group Rights*, 4(2)).

The Lund Recommendations on the Effective Participation of National Minorities in Public Life, http://www.osce.org/hcnm/documents/recommendations/lund/index.php3

The Oslo Recommendations Regarding the Linguistic Rights of National Minorities http://www.osce.org/hcnm/documents/recommendations/oslo/index.php3, (with Explanatory Note and supplemented with scholarly articles: *International Journal on Minority and Group Rights*, 6(3)).

Secondary sources

Bíró, Anna-Mária and Petra Kovács (eds) 2001, *Diversity in Action; Local Public Administration of Multi-Ethnic Communities in Central and Eastern Europe.* Budapest: Open Society Institute.

Bloed, A., ed., 1993, *The Conference on Security and Cooperation in Europe: Analysis and Basic Documents, 1972–1993*, Dordrecht: Martinus Nijhoff Publishers.

Bloed, A., ed., 1997, *The Conference on Security and Cooperation in Europe: Basic Documents, 1993–1995*, The Hague: Kluwer Law International.

Bothe, M., N. Ronzitti and A. Rosas, (eds), 1997, *The OSCE in the Maintenance of Peace and Security; Conflict Prevention, Crisis Management and Peaceful Settlement of Disputes*, The Hague: Kluwer Law International.

Buergenthal, T., 1990, 'The Copenhagen CSCE Meeting: A New Public Order for Europe', *Human Rights Law Journal*, 11, Parts 1–2, 217–32.

Carens, J. H., 2000, *Culture, Citizenship, and Community: a Contextual Exploration of Justice as Evenhandedness*, Oxford/New York: Oxford University Press.

Cohen, J., 1999, *Conflict Prevention in the OSCE: An Assessment of Capacities*, The Hague: Netherlands Institute of International Relations Clingendael.

De Varennes, F., 1996, *Language, Minorities and Human Rights*, The Hague: Martinus Nijhoff Publishers.

Dunbar, R., 2001, 'Minority Language Rights in International Law', *International and Comparative Law Quarterly*, 50: 90–120.

Eide, A., 1999, 'The Oslo Recommendations Regarding the Linguistic Rights of National Minorities: An Overview', *International Journal on Minority and Group Rights*, 6(3): 319–28.

Ghebali, V.-Y., 1996, *L'OSCE dans l'Europe post-communiste, 1990–1996: Vers une identité paneuropéenne de sécurité*, Bruxelles: Etablissements Emile Bruylant.

Holt, S., 2003, 'The Activities of the OSCE High Commissioner on National Minorities: January 2001-May 2002' in European Centre for Minority Issues and EURAC Research (eds), *European Yearbook of Minority Issues*, Volume 1 (2001/2), The Hague: Kluwer Law International, 563–89.

Holt, S. and J. Packer, 2001, 'OSCE Developments and Linguistic Minorities', *MOST Journal on Multicultural Societies*, 3(2) http://www.unesco.org/most/vl3n2packer.htm

Kemp, W., ed., 2001, *Quiet Diplomacy in Action: the OSCE High Commissioner on National Minorities*, The Hague/Boston/London: Kluwer Law International.

Kontra, M., 1999, ' "Don't Speak Hungarian in Public!" – A Documentation and Analysis of Folk Linguistic Rights', in M. Kontra, R. Phillipson, T. Skutnabb-Kangas and T. Várady, (eds) 1999, *Language: A Right and a Resource*, Budapest: Central European University Press, 81–97.

Ó Riagáin, P. and N. Nic Shuibhne, 1997, 'Minority Language Rights', *Annual Review of Applied Linguistics*, 17: 11–29.

Packer, John 1993, 'On the Definition of Minorities', in J. Packer and K. Myntti, (eds) *The Protection of Ethnic and Linguistic Minorities in Europe*. Turku/Åbo: Institute for Human Rights, 23–65.

Packer, J., 1999a, 'Problems in Defining Minorities', in D. Fottrell and B. Bowring, (eds) *Minority and Group Rights In the New Millenium*. The Hague: Kluwer Law International, 223–74.

Packer, J., 1999b, 'The Role of the OSCE High Commissioner on National Minorities in the Former Yugoslavia', *Cambridge Review of International Affairs*, 12(2): 169–84.

Packer, J., 2001, 'The Protection of Minority Language Rights through the Work of OSCE Institutions', in S. Trifunovska, ed., 2001, *Minority Rights in Europe: European Minorities and Languages*, The Hague: T.M.C. Asser Press, 255–74.

Packer, J. and G. Siemienski, 1999, 'The Language of Equity: The Origin and Development of the Oslo Recommendations Regarding the Linguistic Rights of National Minorities', *International Journal on Minority and Group Rights*, 6(3): 329–50.

Van Der Stoel, M., 2000, 'The Protection of Minorities in the OSCE Region', *Address at a Seminar at the OSCE Parliamentary Assembly*, http://www.osce.org/hcnm/documents/speeches/2000/index.php3.

Wilson, D., 2002, *Minority Rights in Education: Lessons for the European Union from Estonia, Latvia, Romania and the Former Yugoslav Republic of Macedonia*. Lund: Raoul Wallenberg Institute of Human Rights and Humanitarian Law.

Zaagman, R., 1999, 'Conflict Prevention in the Baltic States: The OSCE High Commissioner on National Minorities in Estonia, Latvia and Lithuania', *ECMI Monograph # 1*, Flensburg: European Centre for Minority Issues.

Part III
Case Studies

6
Ethnic Germans as a Language Minority in Central and Eastern Europe: Legislative and Policy Frameworks in Poland, Hungary and Romania

Stefan Wolff and Karl Cordell

Introduction

In many cases, language is a vital component of individual and group identity and figures prominently among the aspects by which ethnic minorities distinguish themselves from majority populations in their host-countries. Thus, the very survival of a minority population as a distinct ethnocultural group often depends upon provision for the continued preservation of its mother tongue as a living language. This can normally only be achieved if this language is used in public as well as the private sphere and is taught as a first language at schools, which, in turn, is only possible if political and legal conditions are in place that allow minorities to 'live' in their language. Such conditions include, above all, a commitment by the relevant state not to discriminate against people who speak a language other than the language of the titular nation. However, general non-discrimination legislation and its enforcement are often not enough to enable a minority to preserve its language. The *Oslo Recommendations regarding the Linguistic Rights of National Minorities* emphasise that the legislative framework also needs to provide for complete equality in the use of individual and place names, must allow language use in the practice and profession of religion and religious ceremonies, that it should extend permissively into community life, the media, and public administration and that adequate funding should be provided for the implementation of such laws. Where appropriate, cross-border

cooperation should be permitted with countries to whose populations the members of the minority feel ethnically or linguistically
related (High Commissioner on National Minorities 1998).

Against this background, this chapter examines the legislative and
policy frameworks in three Central and Eastern European states with
German-speaking minorities – Poland, Hungary and Romania. Our
analysis focuses on issues that are particularly significant in connection with the ability of a minority to preserve its language. These
include language laws and other legal provisions regarding the
official status and use of languages, language access in education,
representation of minority languages in and through the media, and
opportunities for cross-border cooperation within one language
community. We contend that the present status of each of the
German minorities and their abilities to preserve their mother
tongue cannot be comprehensively explained without due consideration of a wide range of contemporary and historical factors. Among
the former, legal and policy frameworks are as important as are the
territorial concentration of the minority communities and their age
structures. Among the latter, the policies of assimilation, discrimination and forced migration pursued to differing degrees in all three
countries over the past half century since the end of the Second
World War are equally significant if one wants to account for the present situation and prospects of each of the minorities under discussion. Thus, while Hungary, Poland and Romania have all ratified the
Framework Convention on the Protection of Minorities and Hungary
has additionally ratified, and Romania signed the European Charter
for Regional or Minority Languages (ECRML), the resultant relatively
permissive legislative framework and the minority policies adopted
within may have been too little too late to create conditions conducive to the long-term preservation of German language minorities
in all three countries.

The German minority in Hungary[1]

In the 1991 census, just under 900,000 people in Hungary declared
their nationality or ethnic identity as other than Hungarian, thus
giving minorities a total share of just under 9 per cent of Hungary's
10 million population. The most numerous among them were Roma,
followed by Germans and Slovaks. Smaller minority groups include

Jews, Croats and Romanians, as well as Greeks, Serbs, Slovenes, Armenians and Bulgarians.

After 1945, as in Poland and Romania, the German minority, which can trace its earliest origins to migration and colonisation in the thirteenth century, was held collectively responsible for Nazi atrocities in Hungary during the Second World War. Approximately 200,000 of its members were expelled to the American and Soviet occupation zones immediately after the war before the Allies put a stop to the expulsions. Between 1950 and the early 1990s, another 20,000 ethnic Germans emigrated to the Federal Republic. Preliminary results from census of February 2001 indicate that 62,233 individuals declared themselves to be of German nationality. This number in fact represents an increase of over 100 per cent since the census of 1991, when only 30,824 declared themselves to be German. This data indicates that an identity shift has occurred among some Hungarian citizens. Of those Hungarian citizens who claimed German nationality in 2001, only 33,792 stated that German was their mother tongue. How many of these are fluent in German is an altogether different matter. With regard to the overall number of ethnic Germans, although some would dispute the afore-mentioned figures as erring on the low side, there is little reason to assume that this is the case. There is no evidence to confirm any sup-position that self-declaration of German ethnicity opens a pandora's box of discriminatory practices.

The reduction of the German minority in post-1945 Hungary had a significant impact upon language use and awareness among those who remained in the country, especially as vital community structures had been destroyed. Even in communities where today more than half of the population is ethnic German, the language is rarely used regularly in public life. This includes religious services, where efforts to re-initiating religious services in German have found success in several settlements during the recent years.

Hungarian minority policy 1945–90

As in Poland, albeit on a very different scale, in the immediate aftermath of the Second World War the ethnic German minority experienced a period of collective victimisation and expulsion, when approximately 200,000 members of the minority were expelled from Hungary, adding to the approximately 50,000 who had fled with the retreating German army. Officially, the main criterion for expulsion was membership in the German minority's principal organisation in Hungary, the *Volksbund*, which had been classified as a Nazi organisation. Although this was true for the period from the mid-1930s onwards, the *Volksbund* traced its history back far longer, and in 1945 its membership included many who had been members long before its nazification. In addition to members of the *Volksbund*, many ethnic Germans were also expelled simply because of their German roots or mother tongue. The expulsion of approximately half of Hungary's pre-war ethnic German population deprived the remaining members of the minority of almost their entire intellectual, economic and political elite and made compact and practically homogeneous German settlements in Hungary a thing of the past. It is also important to see the impact that the expulsion of the ethnic Germans in Hungary had on their opportunities to preserve a distinct ethnocultural identity in the wider context of population transfers in Central and Eastern Europe between 1945 and 1950. On a smaller scale, ethnic Hungarians had been expelled in particular from those territories that Hungary had won in the first and second Vienna arbitration awards in southern Slovakia and Romania (Transylvania) and Yugoslavia (Vojvodina). Hungarians expelled from these areas were often resettled in (formerly) German villages, thus adding to the difficulty to maintain viable community structures suitable for the preservation of living German language in the country.

From the 1950s onwards, the communist regime in Hungary primarily pursued a policy of indifference and neglect towards the country's ethnic minorities. There was some limited provision of minority-language education for members of the German minority, but following the expulsions, many ethnic Germans in Hungary embarked on a course of 'voluntary' assimilation, resulting in a rapid language shift towards Hungarian as the principal language within the community, replacing almost entirely local German dialects.

Post-communist developments

From the 1980s onwards, changes towards a more liberal minority policy began to take effect when the communist regime began to open up and gradually transform itself. Today, Hungary has an extensive network of legislation regulating the situation of ethnic minorities in the country. The constitution recognises national and ethnic minorities as integral parts of society and obliges the state to protect them and to ensure their collective participation in public life. The state is also required to create conditions within which minorities can foster their culture, use their mother tongues, and provide school instruction conducted in native languages. The state guarantees the right of minorities to use their names in their own language. The Law on the Rights of National and Ethnic Minorities of 1993 provides a complex system of general regulations, individual and group rights, local and national minority self-government and cultural autonomy, and (with regard the private and semi-public) spheres sanctions the unrestricted use of minority languages. The provisions of this law are backed up by according regulations in the Law on Public Education (1993), in the National Curriculum (1994), in laws regulating the procedures of civil and criminal law, and in laws on the conduct of local authorities. Closely modelled on the bilateral treaty between Germany and Poland, that between Hungary and the Federal Republic of 1992 makes explicit and far-reaching provisions for the protection of the German minority in Hungary, including the possibility of support from Germany. A similar agreement exists between Hungary and Austria.

Within the public education system, the German minority has its own educational structure, comprising native language schools, bilingual schools and so-called language training schools, where efforts are made to teach part of the curriculum in German. The German minority maintains its own native language libraries with support of public libraries of the local community governments. School libraries of educational institutions participating in minority education stock literary and non-literary works in German. Native language education of students from the German minority is provided, among others, by 140 to 150 visiting teachers. For the second half of the 1990s, total student numbers at pre-school and primary school level were just above 50,000. Most of them, however, went to language training schools, with the smallest number attending native language schools (below 1,000). Despite improvements in the provision with school facilities, textbooks, native language teachers and so on, the language skills of most of the younger members of the minority are significantly below those of older generations, particularly because of the functionality of Hungarian in daily life and the attractiveness of English. The lack of situations in which German remains used and useful thus decreases constantly and the language therefore continues to lose its appeal. The Hungarian government makes available about €150,000 worth of extra funds annually for cultural and educational programmes and there is significant support from Germany and Austria.

The cultural life of the German minority is organised at local and national level by private associations and the minority self-government.[2] These private associations include the Association of German Writers and Artists in Hungary, founded in 1990, the German Theatre at Szekszárd, founded in 1986, the *German Nationality Museum*, founded in 1972, the Alliance of School Societies of Germans in Hungary, the Saint Gellért Catholic Association, founded in 1991, and the National Council of German Song, Music and Dance Groups, founded in 1996, which acts as umbrella for almost 400 member organisations. Hungarian Television has broadcast programmes in German since 1978. Since 1998 programmes in German are broadcast daily for 90 minutes at regional level and for 30 minutes at national level, totalling 840 minutes of weekly programming time. This marks considerable progress to the situation before when there was only a half-hour programme every two weeks (Nelde 2000: 126). The German weekly *Neue Zeitung* receives annual subsidies of approximately €100,000, and the German national self-government council in Budapest publishes its own periodicals.

Cross-border cooperation functions well and is encouraged. The two primary legal instruments for bilateral German–Hungarian cooperation are the Treaty between the Republic of Hungary and Federal Republic of Germany on Friendly Cooperation and Partnership in Europe and the Joint Declaration by the Government of the Republic of Hungary and the Government of the Federal Republic of Germany on Assistance for the German Minority in Hungary and on the Teaching of German as a Foreign Language, both of which were signed in 1992. In addition, there are numerous twinning arrangements with villages or towns in Germany and Austria, and the National Self-Government of German Hungarians has also established ties with German minorities elsewhere, including with Germans from Denmark and South-Tyrol. In the context of existing bilateral treaties and agreements, Germany and Austria support the professional and linguistic training of teachers, provide funding for schools, offer assistance for curriculum development, school book design and production and supply scholarships for secondary, college and university education and scientific exchange programmes. Funds are also made available for libraries and the German Theatre in Szekszárd. Some 165 local self-administration offices, set up by the German minority under the provisions of the 1993 Law on the Rights of National and Ethnic Minorities, have been furnished and equipped with German assistance.

The German minority in Poland[3]

Only approximately 2 per cent of Poland's population of over 38 million are considered to be members of an indigenous ethnic minority. Until the results of the census of May 2001 are finally published, we must work with sometimes radically different estimates. What is indisputable is that Poland is ethnically highly homogeneous with the largest minority groups being the Ukrainians, Germans and Belarusians. Other minorities include Roma, Jews, Ruthenes, Lithuanians and Slovaks.

Ethnic Germans in Poland, whose origins as a national minority in the country primarily date back to the territorial revisions after the First and Second World Wars (when large parts of formerly German territory were annexed to Poland), have only since 1989 been a recognised national minority of some 300–500,000 people.[4] They are territorially concentrated in the Opole Voivodship, where German is still used in everyday life, especially in the south and east of the Voivodship. There are also small and declining German communities in parts of the Silesian Voivodship and the Warmia-Masuria Voivodship. The size of the minority has remained largely stable since the early 1990s, but between 1950 and 1992, almost 1.5 million ethnic Germans left the country and emigrated to the Federal Republic. This was primarily a reaction to the severe level of discrimination and the perpetually dire economic situation that they had faced during the era of communist rule.

Polish minority policy 1945–90

As far as the Polish authorities were concerned, the vast majority of post-war citizens who once held German passports or considered themselves to be of German ethnicity were not German at all. This group of people, which may have totalled as many as 1.2 million must be distinguished from a much smaller group, known officially as the 'designated German minority', that numbered no more than 250,000. Official policy geared towards the former group was one of 're-Polonisation'. With regard to the latter group expressions of German cultural identity were permitted, as members of the 'designated German minority' were not considered ethnic Poles.

Following the completion of the expulsion process in 1950, the objective of the Polish government was to perfect the eradication all 'alien' influences from various groups of 'Germanicised Poles' in order to promote their speedy assimilation into Polish society. This entailed establishing an absolute ban on the use of German as a medium of communication in areas where such people resided in number. In order to better promote such policies of assimilation, the physical landscape was itself changed. Wherever possible all traces of German culture were removed. This involved the chiselling out of inscriptions, the eradication of German topographical names and the re-interpretation of history.

However, there is reason to query the efficacy of these policies. First of all, in the 1950s the state and communist party were both weak, even within a comparative Polish context. To what extent they actually possessed wholly effective means through which they could implement such policies is open to question. Enforcing the linguistic ban in schools and within public spaces, particularly in large towns and cities was relatively easy. On the other hand, a large majority of these people lived either in rural areas or de facto inner-city ghettos. Penetration of such closed communities on the part of the communist party was uneven. Moreover, in many cases monolingual German speakers were well past school age. The extent to which they could actually be forbidden to speak German, especially within their relatively closed circles is debatable. This is particularly true of women, as they were less likely to be in paid employment than were their male counterparts, and in general were less likely to engage with wider Polish society. Gradually, however, Polish did become more widespread, partly because it had greater functionality and also because many 'Germanicised Poles' were either to some degree bilingual, or in fact spoke no or little German at all, but had come to identify with the German state and culture despite this apparent linguistic contradiction. This was above all true in the southern part of former East Prussia, today's Warmia-Masuria Voivodship.

In comparison, the situation of the designated German minority was quite different. In the summer of 1945, it became clear to sections of the emergent political elite that in the short to medium-term, skilled German labour would be needed to help run factories, especially in the industrial centres of Lower Silesia. Around 80,000 skilled workers and their families were thus either exempted from expulsion or forced to remain in Poland. Given that this group of people had been recognised by the Polish authorities as being 'indisputably German', they were not subjected to a campaign of re-Polonisation as were their counterparts in rural Upper Silesia, Masuria and East Pomerania. The Polish government moved reasonably quickly to support the maintenance of German language and culture, albeit within narrowly prescribed ideological parameters. Thus, as the memories of war slowly began to diminish, and some kind of normality returned, so the situation of the designated German minority began to improve. Following various legislative decisions, the possibilities for this group officially to maintain its identity grew in scope. German schools together with a variety of tertiary colleges were gradually opened throughout industrial cities in Lower Silesia and, to a significantly lesser extent, Pomerania. In addition, the Polish government, in conjunction with its East German counterpart, embarked upon a series of measures designed to maintain elements of German culture. These included, among others, the establishment of German theatre and dance groups and of a German-language press, but excluded the preservation of any physical traces of the German cultural heritage which were systematically destroyed, either by deliberate action or neglect.

Following the conclusion of the Treaty of Görlitz in 1950, whereby East Germany recognised Poland's western border, the GDR's government assumed a formal protective role for the 'designated German minority'. For example, members of the minority, who had initially been declared stateless, were offered the opportunity of acquiring East German passports. Funding was made available for various cultural activities, and eventually re-settlement was facilitated for those who wished to emigrate when such an alternative became a realistic possibility in the late 1950s.

In the late 1950s, changes in political attitudes coupled with a changed socio-economic situation, spelled the beginning of the end of the 'designated German minority'. In 1957 virtually all restrictions on the minority were removed, and they were placed on the same legal footing as other recognised minorities in Poland. At the same time emigration restrictions were further relaxed as sufficient numbers of Poles were now available to replace the formerly essential German labour. Final regularisation of their position came with the promulgation of the Law on Nationality of 15 February 1962, and the offer of a Polish passport to those who desired it. The vast majority, however, opted for migration to either of the German states.

Post-communist developments

Since the end of communism in Poland, the situation of national minorities, and in particular that of ethnic Germans has much improved. Legal provisions that relate to minority languages and their users in Poland are laid down, among others in the country's constitution of 1997, the Law on Radio and Television (1992), the Law on the Educational System (1991). Article 27 of the constitution stipulates that 'Polish shall be the official language in the Republic of Poland. This provision shall not infringe upon national minority rights resulting from ratified international agreements.' Article 35, Paragraph 1, further states that the 'Republic of Poland shall ensure Polish citizens belonging to national or ethnic minorities the freedom to maintain and develop their own language, to maintain customs and traditions, and to develop their own culture', while Paragraph 2 lays down that '[n]ational and ethnic minorities shall have the right to establish educational and cultural institutions, institutions designed to protect religious identity, as well as to participate in the resolution of matters connected with their cultural identity'. Another part of the reason for the marked improvement since 1989 can be located within the extensive legal framework for cooperation between Poland and Germany in the fields of education and culture. The major legal instruments include the *Treaty between the Republic of Poland and the Federal Republic of Germany on Neighbourliness and Friendly Cooperation* (1991), the *Agreement between the Government of the Republic of Poland and the Government of the Federal Republic of Germany on Polish and German Youth Cooperation* (1991), the *Agreement between the Government of the Republic of Poland and the Government of the Federal Republic of Germany on the Establishment and Operation of the Representative Office of the German Academic Exchange Service* (1997) and the *Agreement between the*

Government of the Republic of Poland and the Government of the Federal Republic of Germany on Cultural Cooperation (1997).

On the basis of national legislation and agreements with Germany, funding for the minority in the areas of education and culture comes from both Polish and German sources. The German government has provided staff support to improve the quality of German language teaching in Poland. The number of teachers sent to Poland has increased from just one in 1989 to over 100 by 1994, and has remained at that level. In addition, four federal government-sponsored experts on German-language teaching have been working in Poland since 1994; the German Academic Exchange Service funds 26 lecturers at Polish universities, and is in the process of establishing a new German–Polish research institute in (collaboration with the University of) Wrocław. In addition, the Goethe Institute has supplied eight lecturers for the further training of Polish teachers of German. However, the chronic lack of teachers of German in German minority schools remains the most important and yet unresolved problem. Very few qualified German school-teachers are prepared to relocate to Poland even on a temporary basis. Since 1993, members of the German minority in Poland have had access to a special grant programme to study in Germany for a period of up to 12 months. The federal government also provides partial funding for TV and radio broadcasts and print media of the German minority and supplies German newspapers and magazines to the cultural organisations of the minority. While the German minority in Poland remains one of the two priority groups supported by the German government, the majority of the funds in the approximately €40 million budget for German minorities in Central and Eastern Europe is assigned to projects in the former Soviet Union, especially in Russia and Kazakhstan. However, declining financial support from Germany is partly compensated by the Polish government which makes about half of all funding for minorities available to the German minority.[5]

Members of the minority have access to educational institutions where German is either taught as a second language or is the medium of instruction. As Polish law requires a minimum of seven students in each class requests such provision be made available, in effect access to German-language teaching, is largely restricted to the Opole Voivodship. As of January 2003, German was the main language of instruction in 182 primary schools and 34 grammar schools in the Opole Voivodship. The Voivodship also played host to two bilingual primary schools. A further four grammar schools provided bilingual classes. In addition German-language lectures are delivered at Opole Polytechnic, and a number of colleges offer teacher training courses in German as a foreign language. Elsewhere in Poland primary and secondary German-language education barely exists outside of a few large cities. Students graduating from all such establishments are guaranteed full and equal access to universities. All Polish universities have departments of German philology.

The German minority in Poland has four print media – the weekly *Schlesisches Wochenblatt*, as well as one monthly, one bimonthly and one quarterly magazine. One regional TV station (in the Opole Voivodship) broadcasts a regular, albeit short programme in German, while a number of others have programmes in Polish aimed at the German minority. Radio Opole broadcasts three times a week in German and bilingually in German and Polish, and four other radio stations have weekly programmes in German.

There are no restrictions on cross-border cooperation, the framework for which is covered by the bilateral treaties and agreements between Germany and Poland. In addition, some members of the German minority have benefited from the establishment of the Praded/Pradziad Euroregion in 1997, which straddles the border between Poland and the Czech Republic. These measures came too late to arrest the decline of the German population and language in the Silesian and especially the Warmia-Masuria Voivodships. There is however, every sign that in the Opole Voivodship the policy of linguistic regeneration has succeeded, in increasing the number of people with a working knowledge of the language. Any increase in German national consciousness is, as much as anything else, the unintended consequence of the botched 're-Polonisation' campaign, and the superior economic performance of the Federal Republic in comparison to Poland.

The German minority in Romania[6]

According to the 1992 census, Romania comprises 16 national minorities within a total population of almost 23 million people, the largest of them being the Hungarian minority, followed by the Roma and German communities. The 1992 census recorded 120 000 ethnic Germans as living in the country. However, due to further emigration since then, the current size of the German minority in Romania is estimated at around 50–70,000.[7] Although scattered over the Romanian Banat area and Transylvania, there remain a large number of predominantly German settlements in which German is used widely and commonly. Other minority groups in the country include Ukrainians, Russians-Lippovans, Turks, Serbs and Tartars, as well as a number of smaller groups with less than 10 000 members.

Historically, the German minority in Romania is made up of two distinct groups. The Transylvanian Saxons, who originated in the Moselle and northern Lorraine areas of present-day France and in Luxembourg and Flanders, arrived as colonists as early as the middle of the twelfth century. The Banat or Danube Swabians began to settle in the so-called Banat area (comprising a region divided by the Treaty of Trianon between Romania, Hungary and former Yugoslavia) in the first decades of the eighteenth century. Just before the beginning of the Second World War, about 750,000 ethnic Germans lived in Romania. Subsequently, several developments effected the decline in size of the minority. These included the *Heim ins Reich* resettlement policies of the Nazi regime, the evacuation of large numbers of Germans from Romania with the retreating German Wehrmacht at the end of the Second World War, a total of about 15,000 war dead (mostly male members of the minority who were conscripted or had volunteered for the SS), and the deportation of about 70,000 ethnic Germans to labour camps after the end of the war, many of whom did not return. In contrast to both Hungary and Poland, Romania did not expel any of its ethnic Germans after 1945, but from the 1970s onwards allowed their emigration to the Federal Republic of Germany. With about 220,000 ethnic Germans left in 1989, many of them in their historic settlements and maintaining functioning community structures (including educational facilities teaching German as a mother tongue), the future of the minority seemed secure. However, the violent toppling of the communist regime in 1989/1990 and the subsequent upheavals during the early period of Romania's transition to democracy led over half of the pre-1989 members of the minority to migrate to Germany. This figure included many of the young and most consciously German among them. Despite this, there are still signs that the remaining members of the German minority have preserved a relatively strong sense of ethnocultural identity.

Romanian minority policy, 1945–90

When compared to the situation of ethnic Germans in Poland and Hungary in the period after the Second World War, that of the German minority in Romania appears to have been significantly better in two respects. For one, there were no expulsions. Thus, even though about 70,000 male ethnic Germans were deported to labour camps in Ukraine and approximately 100,000 fled with the retreating German army, the minority and its social and community structures were left largely intact. Second, until the mid-1960s Romania pursued a relatively minority-friendly policy. This began as early as February 1945, when the reconstituted Romanian parliament passed the so-called minority statutes. These did not immediately apply to the German minority, and the citizenship status of its members remained uncertain for a number of years. However, once the citizenship rights of ethnic Germans had been restored, they had access to mother-tongue education, were allowed their own daily and weekly press and book publications in German and funds were made available for cultural programmes organised by the German minority. In addition, there was airtime for German – language radio and television broadcasts. All of this, of course, has to be seen in the context of a communist regime, which recognised early on that the reach of the communist party could be increased by a more liberal minority policy.

Significant changes to this approach were introduced in the mid-1960s, when the regime unilaterally decided to abandon its 'multicultural' approach and henceforth consider Romania a homogeneous nation-state. The subsequent policy of repressing expressions of different ethnocultural identities and of vigorously assimilating ethnic minorities affected the German community less than other ethnic minorities in Romania. In contrast, in particular to the situation of Hungarians, German continued to enjoy, albeit in a more limited way, opportunities to express, preserve and develop their distinct ethnocultural identity. The main reason for this was the fact that the Romanian communist regime had discovered its German minority to be a source of hard-currency income. In the context of West Germany's *neue Ostpolitik*,[8] over 150,000 ethnic Germans were given exit visas to the Federal Republic between 1977 and 1988, against a per capita fee of between 8,000 and 12,000 Deutschmarks. While on the one hand, pressure was applied on members of the minority to emigrate, the communist authorities at the same time ensured that there were sufficient opportunities for them to retain their German culture. In addition, some structural factors also contributed to the relatively great extent to which the minority managed to preserve its distinct ethnocultural identity. These included the fact that the two elements of the minority – Transylvanian Saxons and Banat Swabians – each lived in relatively compact areas, and they were, for the most part, settled in rural areas, often in almost entirely German villages and small towns where German remained the everyday language of communication. Nevertheless, all post-war censuses show a steady decline in the number of ethnic Germans in the country: by 1966, the number of people who declared themselves to be German had already about halved from the 1930 census (380,000 compared to 750,000). By the time of the next census in 1977, approximately 360,000 ethnic Germans lived in Romania, and after increased emigration over the following decade, by the time the communist regime collapsed in 1989/90, there were only just over 200,000 of them left. By 1996, another 180,000 emigrated, reducing the current number of ethnic Germans in Romania to a dwindling 50,000–70,000. Emigration has also meant that many traditional German settlements have been abandoned completely or in part, reducing the minority even further, with all the knock-on effects that entails for the use of German in daily public life, education and culture. In addition, the opportunity for emigration has been taken up by many more young people, so that the age structure of the minority today is rather unfavourable.

Post-communist developments

Following the initial nationalist turn in minority policy after 1990, a change in government in 1996 enabled Romania to make significant progress in adopting laws and policies aimed at establishing and implementing regulations of minority protection. Several articles in the constitution provide the wider legal framework for this. Article 6 establishes 'the right of persons belonging to national minorities, to the preservation, development and expression of their ethnic, cultural, linguistic and religious identity' even though it denies a right to positive discrimination for members of national minorities on the basis of 'the principles of equality and non-discrimination in relation to the other Romanian citizens'. Article 32 guarantees the 'right of persons belonging to national minorities to learn their mother tongue, and their right to be educated in this language', while Article 59 ensures that 'organizations of citizens belonging to national minorities, which fail to obtain the number of votes for representation in Parliament, have the right to one Deputy seat each', thus securing representation of all recognised national minorities in the national parliament. Article 127 declares that Romanian citizens 'belonging to national minorities ... have the right to take cognizance of all acts and files of the case, to speak before the Court and formulate conclusions, through an interpreter ... ' In addition to these constitutional provisions, there are a number of other bills and regulations pertaining to minority protection in Romania, in particular in relation to media and education. A bilateral treaty between Germany and Romania was concluded in 1992, followed by agreements on cultural cooperation (1995) and school cooperation (1996). These have been the basis for strong and positive relations between the two countries which have also benefited the situation of the German minority in Romania.

In the area of education, members of the Germany minority have access to the whole range of educational institutions existing in Romania, including those that have been specifically established to cater for the needs of mother tongue education in German. In an effort to create an adequate education system for its national minorities, the Romanian government has made provisions for the opening of multicultural schools that have classes for children of the German minority (and/or other national minorities) in addition to classes for Romanian children. In 1997–98, there were a total of 286 such institutions that catered for around 20,000 pupils in Bucharest, as well as in eight counties within areas of significant German settlement. In 1998, a teacher training college was established in Sibiu with financial and personnel support from Germany, and in 1999 the University of Bucharest, in collaboration with the Goethe Institute, launched a course for the training of primary schoolteachers of German. Babes-Bloyai University offers 12 subjects for study in German (including history, applied modern languages, physics, mathematics, biology, chemistry, geography, philosophy, arts). The University College of

Bistrica runs a course in tourism management and German. In 2000, preparations were finalised for the setting-up of a multicultural German–Hungarian–Ukrainian university in Transylvania. A total of over 400 teachers at primary and secondary levels provide instruction in German as a mother tongue, while an additional 60, co-sponsored by the German government, work in teacher training.

The German minority still has a rich cultural life, even though some of the most impressive and long-standing traditions have significantly declined, including an independent German literary tradition from which such important German contemporary writers such as Herta Müller and Richard Wagner originated. Four German cultural centres exist in Iais, Cluj, Sibiu and Timisoara, providing a varied programme of activities and access to resources, such as newspapers, books and films in German. A strong tradition in the area of print and electronic media also continues: several local German newspapers and radio stations exist in areas of minority settlements. In addition, two nationwide cultural magazines are published in German, co-financed by the Romanian government. A total of 24 hours and 40 minutes per week of TV broadcasts by state television are specifically aimed at the German minority; in addition, there is a two-hour weekly German-language broadcast on national television, as well as 45 minutes per week of German-language programming on TV Cluj-Napoca which reaches 10 districts in the northwest and west of Transylvania. This is complemented by approximately 14 hours of German-language local radio programming per week.

The German government has helped the German minority in Romania extensively in the preservation of its cultural traditions. Between 1990 and 2000, it provided a total of approximately €90 million of funds in support of the German minority in Romania. Increasing rapidly in the first half of the 1990s, funding remained relatively stable until 2000, when the federal government decided that the German minority in Romania was no longer a funding priority. Nevertheless, funding, especially in the education and cultural sectors, continues to date, albeit at more modest levels.

Conclusion

Since the collapse of communism in East-Central Europe and the Balkans, the situation of the German minority in each of the countries we have considered has improved immeasurably. In theory, that of the Germans in Hungary is the best. The extensive and intricate minority rights regime affords all minorities a wide degree of protection. Despite a less comprehensive legal code, the German minority in Poland also finds itself in a relatively strong position. With regard to the German minority in Romania, their position is handicapped by their dwindling numbers and heavily skewed age profile. The questionable 'post-communist' credentials of much of the Romanian political elite combined with a consistently woeful economic situation have conspired to make emigration to Germany an attractive option for all but the elderly and those with a fierce attachment to the *Heimat*.

Of the three groups under consideration here, the outlook for the German community in Poland is probably brightest given its sheer size and the fact that approximately 80 per cent of them live in three counties of the Opolskie Voivodship. This territorial concentration has enabled them to preserve viable community structures and a social framework in which knowledge of the German language retains its importance. This has occurred despite the fact that after the Second World War the parents and grandparents of the current generation were classified as 'Germanicised Poles', and subjected to a failed policy of 're-Polonisation'. As in Hungary there has been a great deal of linguistic assimilation. However, the situation in Hungary is less favourable – here the process of language shift from German to Hungarian seems to be unstoppable. This contrasts vividly with the Polish example where some degree of bilingualism is the rule. Nevertheless the German minority in Hungary has managed to preserve a sense of distinct ethnocultural identity, indicating that, while language may be an important factor, it is not the only one that helps determine the survival of an ethnoculturally distinct group. Despite the apparent doubling of the ethnic German population between 1991 and 2001, the pattern of internal German settlement indicates that the maintenance of a distinct German identity in Hungary is becoming ever more problematic.

Finally, we should note that in all three countries, where EU membership is likely to become a reality between 2004 and 2007, English has great functionality as a second language. No matter the desire for younger generations to recover mother tongue skills, in the face of the English language onslaught those who wish to secure the place of German (or almost any foreign language other than English), face formidable problems. To what extent they can be overcome, remains to be seen.

Notes

1. Additional information in this section was found in Government of Hungary (1999), Hungarian Helsinki Committee (1999), Advisory Committee on the Framework Convention for the Protection of National Minorities (2000) and Government of Hungary (2001).
2. According to Act LXXVII of 1993 on the Rights of National and Ethnic Minorities, any minority has the right to establish a minority municipal government or directly or indirectly formed local minority self-governments in townships, towns, or the districts of the capital city, as well as a national minority self-government. Minority self-governments may, among other things, establish and run institutions concerned with culture, education and print and electronic media.
3. This section is partly based on earlier research published in Wolff (2001 and 2002b). Further information was found in Government of Poland (2002) and Polish Helsinki Committee (1999).
4. The main German minority organisation, the *Verband der deutschen Gesellschaften* (VdG) claimed a paid-up membership of 275,000 as of January 2003 but acknowledges that not all ethnic Germans in Poland are members of the organisation.
5. The latest available figures are for the financial year of 2000. Then, the Polish government spent almost €3 million out of a budget of €6.5 million on projects in support of the German minority. Since then, the overall budget, however, has decreased.
6. This section is partly based on earlier research published in Wolff (2001 and 2002b). Further information was found in Advisory Committee on the Framework Convention for the Protection of National Minorities (2001) and Government of Romania (2002).
7. A new census was held in March 2002, but at the time of writing its results had not yet become public.
8. *Neue Ostpolitik*, the new set of policies adopted by the West German federal government under Willy Brandt after 1969, was aimed at achieving rapprochement with the countries in Central and Eastern Europe. It included a policy of humanitarian relief (*menschliche Erleichterungen*) aimed at the populations behind the iron curtain in general, but also at members of ethnic German minorities for whom improved opportunities for emigration to the Federal Republic were sought.

References

Advisory Committee on the Framework Convention for the Protection of National Minorities. 2001. *Opinion on Hungary*. Strasbourg: Council of

Europe.   <http://www.humanrights.coe.int/Minorities/Eng/Framework
Convention/AdvisoryCommittee/Opinions/Hungary.htm>

Advisory Committee on the Framework Convention for the Protection of
National Minorities. 2002. *Opinion on Romania*. Strasbourg: Council of
Europe.   <http://www.humanrights.coe.int/Minorities/Eng/Framework
Convention/AdvisoryCommittee/Opinions/Romania.htm>

Government of Hungary. 2001. *Comments of the Government of Hungary on the
Opinion of the Advisory Committee on the Report on the Implementation of the
Framework Convention for the Protection of National Minorities in Hungary.*
Strasbourg: Council of Europe.   <http://www.humanrights.coe.int/
Minorities/Eng/FrameworkConvention/AdvisoryCommittee/Opinions/
Hungary.Comments.htm>

Government of Hungary. 1999. *Report Submitted by Hungary Pursuant to
Article 25, Paragraph 1 of the Framework Convention for the Protection of National
Minorities.* Starsbourg: Council of Europe. <http://www.humanrights.
coe.int/Minorities/Eng/FrameworkConvention/StateReports/1999/
hungary/hungarian.htm>

Government of Poland. 2002. *Report Submitted by Poland Pursuant to Article 25,
Paragraph 1 of the Framework Convention for the Protection of National
Minorities.* Strasbourg: Council of Europe. <http://www.humanrights.coe.
int/Minorities/Eng/FrameworkConvention/StateReports/2002/poland.
htm>

Government of Romania. 1999. *Report Submitted by Poland Pursuant to Article 25,
Paragraph 1 of the Framework Convention for the Protection of National
Minorities.* Strasbourg: Council of Europe. <http://www.humanrights.
coe.int/Minorities/Eng/FrameworkConvention/StateReports/1999/
romania/Romanianstatereport.htm>

Government of Romania. 2002. *Comments of the Government of Romania on the
Opinion of the Advisory Committee on the Implementation of the Framework
Convention for the Protection of National Minorities in Romania.* Strasbourg:
Council of Europe. <http://www.humanrights.coe.int/Minorities/Eng/
FrameworkConvention/AdvisoryCommittee/Opinions/Romania.Comments.
htm>

High Commissioner on National Minorities. 1998. *Oslo Recommendations
regarding the Linguistic Rights of National Minorities.* The Hague: High
Commissioner on National Minorities.

Hungarian Helsinki Committee. 1999. *Report on the Situation of Minorities in
Hungary.* <http://www.riga.lv/minelres/reports/hungary/hungary_NGO.
htm>

Nelde, P. H., 2000. 'Bilingualism among Ethnic Germans in Hungary', in
Wolff, S., ed., *German Minorities in Europe: Ethnic Identity and Cultural
Belonging.* New York and Oxford: Berghahn, 125–33.

Polish Helsinki Committee. 1999. The Protection of National Minorities in
Poland. <http://www.riga.lv/minelres/reports/poland/poland_NGO.htm>

Verband der deutschen sozial-kulturellen Gesellschaften in Polen.
http://vdg.pl

Wolff, S., 2000. 'German as a Minority Language: The Legislative and Policy Framework in Europe', in National Varieties of German outside Germany, ed. by Gabrielle Hogan-Brun. Bern and New York: Peter Lang, 49–66.

Wolff, S., 2001. 'From Irredentism to Constructive Renconciliation? Germany and Its Minority in Poland and the Czech Republic', in O'Reilly, C.C., *Language, Ethnicity and the State*. Basingstoke: Palgrave Macmillan, 66–90.

Wolff, S., 2002a. 'Changing Priorities or changing opportunities? German External Minority Policy, 1919–1998', in Wolff, S., ed., *German Minorities in Europe: Ethnic Identity and Cultural Belonging*. New York and Oxford: Berghahn, 183–203.

Wolff, S., 2002b. 'The Politics of Homeland. Irredentism and Reconciliation in the External Minority Policies of German Federal Governments and Expellee Organisations', *German Politics*, 11(2) (August 2002): 105–27.

7
Baltic National Minorities in a Transitional Setting*
Gabrielle Hogan-Brun

The dynamics released by the political and economic liberation from Soviet hegemony in the countries of the former East Bloc have triggered major social and linguistic changes, paving the way for previously suppressed languages and cultures to blossom again. As a result, local languages and cultures have been affected in two different ways: at one end of the spectrum we can observe the successful re-instatement of the official status of the titular languages; at the opposite end of the spectrum we see the unleashing of ethnolinguistic tensions and disputes over minority rights. In the face of these two competing, but not mutually exclusive tendencies, the recognition and safeguarding of these re-emerging cultural and linguistic ecologies have become crucial issues of social significance with psychological, cultural, political, legal and economic implications.

This chapter will investigate the means employed by the Baltic Republics in dealing with their national minorities. Further, by focussing on how the Russian-speaking diaspora population is coming to terms with its changed status, I shall consider ways of promoting inclusive policies in support of societal integration in the Baltic.

The Baltic context

The Baltic Republics were the first to break away from the former Soviet Union and swiftly emerged as the leaders in political, economic and social reform amongst their fellow successor states. Their anti-Union struggle in the late 1980s echoed, and fed on, shared memories of 20 years of previous independent statehood between the World Wars: during this crucial period nation- and state-building processes had been initiated which subsequently provided a legal connection and new starting point for locally re-installed constitutions and laws (Chinn and Kaiser 1996: 96).[1]

The restored Baltic States, however, differ sharply from their interwar predecessors: multinational polities had evolved as a result of Soviet immigration policies which had profoundly affected the make-up of the local populations, albeit in different ways. This demographic legacy therefore had become a principal political issue, played out by language and culture, in the struggle for independence, particularly in Estonia and Latvia (ibid.: 4). The reinstatement of the national languages to official status initially met with considerable opposition from the Russian-speaking population[2] who feared that the sudden shift of Russian to minority status would diminish their position in the Republics (Hogan-Brun and Ramonienė 2003b). Alerted to the sensitive nature of minority issues, the emerging governments subsequently sought to guarantee the rights of minority language communities. Whilst essentially confronting similar challenges, the three republics have implemented different policies since the early days of transition to tackle emerging ethnicity-related issues. What follows is a detailed account of the position of and provisions supplied for the national minorities in Lithuania, Latvia and Estonia.

Emerging ethnicities in the Baltic

The Baltic Republics have a long history of multi-ethnicity. From the thirteenth century onwards Danes and Germans, then Swedes and Russians had sought to end their control along the Baltic.[3] Communities of Roma, Jews, Belarusians and, later, Russian Old Believers also settled in the area. Whilst Lithuania came under the influence of the Polish elite, Estonia and the present Latvian territory continued to live under the German landed aristocracy. By the end of the eighteenth century the entire Baltic had been incorporated into the Russian empire, and Russification increasingly replaced earlier attempts of Polonization and Germanization.[4] Large-scale immigration of Russian peasants ensued, particularly to Latvia and Estonia. Following an intensive phase of state-building, the Balts simultaneously seized the opportunity of the collapse of both Russia and Germany to forge their statehoods in 1919.

The ethnic spread in the three inter-war states was complex but not large in absolute terms (see Table 7.1). In Estonia, the Russians formed the biggest group (3.9 per cent), followed closely by Germans (1.7 per cent) (Hiden and Salmon 1991: 46). The number of Russians in Latvia was more substantial (10.6 per cent), and significant percentages of Germans (3.5 per cent), Jews (4.8 per cent) and Poles (2.5 per cent) were settled there too (ibid.). The pattern in Lithuania was different. Here, Jews constituted the largest minority (7.6 per cent), followed by the Poles (3.2 per cent), Russians (2.7 per cent) and Germans (1.4 per cent) (ibid.). These figures prompted leaders of the fledgling inter-war republics to address minority rights in their constitutions; however, the practical implementation of these rights varied under the ensuing authoritarian regimes in the Baltic (Hiden and Salmon 1991: 46). Following the incorporation of the Baltic Republics into the Soviet Union in 1940, Stalinization led to a policy of heavy industrialization in the region, which involved planned mass immigration of (mainly) Russians, particularly to Estonia and Latvia. The Soviet settlers were chiefly military and blue-collar workers, living in urban areas, whilst the rural parts remained inhabited mostly by the members of the titular nations. These

Table 7.1   Changing ethnic composition in the Baltic States from 1923 to 2000

	1923–34 (%)	1989 (%)	2000/01 (%)
Estonia			
Estonians	92.4	61.5	67.9
Russians	3.9	30.3	25.6
Others	3.7	8.2	6.5
Latvia			
Latvians	73.4	52	57.7
Russians	10.6	34	29.6
Others	16	14	12.7
Lithuania			
Lithuanians	84.2	79.6	83.45
Russians	2.5	9.4	6.31
Polish	3.2	7	6.74
Others	10.1	4	3.5

Sources: Gerner and Hedlund 1993: 74; Latvian Census (2000); Estonian Census (2000); http://www.std.lt/Surasymas/Rezultatai/index_pirm_e.htm; Lietuvių enciklopedija, vol. 15 (1991: 57).

migrants had 'little sense that they were living in a foreign land and little desire to acculturate; rather (they) expected indigenes to behave as if they were in the Russian environment' (ibid.: 97). They did not think of themselves as a minority in a 'host' country as they were treated by Moscow as a dominant group. This caused resentment on the part of the local populations.

The resulting demographic changes experienced by Estonia and Latvia were dramatic, less so in Lithuania. By 1989, the indigenous population had sunk to 61.5 per cent from 92.4 per cent in Estonia, to 52 per cent from 73.4 per cent in Latvia and to 83.45 per cent from 84.2 per cent in Lithuania[5] (see Table 7.1). The situation in Latvia was particularly drastic as this country had come to the verge of losing its ethnic majority. Moreover, under their 50 year-long regime, the Soviets had succeeded in shifting the ethnic balance even more acutely as not only people of Russian nationality ended up declaring Russian as the first language, but also many members of other ethnic communities. Russian was considered to be the first language in all three Republics by a sizeable proportion of Belarusians, Ukrainians, Jews and Poles who used it as a lingua franca in both public and private life. At the time of the restoration of independence, the percentages of ethnic groupings across the three states whose first language was Russian were as displayed in Table 7.2.

Altogether, 34.8 per cent of the total population in Estonia, 42.5 per cent in Latvia and 11.66 per cent in Lithuania had Russian as their first language. Indeed, it has been claimed that in some instances the level of the native language had fallen below the competence of Russian (Zinkevičius 1998: 321). Of those who did not consider the national language to be their first language, some (most Russians) were monolingual; others were bilingual (mother tongue/Russian) or trilingual (mother tongue/titular language/Russian). These and subsequent data in this chapter point to the complex nature of language loyalties, as there is no overall congruence between ethnicity and language use in the Baltic (Druviete 2000: 40). However, although intensive Sovietization had partly resulted in the displacement of languages and cultures, this did not lead to the extinction of the national identities of the Balts who forcefully reclaimed their independence in a swell of national protests in the late 1980s.[6]

Today 29.6 per cent of Latvia's ethnic population consists of Russians (Latvian Census 2002). Estonia's major minority groups are

Table 7.2 Proportion of ethnic groups in Lithuania, Latvia and Estonia with Russian as their first language in 1989

Ethnic groups	Proportion (%)
Lithuania	
Lithuanians	0.4
Russians	95.6
Belarusians	59.5
Poles	14.5
Ukrainians	48.9
Latvia	
Latvians	2.6
Russians	98.8
Jews	74.9
Belarusians	64.8
Poles	54.2
Ukrainians	49.4
Estonia	
Estonians	1.05
Russians	98.6
Belarusians	67.1
Poles	66.4
Ukrainians	54.5

Sources: Vaitiekus (1992); Valodas politikas istenošana Latviā (2002: 6); Estonian Census (2001: 150).

Russians (25.6 per cent) and Ukrainians (2.1 per cent) (Estonian Census 2001: 14), and Lithuania mainly hosts Russians (6.31 per cent) and Poles (6.74 per cent) (Hogan-Brun and Ramonienė 2003a).

The issue of integrating these groups into the overall community whilst also granting them space to preserve their own identity and to protect and nurture their language and culture has been successfully addressed in Lithuania but still needs to be worked on in Estonia and especially in Latvia.

Current Baltic language scenes

In 1989 a range of language laws were adopted throughout the Baltic Republics to end the hegemony of Russian and to ensure the position of the titular languages. When Estonian, Latvian and Lithuanian re-acquired official status in the following year, all work in state entities, organizations and enterprises was to be conducted in the respective state languages. The resident ethnic communities were particularly affected by the sudden change, as language proficiency became a key for employment, chiefly in the public sector. To certify professional linguistic competence and as part of naturalization requirements, state language exams were introduced. The implementation of the emerging language laws started to be monitored nationally by language inspectors.

The function of the newly reinstated state languages was deemed not only to enhance national cohesion in the newly independent republics, but conversely it also ensured that all members would be able to fully participate in the life of the nation (Druviete 2000: 39). Full participation crucially involves access to both (tertiary) education[7] and the job market through language support.[8] In order to enable the members from various language communities to function in the changed environment, state language learning curricula had been developed and introduced in all the Republics[9] with a steady take-up rate. Over the years, the language situation in the Baltic has duly changed. Between 1989 and 2000, the total population who speak their titular language has risen to 80 per cent from 67 per cent in Estonia, to 82 per cent from 62 per cent in Latvia and to 94 per cent from 85 per cent in Lithuania (Mežs: unpublished).

Whilst there are no data on actually achieved levels of language competence, these figures coincide with a decrease of those with no knowledge of the state language (by 13 per cent in Estonia, by 20 per cent in Latvia and by 9 per cent in Lithuania; ibid.) during the same period. Several factors account for this overall increase in the command of the titular languages: the steady demand for the naturalization of non-citizens, nationwide work-related language competency certification requirements, the natural decrease in older (monolingual) immigrant settlers and the simultaneous succession of a younger generation who have acquired appropriate linguistic knowledge through schooling, which will be the subject of discussion in the forthcoming sections. These quantitative data however require some qualification as the attitudes towards and amongst the ethnic communities in the Baltic vary considerably.

Lithuanian ethnic communities and their attitudes to integration

In Lithuania, where the ethnic groups amount to nearly 17 per cent (Hogan-Brun and Ramonienė 2003a) positive signs of the consolidation of society have been observed. However, the two largest minorities – Russians and Poles – who both used to belong to formerly dominant groups, have assumed quite different positions towards integration: the latter, who live predominantly in the south-eastern regions, are on the whole keen to protect their own identity and to retain their distinctiveness. The former by contrast, who tend to live more in cities, display less in-group cohesiveness.[10] The upward mobility and perceived assimilationist manner including linguistic accommodation of the Russian population in Lithuania could arguably be motivated by a better lifestyle here than would be possible in their former homeland. With the changes in the socio-political situation, the overall attitude towards the titular language has changed considerably amongst the ethnic groups.[11] Most members now feel positive about using Lithuanian, and 10 per cent of the total population declare it as their second language (as opposed to 5 per cent in 1989; Mežs: unpublished). This rise is partly linked to current practices relating to parental choice of schooling for their offspring: seeing their children's future directly linked to success in the mainstream, many parents from the minority communities have increasingly started to send them to Lithuanian medium schools (Hogan-Brun and Ramonienė 2003b).[12] More recently, new models of bilingual schooling at the primary and secondary levels have been introduced[13] in order to better supply the needs of the changing society through open multicultural education. Ethnic minority schools, where instruction is chiefly held in the community languages, have been retained alongside this new scheme.[14]

The majority of Lithuania's ethnic population was able to acquire citizenship in a naturalization process that offered the 'zero option': this permitted all individuals normally resident in the Republic at the time of the restitution of independence to become Lithuanian citizens (de Varennes 1996: 244). This fact has generated an overall positive attitude towards integration amongst these groups, providing motivation to work towards a common goal.

Towards ethnic consolidation in Latvia and Estonia

The ethnic composition of Lithuania's Baltic neighbours differs and is a direct result of former Soviet immigration policies. In Latvia, Russian speakers – mainly Russian and Ukrainian settlers – make up close to 50 per cent of the overall population (Druviete 2000: 38). This figure amounts to approximately 35 per cent in Estonia (http://www.riik.ee/saks/ikomisjon; see also Estonian Census 2001: 14). In both countries, stricter citizenship criteria have been applied for minorities than in Lithuania,[15] which poses problems in the process of societal integration (see also Zaagman 1999: 34, 45).

Estonia's Russian-speaking population lives predominantly in the major cities of Tartu (13.5 per cent), Pärnu (4.7 per cent), Tallinn (8.7 per cent), and in the industrialized north-eastern region Ida-Virumaa with its major towns Kothla-Järve (13.4 per cent) and Narva (28.9 per cent). These people are predominantly of Russian origin (29.7 per cent), and the remainder (5.3 per cent) are mainly Ukrainians and Belarusians (Estonian Census 2001: 14). The majority of persons who do not speak the national language therefore use Russian. Bilingualism with Estonian is on the increase, and 13 per cent of the total population now declare it to be their second language (compared to 6 per cent in 1989; Mežs: unpublished). Since 1989, there has been a rise of those who can speak the State language by 37 per cent–40 per cent amongst young Russians of 10 to 24 years of age (ibid.). There are several educational factors accounting for this: Increasing numbers of Russian-speaking pupils are attending mainstream schools (as in Lithuania). Overall, an average of 76 per cent of pupils attend schools with state language instruction (ibid.). Other educational models include immersion,[16] bilingual and minority language medium schooling (mainly Russian schools). The latter also provide Estonian as a foreign language but are often badly integrated into Estonian society, and in areas such as north-eastern Estonia many teachers lack appropriate knowledge of the titular language, which students have no opportunity to practise outside school (Estonia's Integration Landscape 2000: 12). Lawmakers foresee the gradual abolishment of Russian-medium upper secondary education (from year nine onwards) as from 2007. However, plans to replace this with Estonian-only schooling have been put on hold due to a lack of popular support,[17] and bilingual education is likely to continue.

In order to bring Russian and Estonian schools closer together and to ensure greater social harmony whilst providing the opportunity for ethnic groups to preserve their identity, mother tongues and cultural traditions, a state programme entitled 'Integration in Estonian Society 2000–07' has been launched (http://www.riik.ee/saks/ ikomisjon/). Politically and financially backed by the European Union (EU), this is based on the 'model of a multicultural society, characterized by the principles of cultural pluralism and a strong common core.[18] Whilst it is acknowledged that languages and ethnic traditions are not necessarily common to all members of society as they belong to the private sphere of individuals, this programme will have to involve a bilateral process: both Estonians and non-Estonians will need to participate equally in this scheme so as to avoid one-sided integration and possible assimilation.

The bulk of Latvia's substantial Russian-speaking population lives predominantly in the cities Riga (65 per cent), Daugavpils (87 per cent). The number of Latvians in Daugavpils currently amounts to just 15.92 per cent, in Riga – 40.98 per cent, in Rezekne – 42.58 per cent, in Jurmala – 49.08 per cent, in Liepaja – 49.38 per cent, in Jelgava – 50.97 per cent, in Ventspils – 51.58 per cent (Central Statistical Board of Latvia 2001: 36), and in the eastern region Latgale, where the long-established non-Latvian population reaches 60 per cent in rural and 73 per cent in urban areas (Dobson 2001: 159). Due to their great ethnic density these people are on the whole not motivated to learn the titular language in many of these areas where the Latvian environment is missing as they can function well in their own language. Yet bilingualism with Latvian is on the increase too, and 20 per cent of the total population claim it to be their second language (compared to 10 per cent in 1989; Mežs: unpublished). In fact, since 1989, there has been a rise of those who speak the titular language by about 43 per cent amongst young Russians of 10 to 24 years of age (ibid.). Apart from the extrinsic factors mentioned before, there are educational reasons accounting for this increase, as non-Latvian schools (amounting to 40 per cent in total) have to teach two to three subjects in Latvian. Drastic changes to the existing system are planned as the 1998 Education Law foresees that all state secondary schools will use Latvian as their main language of instruction by

2004.[19] Whilst the proposed changes are often misunderstood or wrongly explained in the literature on Latvia (e.g. Dobson 2001: 172), it is questionable whether teachers and pupils from areas where Russian is the dominant language will be able to adapt to this system without a decline in the standards of teaching and learning.

To help minority representatives get along with language-related education and employment laws, a National Program for Latvian Language Training was established in the mid-1990s. Using positive and liberal approaches to the teaching of the titular language, they have produced a number of innovative learning materials for a variety of needs. Apart from teacher- and language training and the development of bilingual methodologies they also organize theme-based mixed (Russian/Latvian) camps in Latvian, which have had an effect on the reduction of inter-ethnic prejudices and myths.[20]

Latvia too has been successful in obtaining EU backing to launch a state integration programme. The aims are to promote naturalization and repatriation procedures as well as supporting projects in the areas of language, education, culture and science. The priority set for 2002 is ethnic, social and regional integration amongst the overall population. This stands in contrast to Estonia's aims that target the integration of non-Estonians into mainstream society.

Ongoing debates on minority issues

There has been a continuing debate over language and citizenship issues in the Baltic, especially relating to Estonia and Latvia. Lithuania, which hosts relatively small ethnic communities (Table 7. 1) with an adequate command of Lithuanian, opted for inclusive citizenship policies. Estonia and Latvia on the other hand have chosen a different approach. They introduced much stricter citizenship requirements due to their greater share of Russophone people (Table 7. 1) who tend to have a limited knowledge of the titular languages. Here, automatic citizenship was strictly granted to original (pre-1940) residents and their descendants, excluding the large numbers of Soviet-period Russian-speaking settlers. A rigorous process of naturalization was introduced for non-nationals. On the whole, this involves procedures which are commonly found elsewhere too (Knowles 1999: 53), plus a test on constitutional and historical knowledge, and on language competence.[21] Many speakers of Russian see the latter as discriminatory and a barrier to naturalization. They have received Moscow's support who, evoking international standards in human rights, took the case of the Russian minorities to the UN, OSCE and the Council of Europe (COE) (Trenin, referred to in Ozolins 1999: 20). The exclusive nature of Estonia's and Latvia's citizenship laws and Latvia's delayed introduction of an efficient and open naturalization procedure have since been criticized by the international community (see Ozolins 1999: 23 and Dobson 2001: 160). Under pressure from the OSCE, who closely monitor minority-related issues, these laws have consequently been liberalized to some extent.[22]

Another source of controversy is the restricted rights of Estonia's and especially Latvia's large numbers of 'non-citizens'.[23] These people may neither vote nor stand for election; they have limited rights to public protest and are barred from holding certain types of employment.[24] Such regulations are affecting their socio-economic situation to some extent (Dobson 2001: 166) and present a barrier to integration. A further law concerns language competency. In all three Republics, customers have the right to be served and receive information in the titular language. Ethnic employees in both the public and private sector therefore have to undergo a language test, pitched according to the level of linguistic competence required in their work. Whilst re-takes are offered within a limited period, attendance of language courses is not usually state-supported, which has severe repercussions for the jobless (ibid.). A more recent (1999) addition to Latvia's language legislation further attracted the interest of the OSCE, who advocate the protection of the private sphere for ethnic minorities: this act seeks to extend the use of Latvian into everyday life, including private business, by requesting that all meetings and correspondence should be in the titular language if so requested by one participant (ibid.: 171). This hotly contested law enforcement can arguably have a segregationist effect on the labour market in the private sector.

These language decrees, whose implementation continues to be monitored by national language inspectors across the Baltic,[25] have, on the one hand, been a means to secure the status and to radically expand the sociolinguistic functions of the titular languages. But some of them have also become the subject of much internal and international debate and evolved into a political hot potato, tossed in the struggle for hegemony between Russia and the West.

Conclusions and outlook

The processes of state (re-)formation and re-structuring in the Baltic have involved the interplay between ethnic patriotism and language issues. Even prior to the restoration of independence, the notion of identity has been a central issue in shaping political practice to redress half a century of ethnic engineering endured under Communist rule. As the titular ethnic groups re-instated the official status of their national languages, Russian and its speakers became marginalized. Latvian and, to a lesser extent, Estonian attempts at legislating language and ethnicity-related changes have evoked criticism internally and further afield. Lithuania's national project on the other hand has been more moderate and inclusive as its ethnic and linguistic ecology has remained more intact there during Sovietization.

Latvia's and Estonia's Russophone settler community, initially faced with a crisis of identity, quickly rallied around the issues of citizenship and language rights, which had emerged as the focal point of their concerns (Melvin 2000: 140). But the Russian diaspora has on the whole remained unorganized, particularly in Latvia, and violent confrontations are rare. This may partly be due to the fact that political solidarity and ethnic cooperation had not been encouraged under the previous regime. However, many Russian-speaking people feel discriminated against, especially in employment. Over the years, some degree of (linguistic) accommodation has evolved across the entire Baltic, as evidenced by previous data. To some extent it could be argued that this is the result of competitive assimilation, spurned by extrinsic motivation as a means to obtain material benefits and better jobs through the mainstream society. Other evidence also seems to support a change in attitudes: asked in surveys to reply to the propositions 'people like us should not be made to learn the titular language' and 'should people who want to become citizens have to pass an examination in the national language?', over half the Russophone respondents disagreed with the former and approved of the latter (Ozolins 1999: 29; Baltic Barometer 2000: 48).[26] Whilst some people, then, seemed to accept the legitimacy of the language laws, the remainder, particularly if they are Soviet-period settlers, will be more inclined to support monolingualism and, in Latvia, a two-official-languages policy (Druviete 2002: 39), which would perpetuate asymmetrical bilingualism.

Conflicts over language and citizenship in Latvia and Estonia, overshadowed by international concerns, are continuing. These issues are mainly related to education, language proficiency testing and the protection of the private sphere of minority representatives in Latvia (see Dobson 1999; Ozolins 2001; Human Rights 2002; Zaagman 1999; Poleshchuk 2001a and b). Both countries have somewhat amended their existing legislation on the basis of recommendations received from the European Commission (see Poleshchuk 2002: 2–6) and the OSCE; see Packer 2001: 265). The significant impact of such Western monitoring on existing Baltic policies directly relates to the locally judged importance of the area's acceptance into wider European structures in order to find stability between East and West. Whilst such interaction certainly is to be welcomed on all sides, legal advice will have to continually take into account local re-adjustments to acts of injustice in the past, when ideologies of 'freedom of choice' were non-existent for the members of the titular nations for half a century.[27] Any mediating approaches therefore must consider the complexity of issues in the Baltic and go beyond a purely legal framework. The Baltic Republics have longstanding traditions of multi-ethnicity, as traced earlier in this chapter. However, current modernist trends that rely on the ethnic national ideal still need to evolve in Latvia and Estonia to make way towards Lithuania's initiated support of cultural diversity and linguistic heterogeneity in order to promote social integration and harmony.

Notes

* I thank the British Academy for their support of my visit to the Baltic Republics in June 2002. Sincere thanks also go to Meilutė Ramonienė for arranging the contacts and for supplying the figures for Latvia in table 1 and for Lithuania (1923–34) in Appendix 1.1. For a thorough overview over the Baltic context see Chinn and Kaiser (1996), Dini (1991), Hiden and Salmon (1991) and Smith (1994).

2. In Lithuania, the Polish-speaking people, who amount to 8 per cent of the overall population, felt equally threatened. Many of them joined the *Interfront* movement, which was a product of conservative Communist forces seeking to mobilize the largest minorities for the purpose of continuing the orthodox Communist system (Hogan-Brun and Ramonienė 2003a).

3. Lithuania subsequently strengthened Polish-Lithuanian Commonwealth (1569–1795), thus succeeding in curbing Teutonic advances.

4. Russian became the language of schools, of administration and the government and the local languages were repressed. For more details see Hiden and Salmon (1991: 10).
5. This minor change in the national percentage of ethnic Lithuanians is explained by the fact that the Republic's south-eastern part, including Vilnius, which were under Polish occupation during the inter-war period, had meanwhile been re-absorbed into state territory; the borders in the Klaipeda region too had been shifted then.
6. Initially, these movements were formed to merely demand *some* measure of cultural and economic independence. However, social liberalization spurned by perestroika and glasnost led to active opposition which, coupled with a rebirth of national re-awakening, quickly spread into socio-economic and political arenas, eventually leading to secession.
7. Tertiary education is provided in the titular languages only at public/state universities, in all three republics.
8. Citizenship issues will be discussed below.
9. In Latvia and Estonia, where the language learning needs are greater, these curricula have been elaborated into larger national state language learning programmes.
10. For a more in-depth analysis of this situation (see Hogan-Brun and Ramonienė 2003a).
11. The author of this paper and Meilutė Ramonienė have commissioned a major survey (the first of its kind in the Baltic Republics) to fully investigate the sociolinguistic situation and language attitudes in these Lithuanian communities.
12. The Lithuanian Polish community is an exception in this trend (for more details see Hogan-Brun and Ramonienė 2003a).
13. For an overview of these models and details of the take-up rate (see Hogan-Brun and Ramonienė 2003b).
14. These schools constitute approximately 9 per cent of all education institutions and are mainly located in the south-east of Lithuania, where the density of these language communities is high, and in the biggest cities: the capital Vilnius, the seaport Klaipėda and Visaginas, a new development next to the Ignalina power station (Hogan-Brun and Ramonienė 2003a). In 1989, residents of Russian nationality amounted to 20.2 per cent in Vilnius, 64.2 per cent in Visaginas and 28.2 per cent in Klaipėda (Vaitiekus 1992). No newer data are available yet.
15. Latvia and Estonia are the only post-Soviet republics to have 'denied the resident population of post-war immigrants the same rights as original citizens' (Dobson 2001: 161).
16. These schools follow the Canadian model and aim to provide 50 per cent – 50 per cent instruction in Russian and Estonian respectively by the ninth school year. Currently there are seven such schools (communication by Mart Rannut, Tallinn, 10 June 2002).
17. Such schooling would have failed to work in the north-eastern Narva area where practical difficulties limit the learning of Estonian.

18. 'Common core' is defined as being a means of connecting the members of society with 'general human and democratic values, a common sphere of information, and an Estonian language environment, common state institutions, values based on the knowledge of Estonian history, the nature of Estonian citizenship and the multicultural nature of Estonian society' (http://www.riik.ee/saks/ikomisjon).

19. This system envisages the following steps for secondary schools (grades 10–12):

    (1) compulsory Latvian-medium teaching in six core subjects (foreign language, Latvian, mathematics, history, economy, business studies, information technology)
    (2) up to 30 per cent instruction in the minority language (compulsory)
    (3) tuition in any language (western too) for subjects such as philosophy, history of art ecology.

    All ethnic pupils are expected to be able to fit into the system, whether they come from bilingual, primarily Latvian- or minority-medium primary schools and will have to pass a centralized language exam before doing so (communication by Evija Papule, Department of Integration, Riga, 12 June 2002).

20. Communication by the Director of the program in Riga, Aija Priedite, 12 June 2002. Such camps have also begun to be organized in Estonia; the ensuing information on the Latvian state program has been supplied by her as well.

21. These tests, which have been modified according to IELTS guidelines, are pitched at a lower immediate level, examining reading, writing, listening and speaking skills. Whilst there is a fee attached to such certification, there are also concessions; sample questions are available for public inspection; the elderly are exempt from the listening and written parts, and re-takes are possible (communication by Lilita Danga and Māra Konkia, Naturalisation Board, Riga, on 13 June 2002).

22. Latvia's naturalization procedure, which was introduced relatively late, in 1994, involved a 'window system': this restricted who could apply for citizenship and was abolished in a 1998 amendment to the Law on Citizenship following OSCE recommendations (Dobson 2001: 164). A further key change was the establishment of the right for children of non-citizens, born after 1992, to be conferred citizenship upon parental registration without a language test; this was argued to be an important step to reduce statelessness.

23. This is the term given to those residents who have not undergone naturalization (yet); currently the majority of non-Estonians and non-Latvians are not citizens of their state of residence (Poleshchuk 2002: 5).

24. Employment bans restrict non-citizens from armed positions (police, military) and, chiefly, the Civil Service, as well as careers in medicine and law (for more details on Latvian regulations see Dobson 1999: 165).

25. The remit of the language inspectors' work in all three Republics is mainly to check on the use and correctness of the titular languages in shops and

on goods labels, and on (the authenticity of) language certification. Corrective measures imply warnings, consultations and, at a later stage, the imposition of fines (communication by Agris Timuška, Deputy Director, State Language Centre, Riga, on 12 June 2002).
26. Rose's repeated surveys elicited the first reply in 1994 and the second, which did not include the Estonians, in 2000.
27. I am referring here to the secret act of the infamous Molotov–Ribbentrop Pact in 1939 and its consequences for the Baltic Republics under subsequent Soviet command. Whilst history cannot be held to 'justify' renewed discrimination, dealing with the effects of planned (Soviet-time) immigration encompasses a dimension not encountered in the West where these legal frameworks have been developed.

References

Chinn, J. and Kaiser, R., 1996, *Russians as the New Minority. Ethnicity and Nationalism in the Soviet Successor States*. Boulder and Oxford: Westview Press.
de Varennes, Ferdinand, 1996, 'Language Minorities and Human Rights.' *International Studies and in Human Rights*, 45. The Hague/Boston/London: Martinus Nijhoff Publishers.
Dini, P. U., 1991, L'anello Baltico. Profilo delle nazioni Baltiche Lituania, Lettonia, Estonia. (The Baltic Ring: Profile of the Baltic Nations Lithuania, Latvia and Estonia.) Genova: Marietti.
Dobson, J., 2001, 'Ethnic Discrimination in Latvia', in *Language, Ethnicity and the State, 2, Minority Languages in Eastern Europe Post-1989*, ed. C. C. O'Reilly. Houndsmills and New York: Palgrave, 155–88.
Druviete, I., 2000, *Sociolinguistic Situation and Language Policy in the Baltic States*. Riga: Latvijas Universitate.
Druviete, I., 2002, 'The Future of the Latvian Language in the Enlarged European Union', *Language, Literature and Translation-Manipulations* 1/34: 34–46.
Estonia's Integration Landscape: From Apathy to Harmony, 2000. Tallinn: Jaan Tõnisson Instituut.
Gerner, K. and Hedlund, S., 1993, *The Baltic States and the End of the Soviet Empire*. London and New York: Routledge.
Hiden, J. and Salmon, P., 1991, *The Baltic Nations and Europe. Estonia, Latvia and Lithuania in the 21st Century*. London and New York: Longman.
Hogan-Brun, G. and Ramonienė, M., 2003a, 'Emerging Language and Education Policies in Lithuania', *Language Policy* (forthcoming).
Hogan-Brun, G. and Ramonienė, M., 2003b, 'Changing Levels of Bilingualism across the Baltic', *International Journal for Bilingual Education and Bilingualism* (forthcoming).
Human Rights in Latvia in 2001, 2002. Riga: Latvian Centre for Human Rights and Ethnic Studies (referred to as: Human Rights).

Integratsioonikomisjoni materjalid. (Material of the Estonian Commission for Integration.) http://www.riik.ee/saks/ikomisjon

Integration into Estonian Society 2000, http://www.riik.ee/saks/ikomisjon

Knowles, F., 1999, 'Ethno-linguistic Relations in Contemporary Latvia: Mirror Image of the Previous Dispensation?', in *Language Policy and Language Issues in the Successor States of the Former USSR*, ed. S. Wright. Clevedon: Multilingual Matters, 48–56.

Lietuvių enciklopedija (Lithuanian encyclopedia), 1991, ed. Vincas Maciūnas, vol. 15. Vilnius: Lietuvių enciklopedijos leidykla (1st edition, Boston: Lithuanian Encyclopedia Press, 1968).

Melvin, N. J., 2000, 'Post imperial Ethnocracy and the Russophone Minorities of Estonia and Latvia', in *The Policies of National Minority Participation Post-Communist Europe. State-Building, Democracy and Ethnic Mobilisation*, ed. J. P. Stein. EastWest Institute (EWI). New York and London: M. E. Sharpe, 129–66.

Mežs, I. (unpublished), 'Some Statistics about the Language Situation in the Baltic States.' Riga: University of Riga.

Ozolins, U., 1999, 'Between Russian and European Hegemony: Current Language Policy in the Baltic States', in *Language Policy and Language Issues in the Successor States of the Former USSR*, ed. S. Wright. Clevedon: Multilingual Matters, 6–47.

Packer, J., 2001, 'The Protection of Minority Language Rights through the Work of OSCE Institutions', in *Minority Rights in Europe. European Minorities and Languages*. The Hague: T. M. C. Asser Press, 255–74.

Poleshchuk, V., 2001a, Multiculturalism, Minority Education and Language Policy. European Centre for Minority Issues, Flensburg: ECMI, Report #10.

Poleshchuk, V., 2001b, Social Dimension of Integration in Estonia and Minority Education in Latvia. European Centre for Minority Issues, Flensburg: ECMI, Report #18.

Poleshchuk, V., 2002, *Estonia, Latvia, and the European Commission: Changes in Language Regulation in 1999–2001*. http://www.eumap.org/articles/content/40/402/index_html?print+/

Rose, R., 2000, New Baltic Barometer IV: A Survey Study. Studies in Public Policy. University of Strathclyde, Glasgow (referred to as: Baltic Barometer).

Smith, G., 1994, ed., *The Baltic States. The National Self-Determination of Estonia, Latvia and Lithuania*. London: Macmillan.

2000 Population and Housing Census. Citizenship, Nationality, Mother Tongue and Command of Foreign Languages, 2001. Tallinn: Statistical Office of Estonia (referred to as Estonian census 2001).

2000 gada tautas skaitīšanas provizoriskie rezultāti (2001). Riga: Latvijas Respublikas Centrālā statistikas pārvalde (referred to as the Central Statistical Board of Latvia).

Valodas politikas istenošana Latviā: Valsts valodas centrs 1992–2002 (2002). Riga: Valsts valodas centrs (referred to as Latvian census 2002).

Vaitiekus, S., ed., 1992, Tautinės mažumos Lietuvos respublikoje (Ethnic minorities in the Republic of Lithuania). Vilnius: Valstybinis nacionaliniu tyrimų centras.

Zaagman, R., 1999, Conflict Prevention in the Baltic States: The OSCE High Commissioner on National Minorities in Estonia, Latvia and Lithuania. European Centre for Minority Issues. Flensburg: ECMI, Monograph #1. Flensburg: ECMI.

Zinkevičius, Z., 1998, *The History of the Lithuanian Language*, translated by Ramutė Plioplys. Vilnius: Mokslo ir enciklopedijų leidybos institutas.

8
Politics and Language Rights: A Case Study of Language Politics in Croatia

Vanessa Pupavac

Language and statehood

Eric Hobsbawm argues in *Nations and Nationalism Since 1780* that 'Languages multiply with states; not the other way round' (1992: 63). Since Hobsbawm's book was published a decade ago, we have witnessed the demise of the status of a shared Serbo-Croat language and its multiplication into four separate languages Bosnian, Croatian, Montenegrin and Serbian, alongside the collapse of former Yugoslavia and the creation of new separate states. The language question in the region has been intimately bound up with the state of South Slav relations, often prefiguring political developments (Greenberg 1996). The Croatian linguist Ivo Pranjković has pointedly observed that 'the perpetual politicisation of our standard idioms and Croato-Serbian relations must be borne in mind' (Pranjković 1993: 106).[1] The accordance of language or dialect status has paralleled political aspirations endorsing Hobsbawm's statement. In essence, the assertion of a common language with regional variations has been associated with South Slavism and the aspiration for a common state, while the assertion of distinct languages reflects ethnic divisions and the aspiration for separate states.

This chapter analyses how language debates and linguists themselves have become entangled in politics through a case study of language politics in Croatia. Nevertheless, setting aside politics, linguistics does have general criteria for determining the existence of distinct languages in relation to morphology, syntax and so on. Linguistically, following the sociolinguists Robert Greenberg and

Kenneth Naylor, not only do Croats, Bosniacs and Montenegrins and Serbs share a common language, but they share the same dialect according to where they live or come from, although the ethnicised nature of dialectologists' studies has sought to demonstrate otherwise (Naylor 1992, 1996; Greenberg 1996). Moreover, regional variations were objectively more marked between Zagreb and Belgrade in the nineteenth century than today. However, the more minor distinctions of today loom far larger in the collective imagination than the greater disparities of yesteryear did for their nineteenth-century forebears.

A useful summary for the general reader of the main regional differences in the language appears in Celia Hawkesworth's *Colloquial Serbo-Croat* (1986):

> There are three main dialects of Serbo-Croat, one of which was selected as the literary language in the mid-nineteenth century. This dialect is known as **štokavian** because in it the word for 'what' is **što**. (The other two are known as **kajkavski** and **čakavski** because in them the word for 'what' is respectively **kaj** and **ča**.) Within **štokavian**, there are two major subdivisions, most conveniently described as the Western and the Eastern variant. The main distinguishing feature of these is the way in which a particular early Slavonic vowel sound has evolved: into **e** in the Eastern variant, and **je** or **ije** (depending on the length of the vowel) in the Western variant, e.g. **mleko** (milk) and **mlijeko**. The variants are thus known as **ekavski** and **jekavski** (or **ijekavski**). (There is a further sub-dialect, **ikavski**, spoken mainly on the Dalmatian coast, in which the word for 'milk' is **mliko**. This is not accepted as standard speech, however.) There are certain other differences [...] These inevitably include some lexical variations, resulting from centuries of separate development. For example, the word for the basic foodstuff 'bread' is **kruh** in the Western and **hleb** in the Eastern variant (xviii, bold in the original).

Here one should note the richness of regional dialects within Croatia: for kajkavian belongs to northern Croatia, and čakavian to the Adriatic islands and part of the coast, in addition to the ikavian dialect of the Dalmatian coast. In short, while the standard language of Croatia is the Western variant of štokavian written in the Latin script, there is much regional language variation within Croatia but these differences are not being politicised: underscoring how linguistics is often secondary in determining the status accorded to differences.

Not only is language crucially influenced by national politics, but language politics has played a significant role in national politics. Claims to a distinct Croatian language have been a key part of the Croatian nation-building process in the 1990s.[2] As such, Croatia is a useful case to study Hobsbawm's statement on the influence of politics on language claims and the link between the recognition of language and statehood. Indeed, linguistic disputes first publicly manifested discontent among the Croatian elite in its relations with Belgrade. Accounts of Croatian secession often refer to the language question in the sequence of events.

> First we defended the constitutional provisions on the Croatian language, then we formed an independent Croatian state, then we made the Croatian literary language completely independent, we established a military force and then we created chaos in the once shared language. As our soldiers would say, we crushed Serbo-Croat as a literary language like an old tin can (Pavičić 1995: 18).

This statement by a journalist published in the Croatian newspaper *Vjesnik* encapsulates how the language issue is no arcane academic matter but is central to the national question in the region. The journalist's comments demonstrate how the establishment of Croatian as a separate language is explicitly linked to the Croatian state-building process. In this context, the assertion of a common language is associated in Croatian politics today with claims to a Greater Serbia, although nineteenth-century Croatian intellectuals had pioneered the idea as part of the Illyrian movement.

Codification of a Croatian standard language, as in other languages, involves contention over which linguistic forms are included or excluded. Noting the importance of distinguishing a Croatian language from the formerly shared Serbo-Croat language, this process has involved the exclusion of particular vocabulary or linguistic forms associated with Serbs, rather than words viewed as merely dialect or vernacular. Hence controversy over the norms of the standard language is ethnicised. As a Croatian grammar of the mid-1990s states, the Croatian language 'serves as a way for Croats to demonstrate and recognise themselves as Croats' (Težak and Babić 1994: 27).

However, local politics have not been the only determining factor in the language controversies of the last decade. An additional neglected factor has been the influence of identity politics on international policy-makers and policy assumptions. In brief, the sources of violent conflict are increasingly traced to 'human needs of recognition and identity' (Burton 1997: 31). Consequently, subjective identity claims including language have been treated sympathetically by international organisations in the last decade as part of conflict management. Recognition of Croatian as a distinct language also implies recognition of Serbian as a distinct language, creating a minority language rights question in relation to the ethnic Serbs in Croatia. All across the region, recognition of distinct Bosnian (or Bosniac), Croatian, Serbian and more recently Montenegrin languages has been accompanied by counter-demands by ethnic minorities for distinct minority language rights. In Croatia, the ethnic Serbian politician Milorad Pupovac of the Serbian Democratic Forum, who originally trained as a linguist,[3] has demanded recognition of Serbian language rights (Pupovac 1992: 17). While in Vojvodina, ethnic Croatian leaders have demanded recognition of Croatian language rights and called for the Vojvodina authorities to provide Croatian language classes in schools (Stantić 1997). Likewise in Bosnia, the three main ethnic groups have been demanding to be taught in their own language. In areas following the Bosnian government curriculum, ethnic Croatian leaders have objected to ethnic Croatian pupils being taught in the Bosniac language and demanded that they be taught in Croatian (Ravlić 1995).

The standard language in schools is an obvious theme in language disputes. In addressing the relationship between politics and language, I highlight how political developments are reflected in the changing treatment of the language in Croatian grammars. Official approval is required for textbooks used in schools; therefore they illustrate official policy and the norms of the standard language as well as politics in different periods. That school textbooks embody national identity at a particular moment is evocatively described by the Croatian writer Dubravka Ugrešić in her essay 'My First Primer' (1998). Examination too of continuity and change in authorship, that is, of the officially approved linguists, indicates both continuity and change in the bureaucracy under regime transformation. Certain prominent linguists have managed to bridge regime transformation, not merely adapting their linguistic positions to the contemporary political climate but actually remaining key ideologues of the new politics and its manifestation in linguistic policies.

For reasons of space, my analysis is necessarily brief and can only highlight particular works and issues as representative of official policy and the politicisation of language. That grammars can assume great political significance is illustrated by the political storm surrounding the publication of a *Croatian Orthography* in 1971. The textbook was not regarded by the federal authorities as 'a mere orthographic rule-book', but was viewed by the Central Committee of the Communist Party of Croatia as a 'nationalist act of sabotage' challenging the state of Yugoslavia (quoted in Babić *et al.* 1984: iv). All copies of the text were ordered to be destroyed, and the orthography became a cause célèbre of the Croatian émigré community who sponsored its publication abroad (ibid.).

The 'politics of dialects' in former Yugoslavia (Greenberg 1996) has both historical precedents and contemporary parallels: contention over the relationship between Dutch and Flemish, to name one example, or British and American English, to name another. Yet such parallels are usually overlooked. The present depoliticisation of the language question between America and Britain allows classical accounts of the history of the English language to glide over historical moves for linguistic independence such as Noah Webster's 1783 *A Grammatical Institute of the English Language* or his 1842 *Dictionary of the American Language*. So Robert Burchill's classic work *The English Language* asserts an unproblematic history of English that contrasts sharply with the language politics of the post-Yugoslav states:

> There are no constitutional processes leading to declarations of linguistic independence as there are in politics. No flags are run up as signs or symbols of linguistic sovereignty. There are not governor-generals of language, and no linguistic Boston Tea Parties (Burchill 1985: 160).

Yet Burchill's confident disavowal of linguistic Boston Tea Parties ignores the political significance of past declarations of linguistic independence such as Webster's campaign for an American orthography (Simpson 1986: 52–6). Webster deplored continuing American cultural dependence on Britain and considered that the American Revolution could not be complete unless there was sovereignty 'in manners', cultivated by American publishing (ibid.). Radical declarations of linguistic sovereignty were ultimately overridden by internal politics: the spectre of Babel loomed larger for American intellectuals than the distant British state (Simpson 1986: 46–8). Namely, a linguistic declaration of war against British English norms might lead not to an American standardisation but to anarchy in the language and the state. As Webster himself is often quoted as stating, 'Our political harmony [...] is concerned in a uniformity of language' (in Gustafson 1992: 313). Always tempered by internal political and security concerns, declarations of American linguistic independence lacked momentum once the United States felt securely established as an independent state. Thus later publications symbolised both statements of independence from and reconciliation with British English. 'If the speller was America's Declaration of Linguistic Independence', the language historian Thomas Gustafson declares, Webster's dictionary 'was a linguistic Treaty of Paris wherein Webster maintains that while a difference of language between England and America is inevitable, a sameness is desirable' (ibid.: 320), illustrating the significance of grammars for statehood.

The post-Yugoslav states do not yet feel securely established and are experiencing a 'Thucydidean moment': 'a time when words are perceived to be not a representative sign of ideas but a sovereign duplicitous force' (ibid.). In these circumstances, language debates are dominated by political concerns, rather than linguistic realities, until such time as the new states and the ethnic groups within them no longer feel insecure and threatened. So while the competing demands for language rights may not make linguistic sense and lack linguistic necessity, these demands do make political sense for they help legitimise political claims, both domestically and internationally. In the case of ethnic minorities, language rights claims relate to claims for political inclusion through a specifically recognised status. As such, the proliferation of language rights demands is the logical consequence of both domestic and international politics of recognition and their codification of identity-based rights. In this shared elevation of identity, international responses to the language question in the post-Yugoslav states have tended to endorse nationalist language politics, which international policy-makers are now attempting to unravel.

International officials are, for example, attempted to de-ethnicise the language issue in Bosnian schools by approving language textbooks euphemistically entitled *Naš jezik* [*Our Language*] (Gazibara and Zekić 2002). I begin by discussing post-war Yugoslav language politics.

Language politics in SFR Yugoslavia

Mindful of the experiences of the Second World War, post-war Yugoslavia sought to prevent nationalist politics by depoliticising and defusing ethnicity. Extensive recognition of identity, such as the codification of Macedonian as a literary language, was promoted to accommodate ethnic sentiment. The handling of the Serbo-Croat language spoken by four of the officially recognised nations of Yugoslavia who represented approximately three-quarters of the population was considered of vital significance to the legitimacy and cohesion of the state (Bugarski 1995: 16–17). In the 1950s there were moves to coordinate standardisation of the language in the two ekavian and ijekavian variants, aiming to reconcile the need for a standard with the symbolic significance of the two predominant Croatian and Serbian literary language traditions, representing the two most populous ethnic groups in the country. This standardisation of the language in more than one variant may be observed in relation to Armenian, Greek and Hindi-Urdu (Haughen 1972: 107). In 1954 the Novi Sad Agreement declared that the language was one:

> The national language of Serbs, Croats and Montenegrins is one language, that is, the literary language which developed from its basis around two main centres, Belgrade and Zagreb, united, with two pronunciations, ijekavian and ekavian (cited in *Pravopis* 1960: 9).

The agreement stated that the Cyrillic and Latin scripts were equal and that both scripts should be learnt from the first grade in school. The Novi Sad Agreement was followed up in 1960 with an *Orthography of the Serbo-Croat Literary Language* (Aleksić *et al.* 1960), a joint project involving the universities of Belgrade, Sarajevo and Zagreb and published in ekavian and the Cyrillic script by the Serbian *Matica Srpksa* in Novi Sad, and in ijekavian and the Latin script by the Croatian *Matica Hrvatska* in Zagreb. Joint work was also begun on a *Dictionary of the Serbo-Croatian Literary Language*. Following on from the Novi Sad Agreement, the 1963 Constitutions of Bosnia and Herzegovina, Montenegro and Serbia denominated the official language as Serbo-Croatian, and that of Croatia as Croato-Serbian.

Yet the Novi Sad Agreement only held sway for a decade before the language question was publicly reopened in the mid-1960s with acrimony over the first two volumes of the *Dictionary of the Serbo-Croatian Literary Language* submitted to Matica Hrvatska and Matica Srpska. Croatian academics accused the joint dictionary project inter alia of representing the Serbianisation of the language in its treatment of certain vocabulary in standard use in Croatia as dialect words. At the same time, the existing *Orthography of the Serbo-Croatian Literary Language* (Aleksić *et al*. 1960) was also attacked for not sufficiently taking into account Croatian orthographic practice, although it had received praise when it was first published for its sensitive treatment of the two variants. That the treatment of particular linguistic forms as non-standard should fuel linguistic disputes is unsurprising, given the symbolic significance of inclusion and exclusion of linguistic forms. The treatment of a term as merely dialect, that is non-standard, is to give it an inferior status as language 'excluded from polite society', as Haughen observes (Haughen 1972: 100). However, there was an unwillingness to work on a linguistic solution.

The dispute escalated quickly beyond linguistics and became icons of Croatian intellectuals' general discontent with their position in the state, culminating in the 1967 Declaration on the Name and the Position of the Croatian Literary Language. The Declaration was significant because it was signed by prominent figures: 18 Croatian institutions and 140 Croatian intellectuals including the Croatian writer Miroslav Krleža and others who had signed the 1954 Novi Sad Agreement, as well as members of the Central Committee. In the Declaration Croatian intellectuals rejected the 1954 Novi Sad Agreement as a denial of the Croatian literary heritage and declared Croatian and Serbian to be separate literary languages and demanded that the Constitution recognise four literary languages: Croatian, Macedonian, Serbian and Slovenian. While the Declaration addressed language, the document effectively represented the declaration of the Croatian Spring nationalist movement demanding a revision of Croatia's status within Yugoslavia. The Croatian academic

Radoslav Katičić wrote in the weekly *Hrvatski Tjednik* in 1971:

> This agreement rests on the unsupported assumption of an alleged Serbo-Croat linguistic unity, which has frequently been used to deny the independent existence of the Croat literary language and its historical and territorial continuity (quoted in Babić *et al*. 1984: xvi).

These demands then led to counter-demands by 42 Serbian intellectuals who in a Proposal for Consideration of the same year demanded measures to protect the Cyrillic script from encroachment. This rift was never overcome despite dissenting academics on both sides. Cooperation between Matica hrvatska and Matica srpska over the joint dictionary project was not resumed. While the first three volumes of the *Dictionary of the Serbo-Croatian Literary Language* were published jointly by Matica hrvatska and Matica srpska in 1967, 1967 and 1969 respectively, the subsequent volumes were published in the 1970s by Matica srpska alone. A pattern emerged in dialectology studies of Croatian assertion of a distinct literary language and Serbian assertion of a distinct dialect belonging to ethnic Serbs within Croatia which distinguished them from their fellow Croatian citizens (Greenberg 1996).

Croatian concern to secure the position of the Croatian literary language manifested itself in the revised 1974 constitutional provisions. The provisions of the three other relevant republics shifted towards the idea of a shared hyphenated title or titles for the language. However, the idea of shared hyphenated title or titles was now mistrusted as creeping Serbianisation by the Croatian elite. The constitutional provision for Croatia sought to guarantee officially the existence of the Croatian literary language to appease national sentiment, but at the same time retain the previous constitutional provision 'Croatian or Serbian': 'The Croatian literary language – the standard form of the national language of the Croats and Serbs living in Croatia, which is called Croatian or Serbian'. The Constitutional Court of Yugoslavia held that the provision on the Croatian literary language was ambiguous since it was not clear whether the provision referred to one or two standard languages (discussed in Bugarski 1995: 58–61).

This provisional ambiguity and the cautious response of the Constitutional Court demonstrate how there was nervousness about both the evident politicisation of the language and how this politicisation might be confronted. The authorities vacillated between taking a tough or a more tolerant line. Severe responses were meted out to the use of the term 'Croatian language', leading to the pulping of *Croatian Orthography*. But officials were inconsistent in relation to the term 'Croatian literary language'. Authors found they got contradictory responses from different officials as to whether the term was or was not acceptable. Publication was prevented of a revised and renamed sixth edition of *Overview of the Grammar of the Croatian Literary Language* (1973) (Težak and Babić 1994), which had previously gone under the title *Overview of the Grammar of the Croato-Serbian Literary Language* (Težak and Babić 1966). Yet other works were published using the term 'Croatian literary language'.

Language disputes were not resolved and intensified from the mid-1980s as political divisions manifested themselves in grievances over language rights. In Slovenia, the use of Serbo-Croat as the official language of the Yugoslav People's Army (JNA) and military courts galvanised Slovenian public opinion against the federal authorities in the notorious Mladina trials. In Serbia, the infamous 1986 Memorandum drafted by members of the Serbian Academy of Arts and Sciences singled out Croatian language aspirations as a threat to the language and position of ethnic Serbs in Croatia (Croatian Information Centre 1994: 71). As these language disputes intensified, academics, such as the Croatian linguist Dubravko Škiljan, called for better coordination on the standardisation of the language to ensure valid concerns were addressed. One of the last symbolic initiatives was a special monograph under the title *Language, Serbo-Croatian, Croato-Serbian, Croatian or Serbian* (1988) co-authored by the leading Croatian linguist Dalibor Brozović and the leading Serbian linguist Pavle Ivić. Nevertheless such initiatives had little impact on the course of the disputes or even some of the authors of these joint projects who went on to espouse nationalist positions. Brozović, for example, became politically active in the new regime as a member of Franjo Tudjman's ruling HDZ party and was a member of the Croatian Presidency in 1990 involved in changing the Croatian Constitution. Alongside the new constitution came a new Law on Primary Education (1990) under which it was declared that teaching was to be in the Croatian language. With new language norms came new grammars, although the authors were often familiar names and the grammars re-workings of previous editions.

The next section contrasts the treatment of the language in a sample of Croatian grammars past and present.

Croatian grammars past and present

Official school grammars of the postwar period such as *Grammar of the Croato-Serbian Language* (Brabec *et al.* 1965) followed the position of the Novi Sad agreement. Not only was the language treated as unified in the present, but from its very codification as a literary language. Texts emphasised the joint cooperation between Croatian and Serbian intellectuals in developing the modern literary language. Moreover, primacy was given to the commonality of the spoken word over distinct literary traditions (Babić 1967: 86–7). Regional distinctions in accent and vocabulary were not regarded as significant. In particular, the ekavian and ijekavian distinction was minimalised as subcategories of the shared štokavian dialect adopted by both Zagreb and Belgrade as the standard (Babić 1967: 51 and 90; Brabec *et al.* 1965).

In contrast, authorised grammars of the last decade in Croatia declare the existence of a distinct Croatian language evidenced primarily on the use of ijekavian and the Latin script, and particular vocabulary, morphological and orthographic differences. Cooperation in the establishment of the standard written language is ignored or downplayed. Comparing the diametrically opposed accounts in the post-1990 *Grammar of the Croatian Language* (Težak and Babić 1994) to the earlier editions of *Introductory Grammar of the Croato-Serbian Literary Language* (Težak and Babić 1966) makes interesting reading given that authorship remains the same. The later edition strongly refutes the common language thesis of the earlier editions, stating that the issues of mutual comprehension, shared structure and stokavian dialect are irrelevant and merely obscure the existence of a distinct Croatian language:

> Theoretically, its singularity is obscured by the fact that it is so closely related to the Serbian literary language that they can be understood almost completely without translations. This is because both are based on the stokavian dialect and share a common structure and the main body of vocabulary (Težak and Babić 1994: 16).

Yet, in the face of the official position on ekavian as distinguishing Serbian from Croatian as a language, ekavian is nevertheless regarded as one of the accents of Croatian in their grammar (ibid.: 18–19), underscoring the importance of politics in language debates.

Minority language rights for Serbs?

With the official divorce of the language and the declaration that teaching in schools was to be in the Croatian language, a requirement was logically created under both domestic and international minority rights provisions to provide Serbian language classes to ethnic Serbs in Croatian schools. Human rights advocates from Amnesty International, Helsinki Committee and other organisations have criticised Croatia for not respecting the language rights of its ethnic Serbian minority by not providing special language provision. Yet would one demand special language provision for ethnic Britains in the United States or vice versa? Criticisms of the lack of special language provision and policy proposals for special language rights misrepresent the interests of ethnic Serbs in Croatia and are highly inappropriate for addressing their needs.

The minority rights model ironically endorses the nationalist declarations on the language question as opposed to linguistic criteria. While the work of foreign linguists has not supported nationalists' language claims (Škiljan 2000: 6), the identity rights-approach of foreign diplomats, human rights advocates and conflict mediators has unfortunately tended to legitimise nationalist language claims and minority exclusions. The very designation of a separate minority language status for ethnic Serbs is to be excluded from the standard and thus set apart from mainstream society or 'polite society', borrowing again from Haughen (1972: 100). While ethnic leaders may press for special minority rights and become included in the public sphere as recognised community representatives, it is not advantageous overall for ordinary ethnic Serbs. In the aftermath of a war in which Serbia was regarded by the Croatian authorities as the aggressor, few ethnic Serbs want to bring undue attention to themselves by identifying themselves with the enemy nation.

To illustrate the concerns of ordinary ethnic Serbs, I will briefly highlight issues raised in informal interviews conducted between

1996–98 with ethnic Serbian teachers and parents about schooling. The first group concerns the views of ethnic Serbs in Eastern Slavonia during the period of transition under UN supervision. Ethnic Serbs in Eastern Slavonia form a more cohesive population, than ethnic Serbs elsewhere in Croatia who are politically and socially atomised, and their demands differed accordingly. These ethnic Serbs were still demanding a degree of autonomy during negotiations over the return of Eastern Slavonia to Croatia. International human rights advocates have tended to translate these demands into cultural and language rights. However, the right to cultural self-determination did not motive demands for autonomy, although it may be recalled that certain parts of Eastern Slavonia are ekavian speaking. The main preoccupation of teachers was whether the Croatian authorities would recognise their teaching qualifications or experience recognised by the former Republika Srpska Krajina authorities. The teachers expressed anxiety that if a degree of autonomy were not recognised, the Croatian authorities might sack ethnic Serbian teachers who did not have all the requisite teaching qualifications or experience. It is not uncommon for teachers to lack officially required teaching qualifications because of the war and the brain drain out of teaching to better paid work. As a result of the shortage of qualified teachers, education ministries have allowed the recruitment of staff who have not completed all their training or without requiring them to do so. Consequently, the position of many teachers would be jeopardised were the authorities to insist on the officially required qualifications. Their anxiety was not unfounded given that a previous Croatian minister had recommended only pure Croats should teach the Croatian language (Ugrešić 1998: 62). In essence, their concerns were about equality before the law, not special language rights.

Subsequently, it may be noted that the majority of schools designated officially as teaching in Serbian are located in Eastern Slavonia (Ministry of Education and Sport 2000b: 35). Yet what is the advantage to pupils of separate language provision? Effectively the special treatment marks pupils off from their contemporaries and hinders their acceptance into mainstream Croatian society. That recognition of distinct languages is a barrier to the reintegration of pupils in schools and the reconstruction of ethnic coexistence is an issue international officials have belatedly acknowledged and trying to tackle across the border in Bosnia. One indicator of whether ethnic Serbian pupils in these designated schools feel integrated in Croatian society is whether they decide in the future to pursue higher education and careers in Croatia or opt instead for study and employment in Serbia.

That the minority rights model course might be viewed as problematic as a strategy is suggested by the responses of ethnic Serbs elsewhere in Croatia. Ethnic Serbs outside Eastern Slavonia expressed individualised responses to the issue of schooling. Individual teachers were unenthusiastic about being identified so publicly as ethnically Serb by being designated to teach the separate Serbian language, history and culture classes. Similarly individual parents were reluctant to send their children to such classes which might mark them out for bullying as members of the enemy aggressor nation. So while ethnic leaders may acquire security through a special minority leadership status, ordinary ethnic Serbs are seeking to be treated as ordinary Croatian citizens, many putting themselves down as Croatian in the latest census. They are not demanding special public provision to learn ekavian and the Cyrillic script or Serbian history and culture. Often overlooked by international human rights advocates is that outside of parts of Eastern Slavonia, ethnic Serbs will be ijekavian speakers and use the Latin script as their Croatian neighbours. In areas of Krajina before the war where the population was predominantly ethnically Serbian then locals were more likely to be confident reading in the Cyrillic script, because of the greater number of Belgrade newspapers, magazines and comics on sale locally than other parts of Croatia. However, even in a town such as Knin where the pre-war population was 90 per cent ethnically Serbian, it should be reiterated that people were ijekavian speakers and overwhelmingly wrote in the Latin script. It was only during the war under the Republika Srpska Krajina administration and its nationalist Serbian language policies that there was official adoption of ekavian and Cyrillic for public use. Public buildings and shops and cafes were supposed to change their signs and school textbooks were imported from Serbia. Nevertheless, official language policy was frequently honoured in the breach, not least by officials who were themselves ijekavian speakers or whose staff lacked typewriters with keyboards for the Cyrillic script.

The sort of language recognition required by ethnic Serbs in Croatia is driven by practical needs and issues of equality. In particular, there has been a problem with official reluctance to recognise documents printed or written in Cyrillic such as past entries in municipal registers. Notably, ethnic Serbian refugees have had difficulties with the Croatian authorities recognising birth, marriage or death registry entries from the Republika Srpka Krajina period that appeared in Cyrillic. This has even been the case where it is clear from the official documentation that the same official has been involved in compiling the records through the regime changes, switching language norms as required by the incumbent authorities. Failure to recognise the records has meant in particular that ethnic Serbian children born in the early 1990s in areas under Republika Srpska Krajina control have been denied Croatian citizenship for a number of years. But again politics influences whether these entries are recognised as official records: Serbian language norms have not presented an insurmountable obstacle to ethnic Croats seeking to invoke these entries as official records. The issue here is one of equality before the law as in Eastern Slavonia. Insistence on Serbian minority language rights is not only inappropriate to address the needs of ethnic Serbs in Croatia, but is detrimental to their position in Croatian society.

Depoliticisation of the language question?

I have tried to illustrate here how language politics in Croatia is bound up with a 'Thucydidean moment', a crisis of statehood. A continuing sense of insecurity in Croatia and elsewhere in the post-Yugoslav states means that the possibility of depoliticising the language question in the near future remains elusive. Huge sensitivity in Croatia continues to be expressed about the language issue in the new millennium. A Ministry of Education discussion document warns:

> Given all the negative experience gained through history it is essential to take into account the particular sensitivity of the Croatian School, of teachers and parents towards the need to shape and nurture national identity, particularly in the areas of language, material and spiritual culture, history and authentic heritage, and which is being wrongfully usurped by others (Ministry of Education and Sport 2000a: 18).

Until a sense of statehood is secure then efforts will continue to secure the language against its neighbours. That a sense of insecurity impels language wars and demands for language purification is evident in the historical development of other languages. The depoliticisation of the language question between Britain and the United States suggests the importance of security. It was a sense of secure statehood and improved political relations that facilitated reconciliation of British and American English. The international minority rights model would have complicated and hindered the process of resolution had it applied two centuries ago. International minority language rights initiatives are misdirected and merely compound the politicisation of language. It is time to revisit international minority rights approaches and to examine how they may be unwittingly fuelling the 'Thucydidean moment' and legitimising ethnic divisions.

Notes

1. Extracts have been translated by the author of this paper unless otherwise stated.
2. The Croatian sociolinguist Dubravko Škiljan provides a fascinating account of Croatian linguistic identity. See Škiljan (2000).
3. See, for example, Pupovac's *Jezici i politika* (1988).

References

Aleksić, R. *et al.*, 1960, *Pravopis srpskohrvatskoga književnog jezika: sa pravopisnim rečnikom*. [Orthography of the Serbo-Croatian literary language; with an orthographic dictionary] Novi Sad and Zagreb: Matica hrvatska and Matica srpska.

Babić, S., 1967, *Školski lesikon obćeobrazovne škole: Jezik*. [School lexicon for grammar schools] 3rd edn. Zagreb: Panorama.

Babić, S., B. Finka and M. Moguš, 1984, *Hrvatski pravopis*. [Croatian Orthography] London: Novo hrvatska.

Brabec, I., M. Hraste and S. Živković, 1965, *Gramatika hrvatskosrpskoga jezika*. [Grammar of the Croato-Serbian language] 6th edn. Zagreb: Školska knjiga.

Brozović, D. and P. Ivić, 1988, *Jezik, srpskohrvatski/hrvatskosrpski, hrvatski ili srpski*. [Language, Serbo-Croatian/Croato-Serbian, Croatian or Serbian] Zagreb: Jugoslavenski leksikografski zavod Miroslav Krleža.

Bugarski, R., 1995, *Jezik od mira do rata*. [Language from peace to war] Belgrade: Slovograf.

Burchill, R., 1985, *The English Language*. Oxford: Oxford University Press.

Burton, J. W., 1997, *Violence Explained: The Sources of Conflict, Violence and Crime and their Prevention*. Manchester and New York: Manchester University Press.

Croatian Information Centre, 1994, *Greater Serbia from Ideology to Aggression.* Zagreb: Croatian Information Centre.

Gazibara, S. and Z. Zekić, 2002, *Naš jezik za 5. razred osnovne škole.* [Our language for the fifth year of primary school] Sarajevo: Svjetlost.

Greenberg, R. D. 'The Politics of Dialects Among Serbs, Croats, and Muslims in the Former Yugoslavia.' *East European Politics and Society*, 10: 393–415.

Gustafson, T., 1992, *Representative Words: Politics, Literature, and the American Language, 1776–1865.* Cambridge: Cambridge University Press.

Haughen, E., 1972, 'Dialect, Language and Nation', in *Sociolinguistics: Selected Readings* (eds) J. B. Pride and J. Holmes. Harmondsworth: Penguin, 97–111.

Hobsbawm, E., 1992, *Nations and Nationalism since 1780.* 2nd edn. Cambridge: Cambridge University Press.

Ministry of Education and Sport, Council of Education, Republic of Croatia, 2000a, *The Basis for the Education System in the Republic of Croatia (Proposal for Discussion).* Zagreb, June. http://www.see-educoop.net/

Ministry of Education and Sport, Institute for Educational Development, 2000b, *Croatian Education System, Interim Report.* Zagreb, June. http://www.see-educoop.net/

Naylor, K., 1992, 'The Sociolinguistic Situation in Yugoslavia with Special Emphasis on Serbo-Croatian', in *Language Planning in Yugoslavia* (eds) R. Bugarski and C. Hawkesworth. Columbus: Slavica: 80–92.

Naylor, K., 1996, *Sociolingvistički problemi među južnim slovenima.* [Sociolinguistic problems among the South Slavs] Beograd: Prosveta.

Pavičić, J. 'I Srbi progovorili srpski', 1995 [And Serbs speak Serbian] *Vjesnik* 8 October: 18.

Pravopis srpskohrvatskoga kniževnog jezika. [Orthography of the Serbo-Croatian Language] 1960, Novi Sad: Matica srpka.

Pupovac, M., ed., 1988, *Jezici i politike.* [Language and Politics] Zagreb: Centar Vladimir Bakarić.

Pupovac, M., 1992, 'A Settlement for the Serbs', in *Breakdown: War and Reconstruction in Yugoslavia.* London: Yugofax: 17–18.

Ravlić, I., 'Federacija na ispitu'. [The Federation is tested] *Nedjeljna*, 22 September: 36.

Simpson, D., 1986, *The Politics of American English, 1776–1850.* New York: Oxford University Press.

Škiljan, D., 2000, 'From Croato-Serbian to Croatian: Croatian Linguistic Identity.' *Multilingua*, 19: 3–20.

Stantić, J., 1997, 'No Schools and No Status.' *WarReport*, 57: 32–3.

Težak, S. and S. Babić, 1994, *Gramatika hrvatskog jezika: priručnik za osnovno jezično obrazovanje.* [Grammar of the Croatian Language: textbook for primary language education] Zagreb: Školska knjiga.

Težak, S. and S. Babić, 1966, *Pregled gramatike hrvatskosrpskog jezika.* [Introductory grammar of the Croato-Serbian language] Zagreb: Školska knjiga.

Ugrešić, D., 1998, *Culture of Lies.* London: Weidenfeld and Nicholson.

9

'Minor' Needs or The Ambiguous Power of Translation

Carmen Millán-Varela

Introduction

There is a considerable amount of literature in the field of Translation Studies that emphasises the crucial role played by translation activities in the creation and development of national languages and literatures (see, e.g. Even-Zohar 1978; Cronin 1995; Toury 1995; Woodsworth 1996; Millán-Varela 2000). In an interdisciplinary approach to the study of minorities, such as the one provided in this present volume, attention to cultural aspects, and to translation activities in particular, is of paramount importance. Conceived as a socio-cultural practice, the study of translation provides a privileged space in which to explore, not only the activity in itself, but also the complex nature of the contexts in which they take place, as well as underlying attitudes and conflicts. Drawing on the particular case of the Galician context, this chapter attempts, first, to show the funda- mental, sometimes ambiguous, role played by translations, and translators, in a bilingual context characterised by asymmetrical rela- tions of power. Second, following Toury (1997), it suggests the need for careful attention to issues of policy and planning in translation, and consequently the need to draw translation practices to the atten- tion of both language/culture planners and policy makers.

Translation and/in language planning: a pending issue

Language planning has been variously defined to include different types of activities done to languages in order to change their current situation. The common element in them all is the presence of a deliberate intention to influence 'the behaviour of others with respect to the acquisition, structure, or functional allocation of their language codes' (Cooper 1989: 45). Language planning has also been viewed as managing innovation, as marketing and as a decision process. Thus, innovations are usually introduced through translation processes. The very selection of the sources of influence reveals the presence of some specific, implicit or explicit, policy. Deciding what gets translated, and what does not, will determine the type of material that will be available to access in the native language, that is, the amount of exposure the language gets. Furthermore, the strategies used to translate and coin new terms or expressions (whether transliteration, *calque* or the creation of a new term) are also relevant indicators of underlying domestic policy and planning issues. In terms of marketing, translation is used, for example, to spread and consolidate one particular language variety, as is the case in Galicia[1] or in Quebec (Brisset 1989). As a result, a particular ideology, and a specific type of identity construction is enforced. The language becomes a symbolic good whose production and distribution may reveal conflicts between nationalist and market criteria (González-Millán 1994). As regards decision processes, Toury (1995) views translation as a problem solving activity, the 'solution' to a particular 'need' felt in the target culture. This 'need' is usually related to a situation of perceived 'deficiency'. The very decision to resort to translation is itself both the result of planning and also a planning tool. In Toury's view (1997), translation is usually preferred because it serves 'to try out the potentials of the planned system in an efficient way as well as presenting members of the social group which entertains the culture in question with appealing results'. So, in all the above areas, translation is playing a fundamental role. However, and as pointed out by Toury (1997), there is no single reference to translation in these studies. Similarly, planning issues are rarely the topic of discussion in translation studies. An interdisciplinary dialogue needs to start between these two disciplines. Here I will argue that Translation Studies can offer valuable insights into the understanding of cultural dynamics and domestic conflicts in a particular (minority) context. The heavy contextual determination of translation activities, and cultural activities in general, require a particular effort on the part of the researcher, which needs to combine both contextual and textual factors in order to understand specific practices and processes.

In the case of Galician, translations appear to have a clear planning purpose. In the twentieth century, we find that translation was one of the practices chosen, as well as original writing, to recover and renew the literary language. In the 1920s, for example, in spite of the negative views towards (literary) translation, contact with other (selected) literatures was felt to be beneficial. As we will see next, the selection of source texts and languages (Latin and Greek classics and Irish writers) was not unintentional. Later on, in the 1950s and 1960s, and in spite of the lack of resources (literary) translations continue to be present in the process of social and literary recovery, which culminated in the 1980s, when the production and publications of translations (of literary *and* non-literary texts) boomed. In this last period, in particular, the 'normalising' function of translations became very clear, as they contributed to the spread and consolidation of the official language planning programme promoted by the Galician Government. Thus it would appear that by exploring the role and position of translation activities, it is possible to trace the evolution of the target language, or even further, to assess the aims and objectives of existing language/planning programmes. Throughout the twentieth century, it was the wish to promote the Galician language (and identity) that led to the practice of translation. Such underlying aims reveal that the process of linguistic and cultural normalisation is still an ongoing process.

According to Cooper's terminology (1989), translation has been instrumental for statutory, working and symbolic purposes. In spite of this crucial role as a planning tool, translation has rarely been the subject of 'official' planning. Data from the Galician context (Millán-Varela 2000) shows that (implicit) translation planning is subordinated to the wider aims of an existing language/culture planning programme. However, such disregard can have important implications at various levels. For example, in a bilingual context such as Galicia, where translation is supposed to strengthen the target language, what does the lack of a general translation policy reveal? (Cabana 1990; Verdugo Mates 1998). Can the use of Spanish translations as sources for Galician translations mean anything but weakness and dependence at a cultural level? Furthermore, does the presence (or absence) of translation awards, or exclusive attention to children's literature, reveal a genuine concern on the part of local agents and institutions, or is this type of interventionist practice indicative of hidden agendas in order to fix or control these activities, or perhaps even to mask underlying deficiencies at other (socio-cultural, political) levels? Translation is not a 'transparent' or 'neutral' activity. On the contrary, it is highly subjective and manipulative, hence its 'slippery' nature and unpredictable outcomes. Venuti (2000) refers to this ambiguous power of translation as the 'scandals' of translation, for it 'occasions revelations that question the authority of dominant cultural values and institutions'.

The role(s) of translation in the Galician context

Translation and minorities have a lot in common. Both concepts suggest lack of authority and exclusion from the centres of power (Bassnett and Trivedy 1999). Minority translation, therefore, emphasises even further these aspects of marginalisation and exclusion. The functioning of translation activities in this type of context unveils the complex nature of minority contexts and the contextual determination which shapes and determines cultural life in minority languages.

The Galician case is a good example of the ambiguous role of translation as both an oppressing and empowering tool. Since the fourteenth century, the Galician language has been engaged in a constant struggle for survival against the influence of Castilian. The implantation of Castilian in Galician territory functioned as one of the most powerful instruments to push forward the Castilianisation of Galicia (Santamarina 1988). In the socio-cultural context of Medieval Galicia, the loss of political autonomy led to a progressive substitution of Galician by Castilian, and to an abandonment of literary creation. As a result, from the fifteenth to the nineteenth centuries, Galician was absent from public life and had no written form. Ignored and despised by the newcomers, the native language was only used orally, in family circles, the speech of sailors and peasants. Galicians were forced to remain silenced, immersed in a diglossic situation that lasted for five centuries. In Ramón Piñeiro's words, Galician evolved from being the official language in a monolingual community to being a 'non-written popular language' (Rodríguez 1991: 61). In this context, translation first appeared as one of the signs of Castilian domination, as a textualisation of the unequal power relations between Galician and Castilian. Thus, hybridisation of local Galician place names and proper names by means of translit-eration was one of the instruments to 'Castilianise' the Galician space (Santamarina 1988). We could say that Galicians were forced to live in a translated reality. Translation (from Galician into Castilian) was therefore a conscious strategy on the part of the Castilian monar-chy, a planning strategy for Castilian, which reflected Nebrija's view of language as 'the perfect instrument of empire' (quoted in Robinson 1997: 60). And translation did succeed as an imperial tool, for Galician was not used in writing again until the nineteenth century, and not until 1983 was it legally recognised as the original language of Galicia (as well as Castilian Spanish). Galician, however, also used translation in order to survive, to recover, or (re)create an erased identity. The nineteenth century Galician Renaissance, known as *Rexurdimento*, involved the recovery of the literary prestige and the reconstruction of national consciousness. Appropriation and forgery of Celtic myths became the main sources for the creation/invention of a heroic past for the Galician people, from which the new Galician nation would emerge (see Máiz 1997). Later on in the 1980s, original Galician place names were recovered and re-translated back into Galician (from Castilian Spanish), official documents were published in both Spanish and Galician, and Galician translations of prose fiction, children's books, TV series and of technical manuals started to appear.

From these preliminary observations, and within the inevitable con-tradictions and complexities of minority contexts, the powerful but ambiguous role of translation activities becomes manifest. As we will see next, both the strengthening and self-reflecting functions attached to translation products and practices underscore translation as a sensi-tive issue, and an excellent arena to witness current (political, language, identity) conflicts in this particular context. As regards planning, the history of translation and that of the Galician language go clearly hand in hand. The analysis of both translation repertoires and the discourse on translation allows us to identify 'policy' lines which reveal the exis-tence of some type of planning underlying these translation activities.

Before 1980

The beginning of the twentieth century saw the continuation of efforts started in the nineteenth century in favour of the recovery of a Galician consciousness. During the first three decades, we witness the first serious attempts to plan and intervene in the development of Galician. The agents were an elite of nationalist intellectuals who aimed to transform Galician into the everyday language of Galician people, spreading its presence to all domains. This period is related to the beginning of a political nationalism, but the lack of political recognition, and the absence of infrastructure meant a very limited diffusion of activities carried out in Galician. Most of the cultural activity revolved around literary journals and periodicals, as the world of Galician publishing was underdeveloped at this point.

In spite of a lack of infrastructure, it was possible to find Galician translations of foreign texts scattered throughout numerous pages of these journals. These isolated occurrences, although limited in number, constitute, however, a symbolic and valuable example of planning at this early stage in the development of Galician culture and nationalism. The ideological dimension of translation activities during this period appears clearly reflected in the presence of specific texts and references from literatures which are considered as 'superior' in terms of cultural evolution, mainly French, and those which exclusively belong to 'small' nations experiencing similar circumstances to Galicia. Thus, from the texts published in the nationalist journal *Nós* (1919–36), three main (implicit) policy lines can be extracted: First, there is a strong tendency towards translations from other 'minority' languages, Celtic in particular, as this was supposed to be the mythical origin of Galicia.[2] Thus, we find translations of Irish literature (Yeats, Synge, Joyce), of Breton literature and even a text by an Armenian poet. This reveals the existence of a conscious programme with a clear (nationalist) ideology: the (re-)construction of Galician identity as part of the Celtic community. Second, there is a tendency to translate texts from Greek and Latin Classics, which reflects the more conservative and erudite nature of these agents. Translation from the Classics is perceived as more beneficial than any other type of original writing in Galician. Third, and quite interestingly, we also find foreign translations of Galician works into other languages (French, Italian and Portuguese), which reflects the universal spirit of this generation, their wish to make Galician culture known abroad. It is important to point out the motto of this Group, namely to give direct access to culture without having to 'pass through Madrid'. These policy lines reflect very clearly the nationalist and elitist ideology of these cultural agents.

It is worth pointing out the role attached to the translation of non-literary texts in this period. The translation of philosophical texts in the 1920s, for example, represented a direct attack against the diglossic situation of Galician, and a clear indication of the type of function planned for the Galician language, that is, to become, or rather to recover its function as, a vehicle for the transmission of culture and scientific knowledge, in contrast with folkloric views commonly held at the time. For example, the 1922 translation of *Quod nihil scitur* by the Galician philosopher Francisco Sánchez, was introduced as follows:

> ... o interesantísimo tratado Quod nihil scitur, sigue descoñecido, sendo moito máis citado que leído, a causa de non haber ningunha versión ó castelán. Cómpre dalo a coñecer. Elo a contribuír a tiralo prexuicio de que nós permañecemos aleixados da xeneral axitación do pensamento (Nós, 13 (1922), 6).[3]

A similar policy and nationalist ideology was behind the 1950 Galician translation of Heidegger's 1930 essay *Vom Wesen der Wahrheit*, which appeared earlier than the Spanish version. The reactions created by this translation revealed the negative attitudes towards the expansion of the social functions of Galician. Up until this point, however, the cultural agents in charge of this planning programme for the Galician language were nationalist intellectuals, who did not have, or had limited, access to (political) power. In this sense, as pointed out by Even-Zohar (2002), the chances of success were limited.

With the outbreak of the Spanish Civil War in 1936 and Franco's subsequent dictatorship, all the linguistic and political developments that had taken place became truncated. Spanish became the national language of Spain, and all the other languages of Spain were proscribed. Diglossic attitudes were reinforced and continued during the following decades, creating enormous damage amongst the Galician population. As a result of this climate, written production in Galician in Galicia was minimal. Most of the cultural activity was developed and published in exile. Not until the 1970s, coinciding with the decline of the dictatorship, did the situation begin to show changes, such as the creation of Galician political parties and the publication of the *Decreto de Bilingüismo* in 1977, which allowed Galician to be taught at school.

From 1900 until the 1970s, it was therefore the efforts on the part of a group of intellectuals that contributed to the development of a culture and language planning programme for Galician. Translation activities, in this case, constituted a crucial instrument for the development of this programme. Thus, translation in this period appears to perform various roles by:

- strengthening the linguistic system by using Galician in writing, thus fixing written conventions, although no orthographical norms had been agreed at the time;
- innovating the linguistic (and literary) system by introducing and/or developing different registers, genres and social discourses;
- legitimising Galician as a 'language of culture' along with the rest of the linguistic communities, particularly by recovering the prestige of Galician as a literary language. The decision to translate fragments of Joyce's *Ulysses* as early as 1927 is a clear proof of this role;
- disseminating Galician culture abroad (France, Italy and Portugal, in particular, but also within Spain).

After 1980

The institutionalisation of Galicia as a political unit in 1980 affected the social status of the Galician language, which now acquired an official status and was legally recognised as the original language of Galicia. Being the language adopted by the Galician Government, Galicia became symbolically associated with power. In contrast with the period before 1980, it becomes clear that the political institutionalisation of Galicia contributed significantly to the, at least symbolical, empowerment and social prestige of the Galician language and its speakers. In this new context, translation activities have also been present and contributed to this symbolic association. As a result of the new 'bilingual' situation, there is a legal requirement to promote and defend the use of Galician in all areas. The 1983 the *Lei de Normalización Lingüística do Galego* focused on the promotion of Galician in all areas. From the contents of this Bill, it emerges that one of the main roles of the Galician Government was to secure the use of Galician in the Administration and to provide financial help for the development of cultural activity in Galician. However, there is little specification as to how this is supposed to be done. In the domain of culture, it is interesting to note the relevance given to audiovisual translation by including an explicit reference to dubbing and subtitling whereby the Galician Government must promote: ... a producción, a doblaxe, a subtitulación e a exhibición de películas e outros medios audio-visuais en lingua galega.[4]

In contrast, reference to written translation or interpreting is not explicitly made although it is indeed implicitly present throughout the text. In this new context, and in stark contrast to the previous period, we could distinguish two main types of translation:

- *Translations required by law.* This type of translation contributes to the 'statutory' function of the language, as well as both the 'working' and 'symbolic' functions, in Cooper's terminology (1989). All administrative documents have to be written in both Galician and Spanish, so both languages are given the same symbolic power. However, as pointed out by García Cancela (1995a), the aim of language planning should be to achieve complete proficiency in Galician, complete use of the language in all areas. The translation of administrative and legal documents into Galician, then, should be just a temporary solution within this overall plan. However, the continuous reliance on translation for the production of legal documents in Galician may, in fact, achieve the opposite purpose and actually hinder the acquisition of Galician. Thus, translation into Galician becomes a bureaucratic requirement, an 'obstacle', the last step in the production of documents and the writing of bills. The continuous presence of translation forces Galician to be relegated to the status of second/foreign language within its own territory. García Cancela's concern about the role of translation in Administration, ultimately stems from the blurred aims and objectives of the current Government regarding the language planning process in Galicia. This is a crucial area where the need for a stricter control could be beneficial. The fact that there is no 'controlled' or planned action may be also significant.
- *Symbolic/aesthetic* translation. This category refers to translations whose existence is not legally required but appear to fulfil some type of (symbolic) role within the cultural context.[5] A relevant outcome of the 1983 *Lei de Normalización* was the process of modernisation and diversification experienced by the world of publishing. The new social needs, especially the demand from the

newly created school market, was a crucial factor to determine the type of editorial lines adopted during this period. The creation of the Galician Radio and Television Company in 1985 also meant the presence of imported films and series that needed to be dubbed and/or subtitled. There is therefore a great need for texts in Galician, and it is here where translation had a crucial role to play. Translation in this domain emerged as a quick solution to a situation of deficiency: the lack of texts in Galician. This type of translation is not 'compulsory' but the result of the new social demands which appeared in the Galician context, as a result of the planning programme for Galician. This type of translation is therefore a direct outcome of the existence of an official language planning programme. In this sense, translation contributes to the promotion of the official standard norm and responds to the social demand for texts. Additionally, and as a result of this, translation is also contributing to the development of the social functions of Galician by introducing new genres and registers, by establishing links with Western culture and, above all, by creating a readership for Galician books.

The 1980s represent a boom in translation, and in the publication of Galician books in general. Translation constitutes about 20 per cent of the volume of publications in Galician (see Millán-Varela 2000). The following implicit translation policies can be observed: preference for the Latin and Greek Classics, canonical Western authors, children's literature, and more recently, new genres such as detective-stories and science fiction. In non-literary translation, we also find translations of academic essays, usually related to minority issues.

The relevance of translation during this period has been widely acknowledged. Santamarina (1989) notes the increasing importance of translation during the second half of the 1980s, considering that 'now, translation is more than just testimonial' (Santamarina 1989: 7–8). In his words, the evolution of translation goes in parallel with that of the Galician book in general. He highlights the need for scientific texts since, in his view, this is what determines the degree of maturity of a language, together with translations for children and teenagers. In addition, and confirming the earlier mentioned, he alludes to the need to incorporate the 'great pens of universal literature'. Translation appears constructed here as a decisive instrument for the formation of modern standards of world languages, as an enriching tool whereby Galician will become invigorated. Translation appears metaphorically represented as a type of *'gymnastics'* which all languages have practised, an *'exercise* to which we should *subject* the Galician language' (ibid). Arias (1995), former president of the Association of Galician Translators, considers that translations 'stimulate awareness of one's own identity'. Díaz y Díaz (1993), in turn, views the translation of the classics as a way to have direct access to a universal 'patrimony'. Translation, thus, performs various functions which would contribute to the consolidation and 'normalisation' of a 'Galician' culture. The underlying issue is one of access, direct access, in Galician, to any area of knowledge.

In spite of the increasing volume of translated activity during the 1990s, the impression is, however, that what is available in translation is not enough. As Cruces Colado (1993) and Arias (1995) point out, the decision to translate, and what to translate, seems to be done quite at random, based on publishers' individual tastes, or market demand. Darío Xohán Cabana, celebrated author and translator, was one of the voices urging the Galician Government to organise, and subsidise, a translation programme whose aim would be to translate 'a thousand books into Galician' (Cabana 1990). On a similar note, Arias (1995) considered that the amount of translations published by the private sector was not sufficient and that the Government should take responsibility for establishing a translation 'policy'. So far, no action has been taken in this direction.

The need for a translation policy?

As we have seen earlier, in spite of the amount of translations produced, both the quality and the amount of production do not seem to be satisfactory. There is a clear need for some type of 'official' policy and planning programme, as individual efforts no longer seem to suffice. As is common in the development of status planning, the responsibility for translation practices usually lies at the individual level. The absence of a consistent translation policy results in irregular and erratic representations of foreign languages and cultures. As a result of this, the Galician socio-cultural system is still 'weak' and heavily dependent on the Spanish system to fill 'gaps'.

In a 'minority' context such as the Galician, we need to take into account the socio-economic constraints which render difficult the development of cultural activities. Cabrera, for example (1993: 87) comments on the difficulty to carry out the translation series *Grandes do Noso Tempo*, whose main objective was the introduction of Western contemporary writers into the Galician system:

> A nosa sociedade aínda non asumiu plenamente a posibilidade de acceder á literatura ou ó coñecemento universal dende o propio idioma. É unha das nosas moitas asignaturas pendientes.[6]

There are therefore social constraints resulting from socio-linguistic and economic factors that impede the success of a translation series such as the one earlier mentioned. The question of reading habits is of particular interest here, as Galicians prefer to read in Castilian. According to a 1995 survey (Domínguez Seco *et al.* 1995), the great majority of the people interviewed read always (43.8 per cent) or usually (52 per cent) in Castilian. Galician publishers therefore usually focus on those areas which are sure to bring them benefits, such as children's literature or the school market. The links between language and translation policy and planning meet at this point. Thus, there are strong economic constraints preventing the practice of translation. However, it seems that it will be difficult to implement a particular translation policy without changing language attitudes. Another aspect that needs to be at least mentioned is the question of copyright, which is usually sold to the main publishing monopolies, and creates another hurdle in this context.

The benefits of translation in a context like the Galician are obvious. Thanks to translation, Galician has accessed worlds and domains which have been out of reach until very recently. Thanks to translation, Galician people can access a wide range of knowledge through Galician. And this is one of the most crucial functions of translation: it contributes to the (re-)creation of a network of intertextual relations, in Galician, which will encourage therefore awareness of one's identity by strengthening the bond between speakers and languages. Hence the importance of a solid and coherent policy of translation targeted at all areas of social life, both literary and non-literary.

Translation in language/culture planning

So, can translation be planned? What would translation planning involve? Or what should language planners require from translation? There are two main issues to consider: translation as part of language planning programmes, and the need for planning in translation activities.

When looking at the discourse on translation in Galician, translation appears as a tool to strengthen the language, as well as a vehicle for increasing the social domains in which Galician can be used, creating and/or consolidating registers and contributing to the overall purpose of 'normalising' the language. In this respect, in a sociolinguistic context such as the Galician, a consciously planned translation programme would be of great benefit. The first stage would involve the identification of those discursive spaces where Galician is not present. Due to the absence of original production in these areas, translation could be an efficient way to fill these gaps. Here I am referring to both literary and non-literary genres; popular genres such as magazines, instruction manuals are not represented. However, when dealing with translation, as well as language planning, we inevitably have to consider economic issues, particularly the question of copyrights, and the strong competition of the Spanish market. It is here where the discrimination of minorities becomes more painfully evident. A possible alternative policy would be to identify those publications which are not present in Spanish (Verdugo Mates 1998) and which are not, therefore, not easily accessible. This would have direct economic benefits for Galician publishers, although it would not be addressing the persisting existence of (lexical, register, genre, discourse) gaps in the Galician system. Another possible solution, in line with the previous one, would be to follow the line already adopted by Galician nationalists in the 1920s, namely to concentrate on an 'alternative' market, on texts produced in 'minority' cultures, and which may not be accessible everywhere. This could indeed be a way to break the monopoly of the major publishing houses, although it would still create a problem of access to these cultures, and the thorny issue of having to make use of mediated translations. The Galician case also offers a useful alternative: to exploit the new virtual environment of the Internet by creating a virtual library for translations of literary works. The idea has been developed by the Association of Galician Translators, whose website (http://www.bivir.es) has become a virtual library for literary translations which would not normally attract the attention of publishers.

As well as choices at repertoire level, translation planning requires attention to more practical aspects, such as the choice of source languages/texts and the question of textual mediation. The constant influence, and interference, of Spanish, at all levels, can be considered as a sensitive issue when approaching Galician translation. Although rarely acknowledged, Galician translations have often been influenced and shaped by previous Spanish translations. The negative consequences of such influence, at an ideological and cultural level, are obvious and have been pointed out by Verdugo Mates (1998: 66):

> ... nom se está aproveitando a possibilidade de contruir umha forma específica galega de interpretar o mundo e tampouco se estám a buscar soluçons para paliar as deficiências estruturais do idioma (deficiências que, longe de constituir um fenómeno próprio da natureza intrínseca do galego, som conseqüência da sua marginaçom até épocas recentes).[7]

Translation is seen as a powerful instrument in the planning of a language, but also as an indispensable tool for the creation of the Galician 'Self'. The persistent mediation of Spanish challenges the authenticity and independence of Galician identity. Second-hand, or mediated, translation, a procedure which at some point could have been justified, is no longer acceptable and could be considered as a negative influence.

An area that also needs attention is the actual translation process and product. Translation, as a vehicle for the spread of the standard norm, is carefully 'policed' in order to provide a 'correct' representation of the standard norm, both in terms of orthography, vocabulary and syntax. The role of the proofreader is particularly powerful, especially if we consider that most of them are not necessarily acquainted with the source language of the texts they are correcting. There is therefore a perhaps excessive concern with the form of the translated texts and little consideration has been paid to the actual 'accuracy' of those texts, or their genesis. Toury 1997 also mentioned that 'thinking in terms of planning is bound to affect the very way translating and translation(s) will be tackled and the kind of prescriptions and explanations that will come to the fore'. Here both language and translation aims clearly conflate. Questions such as lexical choice, language variation and the translation of cultural references are all issues which need to be considered. When translating we are not only approaching the 'Other', we are also representing ourselves. This is therefore an opportunity to reflect the Galician 'Self'. Steiner (1992: 381) points out that 'to experience difference, to feel the characteristic resistance and "materiality" of that which differs, is to re-experience identity'. Translating, meeting the Other, forces us to look at ourselves, and to recognise ourselves. A final aspect that needs consideration is the need for institutional intervention (grants, translation prizes) in order to support this type of activity. Similarly, the question of copyrights would need to be reviewed in order to allow further access to minorities.

Final comments

Translation activities offer a different perspective to the study of some pressing areas related to language and identity in minority contexts. Translation enhances the consolidation of one's own identity. However, it exposes the target culture, its weakness, its prejudices, its contradictions. The current translation situation, controlled by 'ad hoc' choices and market criteria, in fact highlights ambiguities and contradictions in the existing language planning programme. For this reason, and because of the potential outcomes of cross-linguistic and cross-cultural contacts, closer attention should be paid to the planning of translation activities. Thinking in terms of translation implies reflecting about the whole language planning process, about the role and function attached to the language. Ultimately, its success depends not only on the quality of the texts, but also on sufficient funding for different projects. In the case of Galician, it is obvious that a solid and serious translation policy would bring enormous benefits. The question is, which needs of Galician speakers are considered when devising language and cultural planning programmes? Are the symbolic needs relevant, or profitable enough, to be taken into account? Can a community survive or be built without translations, without contact with the 'Other'? In view of the globalisation process, the absence of translations may imply the fragmented existence of certain languages, and their continuing dependence on major systems. Are we envisaging a more sophisticated type of diglossia for the twenty-first century? In the end, the question that translation studies poses is: What are the needs that count?

Notes

1. The sociolinguistic situation of Galicia is quite complex. Although there is an official norm, supported by the Government, there is, however, no general agreement over this norm and the written representation of Galician.
2. Since the nineteenth century, the Celtic origin of Galicia has been mystified and used symbolically to reconstruct Galician pride and consciousness, breaking away from Spain and Mediterranean Europe, whose oppressive influence was rejected.
3. The very interesting essay *Quod nihil scitur* is still unknown, being more often quoted than read, as there is no version in Spanish. It is necessary to make it known. This will also contribute to the removal of the prejudice that we still remain isolated from the general intellectual activity [my translation].
4. ... the production, dubbing, subtitling and showing of films and other audiovisual media in the Galician language [my translation].
5. Similarly, Michael Cronin, when analysing the Irish situation distinguishes between the 'pragmatic' and the 'aesthetic' function of translation (Cronin, 1995: 89).
6. Our society has not fully assumed yet the possibility to access literature or universal knowledge from our own language. This is one of our many pending issues [my translation].
7. [...] no advantage is being taken of the possibility to construct a Galician specific way of interpreting the world, and no solutions are being sought for either in order to solve the structural deficiencies of the language (deficiencies which, far from being intrinsic to Galician, are a result of the marginalisation suffered until quite recently [...].

References

Anderson, B., 1991 [1983], *Imagined Communities*. London and New York: Verso. Asociación de traductores de Galicia: http://www.bivir.es
Arias, V., 1995, 'A Traducción no proceso cara a normalización cultural en Galicia', in *Actas do Primeiro Simposio Galego de Traducción*. Vigo: Edicións Xerais, 99–107.
Bassnett, S. and Trivedy, H., 1999, *Post-colonial Translation. Theory and Practice*. London and New York: Routledge.

Brisset, A., 1989, 'In Search of a Target Language: The Politics of Theatre Translation in Quebec', *Target*, 1(1): 9–27.

Cabana, D. X., 1990, 'Unha modesta proposición: traducir mil libros ó galego', *Trabe de Ouro*, 1, 69–82.

Cabrera, M. D., 1993, *Editar en Galicia*. Santiago: Xunta de Galicia.

Cooper, R. L., 1989, *Language Planning and Social Change*. Cambridge, New York: Cambridge University Press.

Cronin, M., 1995, 'Altered States: Translation and Minority Languages', *Traduction Terminologie Rédaction*, VIII: 1, 85–103.

Cruces Colado, S., 1993, 'A posición da literatura traducida no sistema literario galego', *Boletín Galego de Literatura*, 10: 59–65.

Díaz y Díaz, M. 1993 'Blurb' to *Hamlet*. Trans. into Galician by Miguel Pérez Romero. Santiago de Compostela: Xunta de Galicia.

Domínguez Seco *et al.*, 1995, *Usos lingüísticos en Galicia*. Seminario de Sociolingüística, Real Academia Galega.

Even-Zohar, I., 1978, 'The Position of Translated Literature within the Literary Polysystem' in Holmes *et al.*, 1978: 117–127. (Revised version in Even-Zohar,1990, *Poslysystem Studies*. Special issue of *Poetics Today* 11: 1, 45–51.)

Even-Zohar, I, 2002, 'Culture Planning and Cultural resistance in the Making and Maintaining of Entities', *Sun Yat-sen Journal of Humanities*, 14: 45–52.

García Cancela, X., 1995a, 'Traducción Administrativa', *Viceversa*, 1: 155–60.

García Cancela, X., 1995b, 'A Traducción Xurídico-Administrativa en Galicia' in *Actas do Primeiro Simposio Galego de Traducción*, Vigo: Edicións Xerais, 99–107.

González-Millán, X., 1994, *Literatura e Sociedade en Galicia* (1975–1990). Vigo: Edicións Xerais de Galicia.

González-Millán, X., 1996, 'Towards a Theory of Translation for "Marginal" Literary Systems. The Galician Situation', in Coulthard, M. and Odber de Baubeta, P. (eds) *The Knowledges of the Translator*. Lewiston; Lampeter: Edwin Mellen Press, 279–90.

Heidegger, M., 1930, 'Vom Wesen der Wahrheit'. In Heidegger, M. (1967) *Wegmarken*. Frankfurt: Klostermann.

Lefevere, A., 1992, *Translation, Rewriting and the Manipulation of Literary Fame*. London: Routledge.

Máiz, R., 1997, *A idea de nación*. Vigo: Edicións Xerais de Galicia.

Millán-Varela, C., 1998, 'Traducción e apropriación: Joyce en galego'. *Anuario de Estudios Literarios Galegos*, 43–73.

Millán-Varela, C., 2000, 'Translation, Normalisation and Identity: The Galician Case'. *Target* 12: 2, 267–82.

Monteagudo Romero, H., 1995, 'Sobre a polémica da normativa do galego' in Monteagudo, H. ed. *Estudios de sociolingüística galega*. Vigo: Galaxia, 197–230.

Rodríguez, F., 1991 *Conflicto lingüístico e ideoloxía na Galiza*. Santiago de Compostela: Laiovento.

Santamarina, A., 1988, 'Efectos do contacto linguístico na toponimia galega', in D. Kremer ed. *Homenagem a Joseph M. Piel por ocasiao do seu 85 aniversário*. Tübingen: Instituto da Cultura e Língua Portuguesa/Consello da Cultura Galega, 87–96.

Santamarina, A., 1989, 'Prologo', in I. Álvarez García, ed. *O libro Galego, Onte e Hoxe*. Santiago de Compostela: Federación de Libreiros de Galicia, 7–8.

Steiner, G., 1992, *After Babel. Aspects of Language and Translation*. Oxford and New York: Oxford University Press.

Toury, G., 1997, 'Translation and Cutlure Planning', http://www.tau.ac.uk/~toury/works/gt-plan.htm

Toury, G., 1995, *Translation Studies and Beyond*. Amsterdam: Benjamins.

Venuti, L., 2000, *The Scandals of Translation*. London and New York: Routledge.

Verdugo Mates, R. M., 1998, *Indústria editorial em Galiza*. Santiago: Laiovento.

Woodsworth, J., 1996, 'Language, Translation and the Promotion of National Identity: Two Test Cases', *Target*, 8: 2, 211–38.

Xunta de Galicia, 1983, *Lei de normalización lingüística do galego*.

10
On Policies and Prospects for British Sign Language
Graham H. Turner

Introduction

This study is not primarily driven by language data per se, but rather draws upon more impressionistic participation and observation within the minority language community in question. The author is a user of British Sign Language (BSL), engaged socially and professionally on a daily basis with the relevant language community. The issue under investigation relates to the interpenetration of language and social systems, and a close awareness of social and public policy forces and their consequences are applied. The work presented here is aligned with an emerging tradition of scholarship in sign linguistics and builds upon the author's earlier work (Turner 1995, 1996, 1999), drawing on the sociology of language and on anthropological linguistics for analyses of language and identity and on some recent developments in socio-political theory.

The structure of the chapter is as follows: An initial account is given of key contextual factors concerning the social and linguistic circumstances of BSL. Two strands of theoretical frameworking are then drawn together in order to focus subsequent discussion: the first derives from the emergence of sign linguistics as a 'legitimate' area of scholarship in the second half of the twentieth century, while the second identifies the roots of the sociolinguistic perspective adopted. In the light of this groundwork, the 'policy web' that enfolds BSL is then described and its consequences are exemplified. It is further suggested that current social theory offers a persuasive explanatory framework which might constructively be adduced here: the social forces of 'hyper-modernity', as investigated by Heller (1999) in relation to French speakers in Canada, may afford insights into the responses – suggested in the concluding section – which minority language users make to the effects of non-linguistic policies.

BSL: context, consequences and contest

BSL is used as a first or preferred language by between 50,000 and 100,000 people in the United Kingdom, and by more as a second or 'hobby' language. A tradition of scholarship in the linguistics of BSL – owing much to Bill Stokoe (Mather 1996) and the mode of scholarship he established in the 1960s in the United States – has emerged since the 1970s in the United Kingdom and demonstrated persuasively that sign languages are natural languages, evolved through processes of communicative interaction within communities wherever Deaf people were present, and capable of fulfilling all of the functions of any natural human language (Kyle and Woll 1985; Brennan 1992; Sutton-Spence and Woll 1999). Most users of the language do not learn it from their parents; more than 90 per cent of Deaf people do not have Deaf parents. There is no conventional written form of the language (although it can be captured on paper for analytical purposes using a notation system); literacy, for a British Deaf person, means literacy in English or another spoken language. As users of BSL are located within a society in which they form just a tiny minority of the population, they are obliged to deal with English users and texts on a daily basis, and are required to learn the majority language as part of formal schooling. Despite the modality difference, BSL is liable to influence from English: it is possible to combine elements of BSL and English in a mixed system (commonly known within the community as sign-supported English, 'SSE') – for instance, English word-order may be overlaid upon a sequence of signs drawn from BSL (Turner 1995) – and most users do this subconsciously much of the time. The ways in which sign language users position themselves on this issue have come to be regarded very much as 'acts of identity' (in the sense of Le Page and Tabouret-Keller 1985; see Kannapell 1993 and Lucas and Valli 1992 for analyses of the parallel situation for signers in the United States, and Schermer 1992 for one parallel in Europe).

BSL has not been explicitly recognized by the national parliament, although lobbying to achieve this is ongoing. The European Union (EU), too, may have been active in promoting sign languages, but has effectively done little towards the recognition of national sign languages (Krausneker, 2000). One of the major barriers to such recognition is the resistance to meaningful acknowledgement that Deaf people form a linguistic minority group. This notion requires a significant ideological adjustment for hearing people to whom 'being deaf' simply means enduring a form of sensory deprivation, making recognition of what is *present* for Deaf people much harder to achieve than to attract sympathy for what appears to be absent (Davis 1995; Corker 1998). Deaf people are therefore identified in public policy frameworks as 'disabled' rather than as users of a minority language. However, aspects of UK public policy do acknowledge the use of sign language as one possible appropriate way in which to meet the 'needs' arising from Deaf people's 'disability'. In theory, as a minority language, BSL is vulnerable to potential language shift in the face of the dominance of English (Turner 1999). This vulnerability is exacerbated by inexplicit recognition of the language, which permits service providers to 'meet' these needs without consideration of the particular language forms through which services are delivered or enacted. Thus, a Deaf student may be entitled to signed interpretation to ensure access to the curriculum, but the institution may be seen to have discharged its responsibility – to have made 'reasonable adjustments' – by employing as an interpreter someone who signs, whether the signed form is strictly BSL or a more English-influenced form.

BSL and the policy web

This juxtaposition of two radically different perspectives – the view of Deaf people as disabled or as members of a cultural and linguistic minority – helps to make explicit the intense connectivity within the 'policy web' which circumscribes and permeates language activity. In the absence of unified, direct statements on policy as regards BSL, government in the United Kingdom relies implicitly upon other policy frameworks to deal with the issues posed by the presence of sign language users.

Education policy, mediated by Local Education Authorities, has progressively redirected Deaf children from residential schools in which most of the children coming from families that did not sign learn BSL from their peers to mainstream settings wherein the deaf child tends to be a singleton for whom the curriculum is notionally made accessible by a support worker. Here, a policy which has been framed in part to satisfy the demands of other disabled people for integration has deleterious sociolinguistic effects for deaf children who are now at risk of segregation from the language community within which they would be most at home.

Employment policy provides Deaf workers with an entitlement to 'Access to Work' support, again intended to facilitate workplace integration by recourse to human or technological aids to communication.

Within the *broadcast media*, a small handful of programmes designed and produced for the Deaf community have created a space for sign language on television, but government policy has succeeded only in establishing quotas for proportions of programmes for which subtitles and on-screen interpretation must be provided: the vast majority of interpreted programmes are screened between midnight and five o'clock in the morning.

Within a broader *social policy* context, disability discrimination in general has been explicitly outlawed since 1995, with the initial enactment of a law protecting disabled people's access to goods and services. Deaf people are covered by this law, which asserts that 'reasonable adjustment' should be made above and beyond regular provision in order to ensure, in principle, that access to services is not denied. The devil, inevitably, is in the detail, and here the word 'reasonable' is, of course, open to interpretation, with the result that providers regularly make adjustments which are seen to be reasonable whilst nevertheless being measurably ineffectual. A crucial area for social policy intervention should be that relating to family matters, but to date no British government has made provision for the families of deaf children to have a right to the kind of guidance – including BSL skills training for parents – that is advocated by the very Deaf people who have first-hand knowledge of the inadequacies of alternative approaches to family communication.

Some advances have been made with regard to *legal policy*, such that Deaf people may be more assured of fair treatment before the law of the land. Government has taken steps to proclaim that only interpreters reaching certain published standards should be employed in legal matters – but has not followed this through to the extent of ensuring that a sufficient number of interpreters are actually trained and available to undertake the relevant work (see Brennan and Brown 1997 and Harrington and Turner 2001 for discussion on access to the law).

Developments in a number of other policy fields give rise to a climate in which being Deaf and preferring to use BSL may appear to be an increasingly vulnerable sociolinguistic position. *Health policy* inevitably impacts significantly upon Deaf people, despite the fact that Deaf people's self-image is not as medical 'cases', 'suffering' from problems of a pathological nature. The genetic revolution in health-care carries within it the potential for pre-emptive interventionist measures to be taken that will reduce the number of children born deaf. This is not the place to discuss the ethical dilemmas inherent in this situation, but it is relevant to note here the immense cultural threat present in the implication that genetic intervention to prevent deafness is a proper course of action: 'It is not', as Ruth Bailey has written, 'a question of numbers but of feeling secure in one's own and one's collective identity, and I do think that potentially genetic testing could undermine that security' (1997: 20). The implications of health policy choices like this, of course, ripple out to many other institutional contexts of public life – starkly apparent in this matter, for instance, are the policies being considered or, indeed, adopted by insurers and other finance corporations looking at tailoring policies to health criteria and 'lifestyle choices'.

Health policy and developments in *science and technology* are close companions here. Deaf people are treated as 'impaired people' by institutions prepared to justify the spending of large quantities of public money on, for example, cochlear implants (leading-edge technology requiring invasive surgery to enhance acoustic signals to the brain of Deaf 'patients'). At the same time, scientific research on the linguistics of BSL has all but dried up since the 1980s and the kind of low-tech intervention that would be made possible by the provision of human resources (for instance, specialist service providers) to offer access to communication in a language which is biologically natural to Deaf people is a rare and precious commodity within the community.

Much of this situation has been exacerbated by a kind of compliant negligence on the part of national government, which has preferred to divest itself of major social responsibilities by deferring considerable power and influence to non-governmental organisations (NGOs). Doing so, however, does not represent a value-free transfer on the part of government. Influential organizations within the Deaf field include those like *Defeating Deafness* which are dedicated primarily to the exploitation of technology in making audiological disadvantage a thing of the past, and others, such as DELTA (Deaf Education through Listening and Talking) which campaign against the use of sign language in the education of Deaf children. The most influential of them all, RNID (*The Royal National Institute for Deaf People*), claims as its constituency up to nine million people with a hearing loss in the United Kingdom: in the context of such numbers, and of the kind of internal diametric opposition to signing as is implied by the very existence of organizations like those just mentioned, it is no surprise that the RNID is not viewed as much of an ally by BSL-using Deaf people (among whom its initials are sometimes said to stand for *Really Not Interested in the Deaf*). Deaf people are thus not unreasonably sceptical about the messages being received by the Treasury concerning the deployment of resources earmarked for their benefit.

All of this adds up to a situation in which, as I have argued, Deaf people's simple, primary requirement – the enactment of policies giving due recognition to the ongoing significance of BSL within the community – is log-jammed by cross-cutting and disorganized policy responses emanating from different spheres and, all told, resulting in a sociolinguistic environment whose huge complexity makes the 'voice' of BSL users extremely hard to discern and any notion of linguistic self-determination on the part of the collective very difficult to sustain.

An example

Perhaps an example can help to reinforce and clarify the point. Suppose the hearing parents of a deaf child are looking to carry out their responsibilities in securing the most appropriate available education for their child.

- Because *education* policy has centred on an 'integrationist' (mainstreaming) model for disabled children, the region's only residential school for deaf children has closed down. The local authority is responsible for the child's education and agrees to a review meeting.

- The *parents* seek advice prior to the review meeting from local Deaf people, but communication is hampered by the fact that the parents sign very little – they received the clear message in *post-diagnostic counselling*, reinforced by *audiologists* and their early interaction with *social service representatives*, that using sign language was not considered best practice within a home like theirs: a message which they only much later began to challenge, having no ready access to training. The parents cannot access funding to enable the purchase of *interpreting services* for their meeting with Deaf community representatives.

- At the review meeting, an 'interpreter' is provided, but the national shortage of qualified interpreters (Brien *et al.* 2002) – coupled with the educational establishment's tolerance of Communication Support Workers (CSWs: cheaper to employ and professionally much more malleable than qualified interpreters, too) with intermediate-level BSL skills – means that this person facilitates communication only relatively ineffectually.

- The school representatives explain that, since they have other 'hearing-impaired' children in the school who do not use BSL – there are two children with cochlear implants in the class – and resources are pulled in multiple directions at once, they propose that the most efficient use of the funding they will have to support the child's education will be to use CSWs as appropriate during the school day.

- An expert is called in from a *national Deaf organization*. This organization's policy on sign language issues is squeezed considerably by the demands presented by those of its members for whom English is the first language. The latter outnumber signing Deaf members by about 300:1. The advice given serves only to underpin the school's attempted compromise position. The review meeting's decision is that there is no affordable alternative educational placement available.

- An informal appeal to local *social services* for support to pursue the case is dismissed since current policy here has shifted any advocacy burden in relation to Deaf people on to charitably-funded 'community development officers', who lack the professional recognition afforded to a social worker in this role. (There is no policy requirement that social workers specializing in work with Deaf people actually need sign language skills, so communication with the child is here also limited.)

- The local *media* are approached to publicize the parents' dissatisfaction with the position taken. The regional television station has ceased production of signed news bulletins, as their quota of signed programming can now be satisfied with after-midnight showings of mainstream programmes with a translator insert. (They now produce no programmes made directly in BSL.)

- The parents might consider challenging the decision at a higher level, invoking recent *legislation* – but these powers are as yet largely untested in the courts, and the legislation is presented in such a way that BSL, as such, is not a specified requirement of 'appropriate' practice in relation to Deaf people's access to educational services.

- As a result, the family is left knowing that their child will not be exposed to BSL for schooling purposes. Not wishing to complicate the child's formative educational experiences, and having only very inadequate access to BSL-using role models for either themselves or their child, the parents decide to try and use the kind of signing produced by the CSW (i.e. SSE) *at home*.

This is a fictionalized account based on a variety of real experiences. I do not offer it as a representative account; certainly there will be variation in different elements of the picture around the country. It is presented as merely illustrative material, an attempt to paint a brief picture of how it is that a range of policy responses relating to Deaf people coincide in such a way as indirectly to provide a profoundly enmeshed set of structural circumstances which will play a major role in constructing (though not determining) the long-term language choices of the family and the child. The intended consequences of policy decisions and the actual consequences may significantly diverge: this is in large measure due to the agency of local interpretations of policy frameworks, interpretations which are, I would argue, poorly informed by an awareness of the possible convergences and conflicts inherent within poorly co-articulated policy structures.

Whilst I do wish to argue that sign languages are not profoundly distinct from other minority languages in respect of being caught in such policy webs, two aspects of this entire picture seem to me to make sign languages stand out from spoken languages here. First, the weak position of signed languages as minority languages (in Europe and elsewhere) centres above all on the family and home circle, just because so many deaf children are not exposed to fluent, natural signing at home. My reading of Joshua Fishman's work on language shift (1991) suggests that the resulting sociolinguistic vulnerability can be seen as entirely predictable, since Fishman is adamant that without the intergenerational continuity which human societies generate within family groups, the threat of language shift is inevitable. The second peculiarity is the way all of the policy issues are cut through by notions relating deafness to disability, notions marked by an almost inevitable institutional conservatism, resulting in the perpetuation of discredited or inappropriate models of disability-as-pathology. It appears to be impossible, in present circumstances, for Deaf people to be seen as *both* a linguistic minority group *and* as disabled people. The late twentieth century has seen Deaf people struggle to cast off identification as disabled (Padden and Humphries 1988; Lane 1992) in order to highlight their claims to the status of a cultural or ethnic group. However, it is surely not impossible to reconcile and accept the applicability of both aspects of identity, providing that one adopts a more enlightened, progressive disability discourse (Corker 1998), one that presents Deaf people not as medically impaired, but 'disabled by society' because they are disadvantaged in the social world for reasons arising in relation to the salient differences between their physical characteristics and those of the majority of the population. For these reasons, whilst there are arguments for simply treating sign languages like other minority languages within the European Union, I would argue that we are faced with a set of exceptional circumstances to which particular consideration is due.

Language policy and hyper-modernity

At this point, having briefly described the present condition of BSL in its policy context, I turn to its future prospects. One of the most exciting developments in contemporary sociolinguistics is the engagement with current social theory (Coupland *et al.* 2001). Monica Heller's work on French as a minority language in Canada uses such theoretical reflections to shed some very particular light on sociolinguistic issues, and I would now like to explore the parallels with BSL which may be identified. Heller is interested in how we respond as language users to 'hyper-modernity' and to the shape of the twenty-first century as it moves on from structures of economics and governance created for twentieth century purposes. Hyper-modernity is, says Heller (1999: 4), about the transformation to an economy of service and information, not bounded by nation-states, and about the movements of people as they carry out the new economy activities and position themselves to take advantage of (or to resist) what the new economy presents:

> This is particularly important for linguistic minorities, whose linguistic repertoires have value that is radically different from the value they had when a centralizing nation-state and a primary resource extraction based economy defined it. Linguistic minorities used the logic of ethnic state nationalism to resist that older form of power in order to enter the modern world. That modern world uses a different logic, and so linguistic minorities now have to define themselves in order to retain their economic and political gains, but without losing their legitimacy.

What does this mean when applied to BSL (see Padden 1996 and Padden and Rayman 2002 for discussion of related issues in the USA Deaf community)? When BSL first began to be identified in scholarly terms as a language in the 1970s, the language abilities which were seen as having capital value (in economic terms) for Deaf people were English, spoken and written, and English-influenced signed varieties. The development of sign linguistic scholarship saw BSL itself, on the other hand, as providing the 'authenticating value' to the community's claims for group identity and self-determination. The 1980s and 1990s have broadly seen a strong shift here: BSL – because it is the language that has been named, taught, and 'exoticised' (Mairian Corker, personal communication), which has a relatively high public profile, and for which there is an infrastructure of qualifications and regulation; in other words, it has been industrialized – now carries an economic status of its own. English, of course, retains its distinct economic value. However, as we move into the twenty-first century, the vernacular in everyday use within the polity increasingly does not use the same signed forms (Turner 1996) as the 'industry standard' has identified, causing major tensions, not least in relation to notions of 'authenticity' with reference to identity.

A key element in the shifting (or at least uprooted) nature of the relationships between language options for Deaf people is the place of hearing people as signers. Hearing people are now increasingly seeing the economic value of sign language: the policy climate means that opportunities for employment using signing skills are rapidly increasing. This new component, allied to the fact that parents and educators of deaf children have long been predominantly hearing, puts those who are not immediately identified as members of the 'focal population' (in other words, non-Deaf people) in control of the means of sign production and distribution. Lately, too, the teachers of BSL employed by colleges have tended increasingly to be non-Deaf people – because of other aspects of the education policy climate (specifically, increasingly bureaucratic regulatory frameworks for teaching at this tertiary level, requiring levels of paperwork that are daunting to non-native users of English). Thus hearing people – typically non-native signers – increasingly control the linguistic resources, their production and distribution and hold the power to decide which forms will 'count' as valuable or not.

In this context, it is perhaps unsurprising that we see a turn among younger Deaf people that is arguably very much in keeping with notions of hyper-modernity. We might identify – very broadly – four twentieth-century phases of Deaf language ideology in the United Kingdom, each approximately associated with a different 'generation' of Deaf people.

1. The first generation resolutely identifies command of the English language as 'best' or 'most respectable': such an ideological perspective is most commonly associated with older signers.
2. In the formative years of slightly younger signers, manual language (often in the form of fingerspelling) gained a foothold in education and public consciousness (and policy): Deaf people began to look to – or anyway, use – signed forms which displayed their knowledge of English for respectability.
3. As time went by, BSL began to be recognized by researchers and become identified by Deaf people as 'best', in the sense of emblematic as the authenticating characteristic of politicized Deafness.

4. Most recently, the territory has started to shift away from this focus on language and identity: younger people reach maturity via a policy climate which is fraught with conflicting and contested discourses about Deafness, disability, community membership and language choices – but one which increasingly enables them to 'get on' using whatever linguistic resources they have at their disposal. Thus their language choices become contingent – a means to an end, rather than a profoundly symbolic act, where the end is a matter of economic and lifestyle 'success'. Language choice, in this context, becomes one among many decisions about self-presentation taken on a case-by-case, pragmatic basis as people move through their daily lives.

Notice that the language choices Deaf people make in the preceding framework can be seen to run in parallel with other lifestyle and identity choices they make (this resonates with Heller's comment about multiple 'linguistic *and cultural* resources' below). For instance, the younger generation are much more pragmatic or instrumentalist and less ideological about the way they *use* cochlear implants (and tolerant in their attitudes towards others who have them). To switch on or not switch on the power-supply to an implant is not necessarily, entirely or fundamentally any kind of political act so much as it is a pragmatic response to seeking to get on in life, and is therefore dealt with on a moment-by-moment contingent basis; for instance, one might choose to switch on for lectures, but not for parties.

So we see, I suggest, as does Heller (1999: 5), a linguistic minority prepared to abandon the old politics of identity, and hence the problematics of authenticity, in favour of a new pragmatic position which allows them to take advantage of their access to multiple linguistic and cultural resources in order to participate in a globalized economy. Certainly, the politics of identity has made them sensitive to exclusionary practices, of which they do not wish to be victims and will not condone. But in contrast to the predecessor generation – still marching resolutely through London's Trafalgar Square and presenting petitions to the Prime Minister at 10 Downing Street – they have learned from the politics of identity that it is important to fight discrimination not on the old-style grounds of collective rights, but on other grounds altogether. Like the participants in Heller's Canadian studies (1999: 16), Deaf people have mobilized to enter the modern world in order to enjoy its fruits, not to maintain the marginalized and difficult life which was the basis of their solidarity, but which was not much fun. These are not young people longing nostalgically for a close-knit community in which, though undoubtedly oppressed, they could be entirely sure where they stood, sure of who was 'us' and who was 'them'. Having grander ambitions for themselves and the world apparently at their feet, they prefer to alter the discourse, to move it towards something pluralist which might be a way station towards a situation in which they will no longer care about any category that might be used as a basis for social stratification. But they have no desire to alter the fundamental nature of the market or build an alternative one: they want equal access to the dominant one.

This does, however, provoke a crisis of legitimacy for minority institutions, which cannot be ignored. Here, UK Deaf people and Heller's Canadians part company, by my analysis. Heller argues that we see 'the beginnings of the construction of a new basis of legitimacy, one founded not on authenticity and tradition, but rather on pluralism, on the extensiveness of the minority's social networks and on the quality of the linguistic resources the minority possesses' (1999: 5). It is the last element which diverges, I think, because control over the new-found linguistic capital is already passing, or has passed, into the hands of (hearing) non-heritage signers – parents, teachers, CSW, interpreters, plus Deaf people caught in institutional structures and operating in such hybridized Deaf-hearing environments that they have lost their grip on heritage forms too. The example of BSL teaching perhaps provides the clearest glimpse of the latter point. At the same time as the new, paper-driven regulatory mechanisms are imposed upon teaching at tertiary level, a huge range of alternative careers are opening up in a way that was simply inconceivable in the last century, and young Deaf people no longer choose to enter the language teaching profession ('who'd want to do that all day everyday, and where's the financial incentive?').

How did we come to this? In the second half of the twentieth century, the fading power of nations seems to have opened gaps permitting the development of resistance to the domination of the majority. But the same conditions which allowed for linguistic minorities to mobilize to seek the right to self-determination undermine the very logic of mini-nationalisms based on ethnic or other group identity – because 'we're all minorities now, so let's seek unity in diversity and be plural'. In the meantime, there have nevertheless been some very real gains. People who were formerly marginalized now wield power in domains of political and economic activity, and position themselves to take advantage of their skills. The problem, then, is how to preserve these gains while accomplishing a shift to a new basis of legitimacy of that position of power. For this legitimacy is now problematic: having based their claims on the logic of linguistic identity, on the right of a people, identified by its common language, to self-determination, it is difficult to imagine the basis on which these minorities would be able to reproduce themselves having departed altogether from the logic of linguistic 'nationalism'. Monica Heller says (1999: 15) that 'linguistic minorities thus illustrate particularly clearly the crisis of legitimacy that hyper-modernity has brought us to'. In the Deaf case, this shifting of the logic of legitimacy has to be attempted whilst at the same time – just when the claims to 'Deaf identity' may result in some 'civic space' to call their own – Deaf people appear to be disowning the language resources that would legitimate their control of this space, leaving it to be colonized (again!) by Deaf people whose preferred language may *not* be BSL, but who know an opportunity when they see one, and by non-heritage signers.

Notice, though, that this is not to suggest that there is no longer *any* social patterning within young Deaf people's language choices – far from it. Rather, the patterning is richer than we have previously been in a position to acknowledge – Heller uses the metaphor of a kaleidoscope to capture this dynamic complexity. We see a dynamic process whereby the policy climate (structure) provides for language activity (agency) which itself reflects and occasions a re-interpretation of the policy climate and its effects. There are language choice patterns within this generation, but users do not orientate to them as political resources in 'the same old way': rather, they deploy this linguistic capital in a local (situated, contextualized, contingent) manner, within particular communities of language practice.

New century, new developments

One response within Deaf communities to the complex and poorly-articulated conjunctions of policy in relation to language and identity – and a response that appears to be gaining ground – is simply to argue that policy-making affecting these communities should be more closely derived from *within* the relevant population. This deceptively simple assertion has effectively been suppressed within wider civic society by individualistic notions of citizenship firmly rooted in liberal traditions (see Faulks 2000 for discussion). However, alternative perspectives on citizenship have emerged during the latter part of the twentieth century, which centre upon a re-evaluation of pluralism and difference, and Deaf communities are strikingly well-placed to engage with such discourses. Iris Young, for instance, asserts (1990: 184) the following principle:

> A democratic public should provide mechanisms for the effective recognition and representation of the distinct voices and perspectives of those of its constituent groups that are oppressed or disadvantaged. Such group representation implies institutional mechanisms and public resources supporting (1) self-organisation of group members so that they achieve collective empowerment and a reflective understanding of their collective experience and interests in the context of society; (2) group analysis and group generation of policy proposals in institutionalised contexts where decision makers are obliged to show that their deliberations have taken group perspectives into consideration; and (3) group veto power regarding specific policies that affect a group directly.

Related positions are presented by political scientists such as Kymlicka (1995) and, whilst they are, of course, open to critique (Faulks 2000) – including on the grounds of cultural essentialism which are also an issue in relation to Deaf communities (Turner 1994) – it is clear that the kind of comprehensive shift of empowerment which is envisaged in these proposals offers to minority communities a platform for developing claims to language rights which are a great deal stronger than may previously have been the case, precisely because 'ownership' of the policy scaffolding which surrounds language-related decisions would stand to be transferred more-or-less directly to the communities in question.

Whilst alternative notions of citizenship present the tantalizing prospect of minority language users being newly empowered as regards policy-making, it is also possible to imagine that the contemporary preoccupation with recourse to the law as a remedy for all ills may play a significant role in the re-positioning of linguistic minorities, including Deaf people. Of particular salience, perhaps, in the United Kingdom at present is the heightened sensitivity to discrimination arising in the wake of racial tensions which have been identified once again as major national issues. Following the murder of a black young man named Stephen Lawrence in south London, the government-appointed McPherson Inquiry, examining claims that policing on the case had been negligent, chose the term 'institutionalized racism' as a way of highlighting the systematically discriminatory approach towards non-white people which was found to be prevalent throughout the Metropolitan police force.

Racism, of course, is not the only form of discrimination to be found in our societies. The existence since 1995 of a Disability Discrimination Act in the United Kingdom announces the clear intent to prevent discrimination against disabled people, too. One form of such discrimination has been identified in print by Harlan Lane (1992: 43; acknowledging that the term is borrowed from deaf educator and author Tom Humphries) as *audism*.

> Audism is the corporate institution for dealing with deaf people, dealing with them by making statements about them, authorizing views about them, governing where they go to school and, in some cases, where they live; in short, audism is the hearing way of dominating, restructuring, and exercising authority over the deaf community.

It is but a short step to bring these two elements together and to speak of *institutionalized audism*. To do so brings into sudden focus the nature of the often depersonalized – but, for all that, often deeply embedded and therefore deceptively powerful – oppression that is routinely experienced by Deaf people, and centres almost exclusively around ignorance of, and consequent institutionalized mistreatment in relation to, the language choices made by Deaf people. One may have profound reservations about the increasing power of the lawyers to regulate, censor and trim human behaviour in almost every corner of the modern world, but if this is to be our *modus vivendi*, then here, perhaps, is an appropriate cause for the application of legal scrutiny.

Conclusion

This chapter has focused upon the central idea that language policy is always located against a wider, multidimensional matrix of inter-dependent social and public policy frameworks and that these have indirect and frequently unintended consequences to which minority languages may be particularly vulnerable. The case of BSL effectively highlights this point, since explicit linguistic policy in relation to this particular language tends to be conspicuous by its absence. This being so, the 'indirect' effects upon language of other policy decisions can become particularly apparent.

As is often shown to be the case, exploration from such an atypi-cal perspective can shed informative new light upon familiar issues, and I would certainly argue that the particular policy web in which BSL can be located is, in principle, no different to that against which the prospects for any minority language must be analysed. Ultimately, then, this example should encourage analysts to remain fully alert to the potential range of strands in the web. Ideological underpinnings in relation to language, open to re-interpretation in the hyper-modern world, are dynamic by nature, and new theoreti-cal directions in the social and political sciences offer intriguing insights into the prospects for linguistic minority group members in the twenty-first century.

The key conclusion here, though, is that any 'protection' afforded to BSL as a minority language – and, by extension, to other minority languages, signed or spoken – is liable to be less effective than it might be just because insufficient attention is paid to the effects of wider social and public policy-making upon language practices. This is a problem of policy co-articulation and one with potentially major long-term consequences for the prospects of minority languages and their users.

References

Bailey, R., 1997, 'Response to Foundation Paper 3 – A Disability Rights Perspective', *Deaf Worlds*, 13(2): 16–21.

Brennan, M., 1992, 'The Visual World of BSL: An Introduction', in *Dictionary of British Sign Language/English*, ed. D. Brien. London: Faber and Faber.

Brennan, M. and Brown, R. K., 1997, *Equality before the law? Deaf people's access to justice*. Durham: University of Durham.

Brien, D., Brown, R. and Collins, J., 2002, *The Organisation and Provision of BSL/English Interpreters in England, Scotland and Wales.* Dept of Work and Pensions: In-house report 102. http://www.dwp.gov.uk/asd/asd5/IH102.pdf

Corker, M., 1998, *Deaf and Disabled, or Deafness Disabled?* Buckingham: Open University Press.

Coupland, N., Sarangi, S. and Candlin, C. N. (eds), 2001, *Sociolinguistics and Social Theory.* London: Longman.

Davis, L. J., 1995, *Enforcing Normalcy: Disability, deafness and the body.* London: Verso.

Faulks, K., 2000, *Citizenship.* London: Routledge.

Fishman, J., 1991, *Reversing Language Shift.* Clevedon, Avon: Multilingual Matters.

Harrington, F. J. and Turner, G. H., 2001, *Interpreting Interpreting: Studies and Reflections on Sign Language Interpreting.* Coleford, Gloucestershire: Douglas McLean.

Heller, M., 1999, *Linguistic Minorities and Modernity.* London: Longman.

Kannapell, B., 1993, *Language Choice – Identity Choice.* Burtonsville, MD: Linstok Press.

Krausneker, V., 2000, 'Sign Languages and the Minority Language Policy of the European Union', *Sociolinguistics in Deaf Communities*, 6: 142–58.

Kyle, J. and Woll, B., 1985, *Sign Language: The Study of Deaf People and their Language.* Cambridge: Cambridge University Press.

Kymlicka, W., 1995, *Multicultural Citizenship.* Oxford: Oxford University Press.

Lane, H., 1992, *The Mask of Benevolence: Disabling the Deaf Community.* New York: Alfred A. Knopf.

Le Page, R. and Tabouret-Keller, A., 1985, *Acts of Identity; Creole-based Approaches to Language and Ethnicity.* Cambridge: Cambridge University Press.

Lucas, C. and Valli, C., 1992, *Language contact in the American Deaf community.* San Diego, CA: Academic Press.

Mather, S., 1996, *Seeing Language in Sign: The Work of William C. Stokoe.* Washington D.C.: Gallaudet University Press.

Padden, C. A., 1996, 'From the Cultural to the Bicultural: The Modern Deaf Community', in *Cultural and Language Diversity and the Deaf Experience*, ed. I. Parasnis. Cambridge: Cambridge University Press, 79–98.

Padden, C. A. and Humphries, T., 1988, *Deaf in America: Voices from a culture.* Cambridge, MA: Harvard University Press.

Padden, C. A. and Rayman, J., 2002, 'The Future of ASL', in *The Study of Signed Languages: Essays in Honour of William Stokoe* (eds) D. Armstrong, M. Karchmer, J. Vickrey Van Cleve. Washington D.C.: Gallaudet University Press, 303–27.

Schermer, T., 1992, *In Search of a Language.* Delft: Eburon.

Sutton-Spence, R. and Woll, B., 1999, *The Linguistics of British Sign Language.* Cambridge: Cambridge University Press.

Turner, G. H., 1994, 'How is Deaf culture?' *Sign Language Studies*, 83: 103–26.

Turner, G. H., 1995, 'Contact Signing and Language Shift', in *Sign Language Research 1994: Proceedings of the Fourth European Congress on Sign Language Research in Munich* (eds) H. Bos and T. Schermer. Hamburg: Signum Press, 211–29.

Turner, G. H., 1996, 'Language Change at the British Sign Language/English interface', in *Change and Language* (eds) H. Coleman and L. Cameron. Clevedon, Avon: British Association for Applied Linguistics/Multilingual Matters, 64–72.

Turner, G. H., 1999, ' "Ungraceful, repulsive, difficult to comprehend": Sociolinguistic consideration of shifts in signed languages', *Issues in Applied Linguistics*, 10: 131–52.

Young, I., 1990, *Justice and the Politics of Difference.* Princeton, NJ: Princeton University Press.

11
The Changing Status of Romani in Europe

Dieter W. Halwachs

Introduction

The Roma are neither a regional minority nor an immigrant minority; they are – like Germans, Hungarians, Romanians, Sami, Ukrainians, Welsh – one of the indigenous ethnic groups of Europe. Just like all other ethnic groups the Roma have a common history, a common language, a common lifestyle and a shared set of values. Even if some Roma groups are almost completely assimilated to their respective majority population they have preserved at least traces of common cultural characteristics. Primarily, this refers to their binary conception of the world: the Roma and the non-Roma, the clean and the unclean, and so on. Perhaps even more importantly, there is also the common history of the Roma, which comprises their origin and migration from India to Europe and the common experience of stigmatization, discrimination, persecution and genocide.

Romani, the common language of the Roma, the Sinti, the Kale and other European population groups, often subsumed under the pejorative denomination 'gypsies', belongs to the Indo-Aryan branch of the Indo-European language family and is the only New-Indo-Aryan language spoken exclusively outside of the Indian subcontinent (see Figure 11.1). From a linguistic point of view, Romani may be described as a heterogeneous cluster of varieties without any homogenizing standard. The terminology used for the individual varieties is primarily based on the denominations of the respective groups of speakers, which again are highly heterogeneous: Apart from the label *Romungro*, which is – sometimes pejoratively – used for settled

Hungarian Roma, and *Vend* (border) for small groups in the border regions of Austria, Hungary and Slovenia, the central varieties show mainly geographic definitions. The same applies to the southwestern Greek Vlax varieties of *Ajia Varvara*, a suburb of Athens, and of *Dendropotamos*, a suburb of Thessaloniki, as well as the northern Vlax variety of the *Mačvaja*, a group originating in the Serbian *Mačva* which today lives in the United States – primarily in California. Some denominations indicate professions, such as *Bugurdži, Čurara, Kalderaš, Lovara, Sepečides* – drill-makers, sieve-makers, tinkers, horse-dealers, basket-weavers. The denominations *Arli* used for Kosovarian and Macedonian Roma and *Erli* used for a group living in Sofia are indications of the long-lasting settled way of life of these Balkan Roma: the Turkish word *yerli* means 'native'. The name *Gurbet* used for the speakers of a southwestern Vlax variety derives from the Arabic word *gharib* 'strange' which has been transmitted via Turkish. *Rumeli* or *Rumelian Romani* stands for the Turkish variety of Romani recorded by Paspati (1870).[1]

Because of shared conservative linguistic features, Northwestern, Northeastern, British and Iberian varieties are sometimes treated as Northern group of Romani (Bakker 1999). Denominations range from geographical definitions to group names and even one language

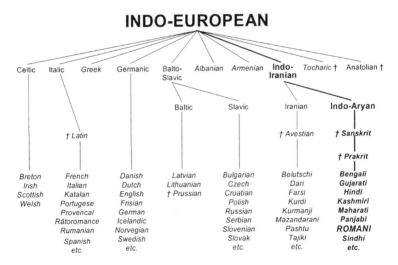

Figure 11.1 The origin of Romani

denomination is used: *Rómanes* is a widespread language name among *Sinte*, a group denomination with unclear etymology. *Manuš* (human being) and *Caló* (black) both are self-designations among Northern groups. The geographical denominations define the current living space – *Lombard Sinte, Finnish Romani* and so on – as well as the country of origin – *Estrexarja Sinte* which in the case of the *Russian Estrexarja Sinte* is the former Austrian Hungarian Empire.

Para-Romani varieties are varieties of the respective majority language with Romani lexicon and, if at all, only a few Romani structural features: *Errumantxela* is a variety of Basque, *Caló* is a variety of Spanish, *Angloromani* of English, *Scandoromani* summarizes Para-Romani varieties based on various Scandinavian languages. The problems with clustering Romani varieties into dialect groups are indicated by the double affiliation of *Dolenjski Romani* spoken in Slovenia in the area of Novo Mesto, which stands between Balkan and Central varieties, and the Hungarian *Gurvari Romani*, which combines Central and Vlax elements.

According to realistic estimates, the number of Romani speakers in Europe amounts to approximately 4.6 million. The percentages,

Table 11.1 Romani-speakers in Europe

Country	Speakers	%	Country	Speakers	%
Albania	90,000	95	Latvia	18,500	90
Austria	20,000	80	Lithuania	4,000	90
Belarus	27,000	95	Macedonia	215,000	90
Belgium	10,000	80	Moldova	56,000	90
Bosnia-Herzegowina	40,000	90	Netherlands	7,000	90
Bulgaria	600,000	80	Poland	56,000	90
Croatia	28,000	80	Romania	1,030,000	80
Czech Republic	140,000	50	Russia	405,000	80
Denmark	1,500	90	Serbia and Montenegro	380,000	90
Estonia	1,100	90	Slovakia	300,000	60
Finland	3,000	40	Slovenia	8,000	90
France	215,000	70	Spain	1,000	1
Germany	85,000	70	Sweden	9,500	90
Greece	160,000	90	Turkey	280,000	70
Hungary	290,000	50	Ukraine	113,000	90
Italy	42,000	90	United Kingdom	1,000	0.5

based on Bakker *et al.* (2000), are summarized in Table 11.1 and indicate the estimated share of the Romani speaking Roma population in each country.

Based on these approximate figures of the Romani speaking Roma population, the total number of Roma in Europe amounts to 6.6 million people. More generous estimates refer to the total number of European Roma to be about 12 million. As the Roma have always been, and still are, a group which demographically can only be identified with difficulty, all numbers are only approximations. The basis for the numbers given in the case of Austria and Spain indicates the problematic nature of any estimates of the extent of migrating populations. The figure 25,000 given for the Austrian Roma includes the autochthonous Roma population and migrants who arrived as so-called guest workers from the middle of the 1960s onwards. It fails to take account of population increases due to recent migrations from the Balkans and Eastern Europe, which were caused by conflict and deteriorating economic conditions in various countries. The number given for Spain only includes the native Roma population, the *Calé*. The same applies to the figure provided for the United Kingdom: only the autochthonous *Romanichal* are included; working migrants, who arrived over the last decades, and recent migrants are not considered. Portugal, although missing from Table 11.1, has, like most Western European countries, a Roma population consisting of an autochthonous group, the *Calé*, which immigrated centuries ago, members of Vlax groups, who came from the late nineteenth century onwards, and recent migrants from Eastern Europe and the Balkans. Despite such unavoidable inaccuracies, the fact is that there are some million Roma and some million Romani speakers in Europe.

The sociolinguistic situation of Romani

Romani is a language that until recently has not existed in a written form as it has exclusively been passed on orally. It has not developed a codified standard and, as a consequence, no prescriptive norms. This linguistic situation reflects the socio-political situation of the Roma: politically, economically and culturally marginalized, ethnically stigmatized, discriminated against and persecuted, the Roma could only survive in small groups, which led to the geographical and social heterogeneity that exists today. Consequently, the Roma have been in no position to build large political–economic structures or to secure their share of political and economic power. Considering that the development of standard varieties generally follows the establishment of political and economic power structures, it becomes evident why Romani does not have a codified standard and why it will not be able to develop one in the near future. This has to be seen in connection with the status of Romani as a non-territorial language. As the Roma were commonly denied ownership of larger estates throughout the centuries and were thus only able to live in small groups – extended families or communities of interest, the so called *kumpanias* – they were unable to develop larger social units which are as a basis for self-contained socio-economic structures. On account of this fact, the Roma have always been dependent on the socio-economic structures of the respective majority population and, therfore, Romani was and is limited to intra-group-communication, inhibiting the emergence of territorial language and the development of a standard form.

To this day, for most Roma their respective Romani variety is reduced to intra-group-communication and thus limited to certain domains. Romani primarily functions as an intimate variety. Nearly all Romani speakers are bi- or multilingual and use the language of the respective majority population(s) for inter-group-communication in public and most often also in informal or partly public domains. As a result, no social stratification can be found within the individual Romani varieties. This repertoire displays the full range of functions as, for example, among some Kalderaš groups where Romani dominates the internal communication and is also used when in contact with speakers of other Vlax varieties. More frequently, however, Romani does not function in the social macrocosm, not even in contact with other Roma groups and is only used as intimate variety in the social microcosm.

These limitations in the functional dimensions together with the lack of a standard and a written variety are the major reasons why Romani has not only very little prestige with the majority population, but also why many Roma consider it inferior as compared to the language of the respective majority population.

The low prestige of the language, reduced domains, multilingualism and the pressure to assimilate on the part of the majority culture make Romani a dominated language whose relationship with the contact languages has never been one between equals. As a result, various phenomena of language contact and language shift occur ranging from lexical borrowings from the majority language to monolingualism in the majority language. This way, some Roma groups have given up Romani without, however, losing their ethnic awareness. For example, many Roma with Romanian background living in Greece, Hungary, Serbia and Romania have adopted varieties of Romanian as their mother tongue, but they still identify with the Roma in an ethnic and cultural sense. Of course, there are also groups whose ethnic awareness was lost when language shift occurred.

Language attitude and self-organization

Changing language attitudes of some Roma groups have occurred because of a decrease in language use. As long as Romani dominates group-internal communication, it is perceived as a matter of course and therefore almost not consciously considered an identity factor. Romani is attributed a conscious status at most as a secret language which must not be revealed to group outsiders; this attitude to language is very prominent among the Sinti. If the use of Romani decreases because of strong pressure for assimilation from the dominant culture, such a development is only perceived consciously when group self-organization takes place according to the guidelines of the majority population. It is via this self-organization that the common criteria of 'nation' or 'ethnic group' are adopted, and language becomes the primary factor of identification. As a consequence of this development, a decrease in the use of Romani is perceived as a loss and, ultimately, as a threat to the continued existence of the group.

This process took place among the Roma of Burgenland (Austria) during the last decade. Initiated externally, language awareness has grown through self-organization and contacts beyond the community, which can be illustrated with a few examples of incidents that occurred during the period since the foundation of the association 'Roma' in Oberwart.

- At the foundation of the association (1989), Ceija Stojka, a famous member of the Austrian Lovara, was invited. She spoke

Romani on this occasion, which made a deep impression on the assembled Roma of Burgenland.

- Thanks to the foundation of the association, the representatives of the Roma of Burgenland entered into contact with other groups, such as the Kalderaš living in Vienna, among which Romani dominates in intra-group-communication. Due to such experiences, language awareness has developed and its underuse began to be felt as a loss and a threat to the persistence of Romani.
- New language awareness was strengthened, among other things, by the wish of the governor of Burgenland that he be told a fairy tale in Romani and German which was then presented in both languages on the radio and finally published in a journal.
- Also, the experience of Romani as a medium of communication and thus as a cohesive element that is shared with neighbouring Roma in Hungary and Slovenia has lead to the fact that now, for the Roma of Burgenland, the maintenance and revival of Romani has become an issue of primary concern, at least at the level of the association.

It is, however, unclear to what extent such newly developed language awareness will have the potential to counteract the continued decrease in language use. It is also not certain that codification, which, at the level of the association, has already resulted in teaching activities at primary schools, in the training of adults and in the production of journals and radio broadcasts, can help to prevent processes leading to language death. At best these developments will decrease the probability that Burgenland-Romani will vanish completely over the next few decades.

As this example shows, decrease in language use, however, is not the main factor for Romani to become the primary identity marker of the community. In fact, the trigger is self-organization in line with the guidelines of the dominant culture, a process which may be described as emancipation by means of organizational assimilation. In the course of this organizational assimilation, the socio-cultural concepts and values of the majority are adopted and, according to the European nation-state ideology, become the primary identity factor for the respective Roma group. Only in exceptional cases does self-organization extend beyond the traditional group boundaries. This has also meant that national and international Roma organizations are not to be considered as umbrella associations of Roma groups and Roma associations, but more or less as loose structures run by a group of Roma activists who are trying to extend their self-organization and to create national or international levels of representation in order to improve their advocacy opportunities. Nevertheless, in view of the fact that the Roma have hardly any share in political and economic power, this is an important interim step of a heterogeneous ethnic group towards self-organization.

In the context of this process of self-organization, Romani plays a key role. The Roma themselves, as well as the institutions of the majority population, attribute to Romani a much higher status today than they did only a few decades ago. While it is true that this development had originally been triggered by their self-organization, today it is determined by an interplay of inside and outside forces. On the one hand, there are the endeavours and requirements of the Roma themselves; on the other hand, this is complemented by the support and the requirements of the majority population. As a consequence, the internal and external statuses of Romani are in permanent interaction. This finds its expression not only in terms of language policy but it has also determined the linguistic development of Romani over the last decades.

Internal status

As far as internal status is concerned, Romani has developed from a little perceived language to maybe the most important cultural parameter of the Roma. As such, Romani determines group-internal as well as group-external ethnic identity.[2] This change in the sociocultural status has resulted in the endeavour to bring Romani in line with other European languages in terms of both structure and function. A consequence of these endeavours is the codification and expansion of Romani in its functional dimensions, which also entails a pragmatic-functional expansion.

Codification

Codification is to be regarded as a means of emancipating Romani *vis-à-vis* other European national minority languages. Individual attempts of codification lie between the tensions of regional and global approaches resulting from the heterogeneity of Roma and

Romani. Regional or group-specific approaches take into account the requirements of single groups of speakers and therefore are primarily orientated towards establishing a communicative basis, whereas global approaches are more or less politically motivated.

The promotion of a written form of Romani is the first step needed in any codification initiatives. According to Matras (1999: 488), there are two types of global codification approaches in contrast to the regional, group-specific ones: 'Codification for the purpose of academic documentation of speech' and 'codification in the service of unification and language engineering' are to be considered as global approaches. Whereas 'codification for the purpose of transposing oral usage into texts directed at audiences' is determined by communicative aspects on a group-specific level.

Though never conventionalized among Romani linguists, a type of academic norm has developed in recent years. Attempts at codification in the service of unification choose character sets which stress the status of Romani as an independent language and which are able to cover all possible phenomena of Romani. As they frequently involve linguistically orientated innovations, they get only little acceptance by the average Romani user. In contrast, the group-specific, communicatively oriented codification approaches gain higher, albeit regionally limited, acceptance. These approaches range from using the conventions of the written language of the respective majority language to partly adapting to global approaches. They combine the familiar writing system of the majority language with Romani-specific innovations.

Expansion

The contrast between global and regional approaches characterizes the lexical expansion of Romani, too. Up to a few decades ago, Romani was primarily used as an intimate variety. Only with the self-organization according to the model of the majority culture was this limitation perceived as a shortcoming. At the same time, the first attempts to use Romani as a language in the media were launched. These attempts nurture the efforts of expanding the language into formal domains, which is most evident on the lexical level where an enormous amount of technolectal designations are lacking in Romani. A dearth of these definitions has not created a communicative problem until the attempt to change the status of Romani. Romani has a very productive set of morphological markers which renders it possible to adopt each word from the respective majority language and to integrate it morphologically. This advantage of Romani is considered as a disadvantage in view of attempts to emancipate the language on the basis of 'purity demands'.

At the beginning of the codification of Burgenland-Romani, the representatives of the Burgenland-Roma, for example, requested to substitute all Slavonic, Hungarian and German elements of their Romani variety with Indian or even Sanskrit lexemes. Only a laborious demonstration of the etymological heterogeneity of other European national languages could neutralize this demand. A similar attempt was made in the course of the codification of a Macedonian variety of Romani. In this case neologisms from Hindi were adopted, which – among others – has resulted in the adoption of *komando* 'command' to Romani as borrowed from Hindi, because their real origin was not clear. These and similar attempts to purify Romani from European vocabulary aim to increase the prestige of Romani. Similar intentions lie behind the strategy to take over missing lexemes from English. This way of proceeding is found in a newspaper published in Prizren in the Kosovo. If in this case the international value of English is meant to further the prestige of Romani in the two examples mentioned earlier, it is hoped to achieve the same result by using Sanskrit or Hindi which sometimes is felt to be the 'language of the mother country'. In other words, increasing the prestige of the language by adopting lexemes from high-prestige languages represents one of the global strategies for the expansion of Romani.

Which of the two strategies for codification – regional or global – is the predominant one in a given context depends on a variety of factors. Without going into a detailed examination of individual cases, the general tendency is that if the 'trigger' of the codification process is an international organization, global strategies will prevail. The same is true for groups with a strong international spread. Communities which have been settled for a longer period and which therefore are partly assimilated, on the other hand, generally apply regional strategies and mainly borrow from the primary contact language.

Emblematic and mobilising functions

Parallel to codification and lexical expansion, Romani has also experienced changes and expansion on the pragmatic level. The new internal status of Romani as a primary identity marker alongside its communicative function implies that the emblematic and mobilizing functions are the primary aspects that need to be considered for the written use of Romani.

Matras (1999: 495) defines emblematic texts as texts 'which are not intended to enhance the addressee's knowledge in order to promote action on his part, but rather to elicit emotional identification on the part of the addressee through the aesthetic symbolism of the text in its particular language-external context'. On a micro level, the emblematic function is attributed to the occurrence of single Romani words in texts in the majority language. There are numerous newspapers and magazines with Romani titles, such as the Austrian magazine *Romano Kipo* 'Roma picture', published quarterly, which is almost exclusively written in German. Example 1 provides an extract of an emblematic text in Rómanes, the Romani variety of German Sinti:

Example 1   (Matras 1999: 496)

I Rikeripaske ap u Sinti de Roma, mare Mulenge, gei weian maschke 1933 de 1945 mardo an u Manuschengromarepen.	In memory of the Sinti and Roma, our dead, who were murdered in the Holocaust between 1933 and 1945.

This sentence was displayed together with its German translation at the end of a commemorative exposition about the Holocaust. It uses regional group-specific codification and German writing conventions. The neologism *Manuschengromarepen*, literally translated as 'striking dead of people', was used for 'Holocaust'.

On a macro level of emblematic texts, there are translations of the Bible and other highly symbolic texts.[3] Such translations demonstrate to the majority population that Romani is suitable for long complex texts; they also have a positive effect on the appreciation of the value of Romani by the Roma themselves. This consequently strengthens their identification with their own language and culture (cf. also Millan-Varela, this volume).

As mobilizing-rallying functions, Matras (1999: 496) defines 'the shaping of a text in such a way that it would demonstrate ideological commitment and political allegiance and identification'. Example 2, which is taken from the minutes of a meeting of Romani delegates at an international conference in June 1994, shows the use of a global approach to codification in relation to the mobilizing function.

Example 2   (Matras 1999: 497)

maśkarthemutne bi-raipne oganizàcie...	international non-governmental
buti vaś-e Manuśkane Ha-kaja p-o	organizations ... human rights
maśkarthemutno nivo. ...	activities at the international level ...

Eventually, conventions on an official Romani standard was established at the Fourth Romani World Congress in April 1990 in Warsaw. In the following years, the proponents of this decision have used the conventions defining the criteria for the implementation of a written language set by the Warsaw decision. By using these conventions, ideological commitment as well as political allegiance and identification with the Romani Union, its resolutions and its decision makers was demonstrated.

External status

The changes within the pragmatic functions of Romani, lexical expansion and codification initiatives all affect the external, public status which the institutions of the majority population grant Romani. Positive changes in the external status contribute to improving the internal language status, while negative developments or a stagnation in the improvement of the external status, on the other hand, stop and impede internal status improvements.

Until the second half of the twentieth century Romani was of interest, apart from philologists and linguists, only to the police and justice. This fact to a certain extent explains the status of Romani as a secret language. Later on, self-organization and the resulting opening towards the world of non-Roma, as well as changes of the language's internal status, have initiated a positive development in terms of an improved external status. Gradually, Romani has become to be perceived as the Roma's primary cultural identity factor by the majority population and increasingly, the public recognizes its status as a language. The previously dominant opinion that regarded it as gibberish, as jargon of fringe groups and as an idiom of crooks is slowly losing ground. One result of this change of opinion has resulted in moderate official attention attributed to Romani as a European minority language.[4]

As can be expected, Romani is not an official language in the European Union and only a few states have recognized it as an official minority language. The following international organizations have expressed their support for the recognition of Romani (Bakker 2001):

- In 1981, the Standing Conference of Local and Regional Authorities in Europe called upon the governments of their member states to recognize Roma and other specific nomadic groups as ethnic minorities and consequently grant them the same status and rights that other minorities may enjoy, in particular concerning respect and support for their culture and language.
- In 1983, the Council for Cultural Cooperation recommended that the Romani language and culture should be used and accorded the same respect as other regional or minority languages and cultures.
- In 1989, the Council of Europe (CoE) and the Ministers of Education stated that the culture and language of the Roma and Travellers have formed part of the communities' cultural and linguistic heritage for over 500 years; their aim was to stimulate the development of teaching methods and materials on the history culture and languages of Roma and Travellers and encourage research into their culture, history and language. In the same year, the CoE adopted a resolution on school provision for Roma and Traveller children.
- In 1990, during the Copenhagen meeting of the Conference on the Human Dimension of the Conference on Security and Cooperation in Europe (CSCE), the participants explicitly recognized the particular problems of the Roma. They further stated that persons belonging to national minorities, notwithstanding the need to learn the official language or languages of the State concerned, should have adequate opportunities for instruction in their mother tongue.
- In 1992, the Charter for Regional or Minority Languages (CRML) was approved by the CoE. It specifically mentions non-territorial languages. In the Explanatory Report, Romani is explicitly referred to as an example of a non-territorial-language.

- In 1993, the Parliamentary Assembly of the European Parliament approved a recommendation on Roma in Europe, stating that as a non-territorial minority, they greatly contribute to the cultural diversity of Europe, among other aspects through their language.
- In 1996, the Universal Declaration of Linguistic Rights was approved by a host of institutions and NGOs. Article 1.4 considers nomade peoples within their historical areas of migration and peoples historically established in geographically dispersed locations as language communities in their whole territory. In this sense, the territory of the Roma and of Romani can be understood as encompassing the whole of Europe.
- In 2000, the Committee of Ministers of the COE stated that in the countries where the Romani language is spoken, opportunities to be instructed in their mother tongue should be offered at school to Roma children.

Perhaps the most important document is the European Charter for Regional or Minority Languages (ECRML) of 1992, which is now operative in the states that have ratified it (cf. Nic Craith, this volume). Not all of its signatory states mention Romani in the list of languages to which the Charter applies on their territory. While Austria, Finland, Germany, the Netherlands and Sweden have listed Romani as a minority language in their area, Norway, Switzerland, Croatia and Hungary have not done so, although the latter two are hosts to a sizeable Roma minority. Such attitudinal differences may have arisen due to the non-territorial nature of Romani. However, recognition of Romani would also imply its promotion and consequently lead to a financial commitment in support of the Romani population, which some governments want to avoid. In the case of the Roma there is no territorital representation and no accepted authority which would be able to lobby effectively for them.

Conclusion

Romani as a non-territorial minority language reflects the socio-political status of its speakers. Marginalized and stigmatized, the Roma never had the possibility to develop social structures beyond extended families and consequently never developed a linguistic standard. They still are a heterogenous nation, a fact which is reflected by their language: Romani is a heterogenous cluster of varieties with a core of common morphological features and approximately one thousand lexemes of Indian, Iranian, Armenian and Greek origin of which some one hundred are part of the lexicon of every single Romani variety. Romani is a dominated language which has no written tradition and has been passed on orally up to now. In most cases it only functions within the social microcosm, as intimate variety in the everyday life of socially marginalized and stigmatized families and clans. Until recently, Romani was not even recognized as a language by many governments and other public institutions.

Due to self-organization and the resulting acknowledgement of these Romani organizations by national and international institutions, the status of Romani is slowly improving. But it is yet unclear whether recent developments will fundamentally contribute to its conservation and recognition as one of Europe's minority languages.

In view of the fact that the Roma have been subjected to long-term pressures to assimilate into their host-societies, the ethnolinguistic vitality of Romani and its varieties still is remarkably intact. This vitality, together with the changes in its internal as well as external status, raises hopes that Romani will continue to form part of the linguistic and cultural diversity of Europe. For this goal to be achieved, it is vital that its speakers will finally be granted equal rights and treatment, which they have been denied for centuries.

Notes

1. The same convention in terms of denominations characterizes the *Welsh Romani* documented by John Sampson in 1926. Up to now this description by Sampson is one of the standard works in terms of Romani linguistics. The second British variety, Angloromani, nowadays is a so-called para-Romani variety, which means that it is a variety of English with lexical elements of Romani. As a consequence of the migration of Vlax groups from Romania from the second half of the nineteenth century onwards and as a result of intra-European migration in recent decades, there are also speakers of Balkan, Central and Vlax varieties in the United Kingdom.
2. Group-external identity means that the Roma perceive Romani as the main factor that constitutes group identity *vis-à-vis* outsiders. For the majority of the non-Roma populations, however, stereotypes and prejudices remain as the main markers or identifiers.
3. The translation of the *Ramayana* by Leksa Manuš (1990) is worth mentioning for its high quality.

4. This process is more relevant in countries where Romani has the status of a recognized minority language, as for example, in Austria, Sweden, Finland and other countries who have ratified the *European Charter of Regional or Minority Languages*.

References

Bakker, P., 1999, 'The Northern Branch of Romani: Mixed and Non-mixed Varieties', in *Die Sprache der Roma. Perspektiven der Romani-Forschung in Österreich im interdisziplinären und internationalen Kontext* (eds) D. W. Halwachs and F. Menz. Klagenfurt: Drava, 172–209.

Bakker, P. *et al.*, 2000, *What is the Romani Language*, Hatfield: University of Hertfordshire Press.

Bakker, P., 2001, 'Romani in Europe', in *The Other Languages of Europe* (eds) G. Extra and D. Gorter. Clevedon: Multilingual Matters, 293–313.

Halwachs, D. W., 1993, 'Polysystem, Repertoire und Identität', *Grazer Linguistische Studien* 39–40, 71–90.

Manuš, L., 1990, *Romani Ramayana vaj Pheniben pal e Ramaste – Romany Ramayana or the tale about Rama*, Chandigarh: Roma Publications.

Matras, Y., 1999, 'Writing Romani: The Pragmatics of Codification in a Stateless Language', *Applied Linguistics*, 20/4, 481–502.

Matras, Y., 2002, *Romani: A Linguistic Introduction*, Cambridge: Cambridge University Press.

Paspati, A., 1870, *Études sur le Tchinghianés ou Bohémiens de l'Empire Ottoman*, Constantinople: Karomela.

Sampson, J., 1926, *The Dialect of the Gypsies of Wales. Being the Older Form of British Romani Preserved in the Speech of the Clan of Abram Wood*, Oxford: Clarendon Press.

Part IV
Conclusion

12
Language, Nationalism and Democracy in Europe[1]

Stephen May

Introduction: Europe and the rise of the nation-state

One need not look far into history or, for that matter, the burgeoning academic literature on nationalism, to find that Europe has provided us with the model of the modern nation-state as we know it today. The French Revolution of 1789 and its aftermath created the precedent for a form of political organisation not countenanced before – a polity represented and *unified* by a culturally and linguistically homogeneous civic realm (May 2001). Previous forms of political organisation had not required this degree of linguistic uniformity. For example, empires were quite happy for the most part to leave unmolested the plethora of cultures and languages subsumed within them – as long as taxes were paid, all was well. The Greek and Roman Empires are obvious examples here, while 'New World' examples include the Aztec and Inca Empires of Central and South America respectively. More recent historical examples include the Austro-Hungarian Empire's overtly multilingual policy. But perhaps the clearest example is that of the Ottoman Empire which actually established a formal system of 'millets' (nations) in order to accommodate the cultural and linguistic diversity of peoples within its borders (Dorian 1998). Nonetheless, in the subsequent politics of European nationalism – which, of course, was also to spread throughout the world – the idea of a single, common 'national' language (sometimes, albeit rarely, a number of national languages) quickly became the *leitmotif* of modern social and political organisation.

How was this accomplished? Principally via the political machinery of these newly emergent European states, with mass education playing a central role (Anderson 1991; Gellner 1983). The process of selecting and establishing a common national language usually involved two key aspects: legitimation and institutionalisation (Nelde *et al.* 1996; May 2001). Legitimation is understood here to mean the formal recognition accorded to the language by the nation-state – usually, by the constitutional and/or legislative benediction of official status. Institutionalisation, perhaps the more important dimension, refers to the process by which the language comes to be accepted, or 'taken for granted' in a wide range of social, cultural and linguistic domains or contexts, both formal and informal. Both elements, in combination, achieved not only the central requirement of nation-states – cultural and linguistic homogeneity – but also the allied and, seemingly, necessary banishment of 'minority' languages and dialects to the private domain (see also section 'A multilingual European Union'). In short, these processes ensured that both national and minority languages were literally 'created' out of the politics of European state-building not, as we often assume, the other way around (Billig 1995).

Of course, this also helps to explain why some languages are mutually intelligible while some dialects of the same language are not (see also Nic Craith, this volume). The example often employed here is that of Norwegian, since it was regarded as a dialect of Danish until the end of Danish rule in 1814. But it was only with the advent of Norwegian independence from Sweden in 1905 that Norwegian actually acquired the status of a separate language, albeit one that has since remained mutually intelligible with both Danish and Swedish. Contemporary examples can be seen in the former Czechoslovakia, with the (re)emergence in the early 1990s of distinct Czech and Slovak language varieties in place of a previously common state language. In the former Yugoslavia, we currently see the (re)development of separate Serbian and Croatian language varieties in place of Serbo-Croat (see also O'Reilly, Pupavac, this volume). In short, independence for Norway and the break-up of the former Czechoslovakia and Yugoslavia have precipitated linguistic change, creating separate languages where previously none existed.

If the establishment, often retrospectively, of chosen 'national' languages was therefore a deliberate, and deliberatively political act, it follows that so too was the process by which other language varieties were subsequently 'minoritised' or 'dialectalised' by and within these same nation-states. These latter language varieties were, in effect, *positioned* by these newly formed states as languages of lesser political worth and value. Consequently, national languages came to be associated with modernity and progress, while their less fortunate counterparts were associated (conveniently) with tradition and obsolescence. More often than not, the latter were also specifically constructed as *obstacles* to the political project of nation-building – as threats to the 'unity' of the state – thus providing the *raison d'être* for the consistent derogation, diminution and proscription of minority languages that have characterised the last three centuries of nationalism. As Nancy Dorian (1998: 18) summarises it, 'it is the concept of the nation-state coupled with its official standard language ... that has in modern times posed the keenest threat to both the identities and the languages of small [minority] communities'. Florian Coulmas (1998: 67) observes, even more succinctly, that 'the nation-state as it has evolved since the French Revolution is the natural enemy of minorities'. Not surprisingly, this state-led 'ideology of contempt' (Grillo 1989) towards minority languages has also contributed centrally to their significant and ongoing decline, as minority language speakers have shifted over time, and in exponentially increasing numbers, to speaking majority national languages as their first language (Skutnabb-Kangas 2000; May 2001).

Europe, supranationalism and the 'Decline' of the nation-state

If Europe was the locus of the modern nation-state, it is also currently a prominent example of the rise of supranationalism. Most notable here of course is the growing influence of the European Union (EU) which currently comprises 15 European nation-states and which is set to expand in 2004 to 25, as it begins to incorporate further nation-states from southern, central and eastern Europe. The EU has proved to be a focus of controversy in the politics of some European nation-states, Britain being one prominent example, for its avowed agenda of greater European integration. Anti-European parties in Britain, and elsewhere, have made much of the EU's potential to 'supersede' the sovereign functions of the traditional nation-state. The particular concerns of anti-European groups, which are usually, but not exclusively, on the right of the political spectrum, tend to focus on two key areas. One is the impending loss of economic sovereignty, a prospect that has been made more likely by the recent establishment of the 'Euro' as pan-European currency in 11 of the member states of the EU. A second focuses on the potential loss of political sovereignty, via the increasing incorporation of member states into the legal, administrative and political structures and functions of the EU bureaucracy.

These ongoing debates are not of principal concern to me here, except perhaps in as much as they point to the growing influence of supranational organisations such as the EU on the affairs of nation-states. However, unlike political opponents of the EU, as well as some academic commentators (e.g. Hall *et al*. 1992; Robertson 1992; Bauman 1993; Soysal 1994; Held 1995), I do not believe that it signals the end of the modern nation-state as we know it. Of course, nation-states are clearly subject to wider trends towards greater economic and political interdependence in this age of late capitalism, not least because of the rapid growth of globalisation. To suggest otherwise would be foolish. But the idea that this is an entirely new phenomenon would also appear to be misplaced, since nation-states have always been subject to wider economic and political forces of one form or another. As Hinsley (1986: 226) observes, the idea of complete economic and political sovereignty is a 'situation to which many states may have often aspired, but have never in fact enjoyed'. Moreover, it can be argued that, far from replacing nation-states, supranational organisations such as the EU may serve, at least in some key respects, to reinforce them. Certainly, the two countervailing political views on European integration that have been promoted over the last decade – the idea of the federal European 'super state' versus the national 'opt out' – both perpetuate the notion of nationhood. The former simply transfers nationhood to a wider entity, adopting in the process many of its key political apparatuses and symbols (territorial boundaries, immigration controls, parliament, currency and an electorate). The latter continues to define membership of the EU in terms of existing nation-states and national boundaries (Shore and Black 1994; Billig 1995; Smith 1998). Indeed, some have gone so far as to argue that the EU has been a key bulwark of the nation-state. As Milward (1992: 3) argues, 'it has been its buttress, an indispensable part of the nation-state's post-war construction. Without it, the nation-state could not have afforded to its citizens the same measure of security and prosperity which it has provided and which has justified its survival'.

Thus, the impending demise of nation-states via the emergence of supranational organisations may be overstated, although such organisations can also clearly act both as catalysts and as intermediaries in relation to other forms of identity – particularly at the local and regional level. The latter is apparent within the EU in the growing emphasis on regional identities, and the allied promotion of greater political devolution and regional control within EU member states (Petschen 1993; Bullman 1994; Jones and Keating 1995). As we shall see, such developments provide a potential political 'space' in which alternative identities, including those of minority language speakers, may be promoted.

A multilingual European Union?

Be that as it may, the record of the EU with respect to minority languages is not a strong one, not least because as Nelde *et al.* (1996) clearly outline, as many as 48 minority language groups within the EU are currently seriously threatened. One reason for this is that many EU member states continue at national levels to ignore and/or oppose the extension of minority language rights on the basis of the national(ist) principle of cultural and linguistic homogeneity, discussed earlier. This opposition – perhaps most clearly evident in France, the first and archetypal modern nation-state – continues even in the face of recent developments in pan-European law which have seen the adoption of a more favourable position towards the recognition of minority language rights. The result, not surprisingly, is significant qualification of the latter. Thus, in relation to the European Charter for Regional or Minority Languages (ECRML) adopted in 1992, individual European nation-states retain considerable discretion over the level of recognition they provide, on the basis of both local considerations and the size of the group concerned. European nation-states also retain considerable scope and flexibility over which articles of the Charter they actually choose to accept in the first place. In this respect, they are only required to accede to 35 out of the 68 articles (see also Nic Craith, this volume). A similar pattern can be detected in the Framework Convention for the Protection of National Minorities, which was adopted by the

Council of Europe in November 1994 and finally came into force in February 1998. The Framework Convention allows for a wide range of rights for national minorities,[2] including language rights. It also asserts at a more general level that contributing states should 'promote the conditions necessary for persons belonging to national minorities to maintain and develop their culture, and to preserve the essential elements of their identity, namely their religion, language, traditions and cultural heritage' (Article 2.1). That said, the specific provisions for language remain sufficiently qualified for most states to avoid them if they so choose.

There is obviously still considerable scope for improvement in the recognition of minority language rights within the EU and its member states. In addition, there is the tricky question of accommodating language rights and multilingualism within the formal workings of the EU itself. At one level, the accommodation of multilingualism is clearly quite extensive, not least because the European Parliament formally adopted in 1990 the 'principle of complete multilingualism'. The treaties of accession guarantee that speakers of the 11 official languages of the EU (in effect, the dominant languages of the 15 current member states) have the right to use these languages in the European Parliament and the European Commission, the administrative centre of the EU. Similarly, official EU documents must be made available in all of these languages, where required. The result is that the EU has the largest translation and interpretation service in the world (Labrie 1993; Phillipson 1998). But with its ongoing further expansion, the prospect of maintaining this degree of multilingualism seems less and less likely. Even now, it is hardly sustainable, with 40 per cent of the EU administrative budget committed to translation and interpretation alone (Skutnabb-Kangas 2000). As Fishman (1995) observes, the logistical cost of interpretation to and from all official languages in the EU is formidable, with currently already 210 possible combinations for the 15 member states. With the inclusion of ten new member states in 2004, this would grow to 600. Add to this those states still wishing to join the EU, notably Romania, Bulgaria and Turkey, as well as the successor states of the former Yugoslavia and some of the newly independent states on the territory of the former Soviet Union, and the potential combinations would quickly exceed 1,000.

Given these difficulties, we already see in the EU a retrenchment of formal multilingualism with, for example, the European Commission adopting only English and French, and to a lesser extent German, as its working languages for all internal documents. While the Parliament and Council of Ministers still use all 11 official languages for formal sessions and key documents, this rule is usually abandoned in less formal situations, where English and French dominate. In effect, English and French are now the principal languages within the EU – English because of its global reach, and French because many of the EU institutions are situated on French-speaking territory. Thus, even within the multilingual apparatus of the EU, linguistic rationalisation in favour of dominant languages is at work. Consequently, the working languages of the EU are increasingly facing the same scenario at the supranational level that many minority languages face at a national level – linguistic marginalisation and allied perceptions of lower status, value and use (Phillipson 1998, 2003).

But there are also countervailing tendencies in favour of multilingualism and minority language rights within the EU. The Committee of Regions and the Bureau for Lesser Used Languages are both active in promoting regional identities, and regional and other minority languages, respectively. More significantly perhaps, the EU has allowed national minority groups within Europe an alternative political forum in which to operate, independent of (or at least in conjunction with) the nation-states in which they are currently subsumed. As Esteve (1992: 259) notes, 'the dynamics of the present-day situation suggest that Europe may evolve into a complex association of autonomous communities in which the supranational unifying process is accompanied by a reinforcement of ... regional autonomies'. One prominent example here is Catalonia, which is currently one of the 'autonomías' (autonomous regions) of the Spanish state. However, the Catalonian *Generalitat*, or government, is also a vocal supporter of the Europe of the Regions and, within the narrow constraints of the intergovernmental system of policy-making, participates as fully as it can in the formal workings of the EU (Keating and Hooghe 1996; Keating 1996, 1997). Wales and Scotland, both of which have recently been granted devolved political and economic powers within Britain, are currently less active in European affairs, but are nonetheless increasingly looking to Europe as an alternative sphere of influence (McCrone 1992; May 1999; Taylor and Thompson 1999). These developments at the sub-state level may also provide considerable scope and institutional space for the fostering of minority languages. Again, both Catalonia and Wales are exemplars here of just what can be achieved in this respect since the move towards greater devolution in the once highly centralised states of Spain and the United Kingdom has facilitated the (re)legitimation and institutionalisation of Catalan and Welsh, respectively, in the civic realm, after centuries of derogation and proscription of these languages.

Addressing the problem of public support: the case of Catalonia

Catalonia and Wales are regarded, at least in the European context, as examples of regions which have successfully re-established a public role and place for languages that had previously been minoritised and peripheralised by the larger states in which they had been subsumed. But even here, opposition to the legitimation and institutionalisation of these (minority) languages continues. I have discussed the Welsh context in this respect at length elsewhere (May 2000), so I will confine myself in what follows to recent developments in Catalonia.

In Catalonia, initial moves in the post-Franco democratic period to establish Catalan as the language of civic administration and education – via initially voluntary Catalan language immersion programmes – enjoyed widespread support, both within Catalonia and Spain as a whole (Woolard 1989; Miller and Miller 1996; Artigal 1997). But more recent attempts to extend the legal status and institutional reach of Catalan have proved to be considerably more controversial (Hoffmann 1999, 2000). These developments have included the adoption of a unified model of Catalan-medium education, with limited opportunities for opting out, and have culminated in the 1988 Catalan Linguistic Policy Act.

The Catalan Linguistic Policy Act has three main objectives. The first is to support the legal consolidation of Catalan language policies in schools and the wider civil service, the former by fully implementing unified Catalan immersion education, the latter by further strengthening formal Catalan language requirements for civil servants working in the Catalonian *Generalitat* (government) and in local authorities. The second objective is to increase the presence of Catalan in the media and commerce fields (in which Castilian Spanish remains dominant), principally via the introduction of minimum Catalan language quota systems in the media, and the requirement of bilingual service provision in the commercial sector. In this latter respect, the Act specifically calls for private companies to implement programmes and measures in support of the further use of Catalan at work. The third objective of the Act is a more broad-based one, to achieve full equality or comparability between Catalan and Spanish in all formal language domains. This includes not only the devolved areas of administration currently regarded as the responsibility of the Catalonian *Generalitat* but also those areas that still remain under the jurisdiction of the Spanish central government, notably the judicial system, law and order and tax administration (Costa and Wynants 1999).

The Catalan Linguistic Policy Act constitutes, in effect, the 'next stage' of the legitimation and institutionalisation of Catalan within Catalonia – with a clear movement away from the more gradualist, 'politics of persuasion' approach that typified earlier language measures (Woolard 1989). The controversy and opposition that has attended these more recent developments is notable for being initiated and fostered principally from elsewhere in Spain, rather than from within Catalonia itself. It has also tended to be firmly located within a broader conservative political agenda advocating the return of a traditional centralist Spanish nationalism exemplified in the majoritarian model of the linguistically homogenous nation-state (DiGiacomo 1999). Thus, Catalan language laws, as the most visible manifestation of an alternative Catalan nationalism and as a demonstrable example of the wider federalism of Spain, have become something of a *cause célèbre* for these traditional Spanish nationalists. Before proceeding to a brief analysis of their campaign, I should point out that these oppositionalists almost never actually see themselves as nationalists – their avowedly 'anti-nationalist' stance obviously does not extend to a critique of their own. The subsumption of majoritarian forms of nationalism at work here is a process that Billig (1995: 17) describes as 'banal nationalism' where the nationalism of the dominant ethnie 'not only ceases to be nationalism ... it ceases to be a problem for investigation'. As Susan DiGiacomo (1999: 131) observes of this in specific relation to the Catalan case, while drawing on the Benedict Anderson's well-known concept of the nation as an 'imagined community': 'It is the ironic condition of stateless nations like Catalonia that the "imagined community" ... is always challenged, by putatively objective scholarship as well as by the state and those who share its interests, as merely imaginary, while the imagined community of state nationalism is treated as objectively real, part of the natural order.'

The campaign mounted against Catalan language laws has been played out in the Spanish media and in the Spanish courts over the course of the last decade (DiGiacomo 1999). The general tenor of this campaign is captured well by the following banner headline in a national Spanish paper in 1993: 'como Franco pero al revés: Persecución del castellano en Cataluña' (The same as Franco but the other way round: Persecution of Spanish in Catalonia) (quoted in Costa and Wynants 1999). The inference here is abundantly clear – minority language rights constitute 'special treatment' and may well be illiberal. Consequently, much of the subsequent vocal and often vituperative debates on Catalan language laws have focused on the supposed threat they pose to the right to speak the majority language (Castilian) Spanish. In this respect, oppositionalists have termed themselves, without any degree of irony it seems, 'bilingüistas' (see Strubell 1998). I say without any degree of irony because while opponents of Catalan language laws ostensibly couch their arguments on the basis of wanting to ensure some form of institutional bilingualism, they are, more often than not, simply arguing for the right of majority (Spanish) language speakers to remain monolingual.

Thus, when the single model of Catalan immersion education was adopted in 1993, opponents took the Catalonian *Generalitat* to the Spanish Constitutional Court, arguing that the measure contravened the individual language right to speak Spanish, enshrined within the Constitution. Unfortunately for the plaintiffs, the Constitutional Court ruled in December 1994 that the Catalan immersion education model *was* constitutional, given that its stated aim was the acquisition of both Catalan and Spanish, and given that this goal is clearly reached because of the broad presence of Spanish in the wider social milieu (Artigal 1997: 140). This particular decision was broadly congruent with a previous one reached by the same Court in February 1991, concerning the formal requirement of a working knowledge of Catalan within the civil service in Catalonia. Catalan language opponents had also argued before the Court on that occasion that such a requirement discriminated against Spanish speakers on the grounds of language, while limiting the freedom of movement that the Spanish Constitution guarantees all its citizens. However, the Constitutional Court ruled that the command of an official language within a given autonomous region was neither an unreasonable nor disproportionate requirement (Miller and Miller 1996).

These legal setbacks have not stopped opponents of the language laws continuing their campaign on other fronts, most notably in attempting to complicate the language question in Catalonia by recourse to class. Here, the approach has been to argue that the denial of language rights to 'immigrants' within Catalonia (by which is almost always meant, Spanish-speaking in-migrants from other areas of Spain) is a reflection of class as well as linguistic discrimination, since such immigrants are also invariably working class. In contrast, Catalan speakers are strongly represented in the middle classes (Hoffmann 1999). These arguments are almost certainly disingenuous, not least because the majority of in-migrants actually accept and support 'Catalanisation' policies (Keating 1997; Strubell 1998; Costa and Wynants 1999; DiGiacomo 1999). But they have nonetheless proved useful as another potential cause of friction with respect to Catalan language laws (Atkinson 1997, 1998).

If there is a valid point to be made in relation to the language claims of 'immigrants' within Catalonia, it is not one made by opponents of the Catalan laws, nor is it about Spanish. Rather, it is that the promotion of Catalan, while not necessarily problematic in itself, does not as yet extend to the *active* recognition of other minority languages and cultures within Catalonia. In this respect, there have been long-settled communities of Roma in Catalonia (Tarrow 1992; see also Halwachs, this volume) and, more recent migrants from North Africa (Hoffmann 1999), whose languages and cultures have been almost entirely ignored. In other words, like many other European minority language policies, the pressing claims of particular national minorities have meant that wider multicultural claims have been given far less priority (see also Nic Craith, this volume).

This important caveat aside, the clear weight of evidence in debates on Catalan language laws suggests that the arguments of oppositionalists are almost entirely invalid. The formal promotion of Catalan does *not* threaten either the position of Spanish or the rights of Spanish speakers. Unlike Québec's formal proscription of English in commerce and advertising for example, Spanish has never been officially proscribed in Catalonia in any domain (not least because the Spanish Constitution forbids it), nor for that matter has any other language. Indeed, Spanish is specifically enshrined as the *only* official language of the *whole* Spanish state, while Catalan only has co-official rights within the autonomous region of Catalonia. And Spanish still remains the dominant language in the media, as well as in fields such as justice, commerce and taxation within Catalonia. As Yates (1998: 207) sensibly concludes, 'by any objective standards, Catalan is still a subordinate language in a process of "reverse shift," with a long way to go towards normalisation in key areas'. One might also add here the rather obvious point that if Spanish speakers in Spain can regard the formal recognition of their language, within their own historic territory, as an inalienable right (with no question of illiberality), why cannot Catalans as well?

Be that as it may, this often-vituperative campaign against the further institutional normalisation of Catalan highlights graphically that minority language rights will always be controversial, no matter how valid the arguments in their favour or, for that matter, how well-established the minority language policy itself. Indeed, such opposition – most often, although by no means exclusively articulated by majority language speakers – should not surprise us. After all, as Stacy Churchill (1986: 33) has observed, any attempt to modify or deconstruct the organisational principle of cultural and linguistic homogeneity in order to better address 'the needs of linguistic and cultural groups outside the majority group... poses a serious threat to the status quo ... '. More sceptically, John Edwards (1994: 195–6) comments:

> The brutal fact is that most 'big' language speakers in most societies remain unconvinced of either the immediate need or the philosophical desirability of officially-supported cultural and linguistic programmes for their small-language neighbours. Some among the minority also share this doubt and it is, in many instances, a minority within a minority who actively endorse [minority language promotion as a form] of social engineering.

Setting aside the rather obvious point which seems to escape Edwards – namely, that the *exclusion* of minority languages from the public or civic realm is just as much a process of social engineering as its promotion – the issue of majority support remains a crucial one for minority-language policy initiatives. In effect, the long-term success of such initiatives may only be achieved (or be achievable) if at least some degree of favourable majority opinion is secured. On this basis, what is needed is a greater degree of 'tolerability' (Grin 1995) on the part of wider public opinion towards specific minority language policy initiatives. And the issue of tolerability towards minority language policies, problematic at the best of times, is clearly made more difficult when a politics of consensus is replaced by a politics of legislative enforcement – the implementation of the 1998 Catalan Act suggests as much (Yates 1998; Hoffmann 1999, 2000; Myhill 1999). But critics of the latter also presuppose that consensus, left to its own devices, will achieve the same result, albeit much more slowly – a position which in light of the ongoing social and political asymmetries of majority and minority languages in the context of European (and other) nation-states is simply naïve.

Prospects for greater ethnolinguistic democracy in Europe

So how might we proceed in light of these challenges to secure a greater public role for minority languages within Europe, and beyond? One potential avenue would be to point out that in this age of increasing globalisation, and with the burgeoning spread of English as the current world language, the question of retaining cultural and linguistic distinctiveness is increasingly becoming an issue for national majority groups as well as for minorities. This is evidenced in the EU, for example, where its Parliament adopted in December, 1990 the 'principle of complete multilingualism ... consistent with the respect which is owed to the dignity of all languages which reflect and express the cultures of the different peoples who make up the [EU]' (cited in Fishman 1995: 49). The central principle involved here is the recognition of state languages as a symbolic reflection of the people who speak them. What is pertinent for our purposes is that this principle can be applied equally to *intra*state languages as to *inter*state languages (see also O'Reilly, this volume). If the Netherlands can argue that Dutch has a right to be represented as a working language of the EU then, by implication, Frisian has a right to be represented as a working language of the Netherlands. After all, it is clearly a national minority language which is predominantly spoken in the area of Friesland in the Netherlands (Fishman 1995). In this way, the language rights of national majorities and minorities can be usefully allied while, at the same time, highlighting the inconsistencies between current interstate and intrastate language policies (Dorian 1998).

More broadly, we can apply the tenets of international law to the issue of minority language rights. With regard to language, for example, three key tenets can be highlighted. The first principle, which is widely accepted, is that it is not unreasonable to expect from national members some knowledge of the common public language(s) of the state. On this basis, it is possible to argue for the legitimation and institutionalisation of the languages of national minorities within nation-states, thus making available to them at least some of the benefits that national languages currently enjoy. Conversely, it needs to be made clear that the advocacy of minority language rights is not about replacing a majority language with a minority one. Quite the reverse in fact, it is about questioning and contesting why the promotion of a majority (national) language should necessarily be at the expense of all others. By this, the principle of cultural and linguistic homogeneity that has for so long underpinned the language practices of nation-states, and which has clearly resulted in the cultural and linguistic marginalisation (not to mention social and political marginalisation) of minority groups, can be effectively challenged and contested.

A second principle is that in order to avoid language discrimination, it is important that where there is a sufficient number of other language speakers, these speakers should be allowed to use that language as part of the exercise of their individual rights as citizens. That is, they should have the opportunity to use their first language if they so choose. As Fernand de Varennes (1996: 117) argues, 'the respect of the language principles of individuals, *where appropriate and reasonable*, flows from a fundamental right and is not some special concession or privileged treatment. Simply put, it is the right to be treated equally without discrimination, to which everyone is entitled' (my emphasis; see also Henrard, this volume). Again, this principle can clearly be applied to minority language speakers within particular nation-states. Ostensibly, this can also be applied to majority language speakers on the same grounds. However, a crucial caveat needs to be added here. The formal promotion of a minority language does not preclude the ongoing use of the majority language, given that it is most often dominant anyway in all key language domains. Thus, what is being promoted is not a new monolingualism in the minority language – indeed, this is usually neither politically nor practically sustainable – but the possibility of bilingualism or multilingualism. As such, the claims of language discrimination by majority language speakers, as in the Catalan case, are both misplaced and inapplicable. The majority language is not generally being precluded from the public realm, nor proscribed at the individual level, nor are majority language speakers actually penalised for speaking their language.[3] Rather, monolingual majority language speakers are being asked to *accommodate* to the ongoing presence of a minority language and to recognise its status as an additional language of the state – a process that I have described elsewhere as 'mutual accommodation' (May 2001).

The third principle arises directly from the previous one – how to determine exactly what is 'appropriate and reasonable' with regard to individual language preferences. Following the prominent political theorist, Will Kymlicka (1995), it can be argued that only national minorities can demand *as of right* formal inclusion of their languages and cultures in the civic realm. However, this need not and should not preclude other ethnic minorities from being allowed at the very least to cultivate and pursue unhindered their own historic cultural and linguistic practices in the private domain. In relation to language, this has been articulated by Kloss (1977) as the distinction between tolerance-oriented and promotion-oriented rights. Tolerance-oriented language rights ensure the right to preserve one's language in the private, non-governmental sphere of national life. These rights may be narrowly or broadly defined. They include the right of individuals to use their first language at home and in public, freedom of assembly and organisation, the right to establish private cultural, economic and social institutions wherein the first language may be used, and the right to foster one's first language in private schools. The key principle of such rights is that the state does 'not interfere with efforts on the parts of the minority to make use of [their language] in the private domain' (Kloss 1977: 2).

Promotion-oriented rights regulate the extent to which minority rights are recognised within the *public* domain, or civic realm of the nation-state. As such, they involve 'public authorities [in] trying to promote a minority [language] by having it used in public institutions – legislative, administrative and educational, including the public schools' (Kloss 1977: 2). Again, such rights may be narrowly or widely applied. At their narrowest, promotion-oriented rights might simply involve the publishing of public documents in minority languages. At their broadest, promotion-oriented rights could involve recognition of a minority language in all formal domains within the nation-state, thus allowing the minority language group 'to care for its internal affairs through its own public organs, which amounts to the [state] allowing self government for the minority group' (Kloss 1977: 24).[4]

What tolerance- and promotion-oriented rights usefully highlight is that a more active promotion of minority language rights can still distinguish effectively between the linguistic entitlements of different minority groups, thus avoiding the problem of 'equivalence', a charge often levelled by critics of minority language rights.[5] In short, greater ethnolinguistic democracy is not necessarily the same as ethnolinguistic equality for all linguistic minority groups. Similarly, a call for greater ethnolinguistic democracy clearly does not amount to asserting linguistic equivalence, in all domains, with dominant, majority languages. Majority languages will continue to dominate in most if not all language domains, since, as I have already made clear, that is the nature of their privileged sociohistorical, sociopolitical position(ing).

Conclusion

It is clear that nation-states remain the bedrock of the international interstate system and look likely, despite many predictions to the contrary, to be around still for some time to come. Like Mark Twain's famous retort to the premature media report of his death, the imminent demise of nation-states is obviously greatly exaggerated. But if this is the case, it certainly does not necessarily follow that the traditional organisation of nation-states should remain unchanged. Indeed, the forces of economic and political globalisation, and the concomitant rise of multinational companies and supranational organisations, have already had a considerable effect in renegotiating the parameters of the economic and political sovereignty of nation-states. This is all well and good. But my argument is that, if we accept this process of change for the nation-state from above so to speak, there is no reason why we should not accept pressure for change from below as well. In this latter respect, the principle of cultural and linguistic homogeneity – itself the specific product of the political nationalism of the last three centuries – has been brought increasingly into question by national and ethnic minorities within European (and non-European) nation-states. What such minorities are asking is simple and direct – why should the notion of a homogeneous national identity, represented by the language and culture of the dominant group, invariably replace cultural and linguistic identities that differ from it? This 'intolerance of difference' (Billig 1995: 130) embedded within the structural organisation of nation-states has resulted in the historical subjugation and, at times, evisceration of the traditional languages and cultures of minority groups. For centuries this process has been 'validated' on the basis that it is necessary for establishing social and political cohesion within the nation-state. But it is a cost that many minority groups are simply no longer prepared to pay.

The challenge, therefore, is to rethink nation-states in more plural and inclusive ways. A key means by which this can be achieved, as I have argued here, is to legitimate and institutionalise national minority languages within the civic realm of nation-states, supported, where possible, by comparable developments at the supranational level, and via the principles of international law. Thus the extension of ethnolinguistic democracy already evident within the EU at the interstate level can be usefully allied to intrastate policies, while at the same time highlighting the discrepancies between the two. Such a process allows for the prospect of more representational multinational and multilingual states in this new century by directly contesting the historical inequalities that have seen minority languages, and their speakers, relegated to the social and political margins. As James Tollefson (1991: 202) concludes,

> the struggle to adopt minority languages within dominant institutions such as education, the law, and government, as well as the struggle over language rights, constitute efforts to legitimise the minority group itself and to alter its relationship to the state. Thus while language planning reflects relationships of power, it can also be used to transform them.

Changing the language preferences of the state and civil society, or at least broadening them, would better reflect the cultural and linguistic demographics of most of today's multinational and multilingual states. Not only this, it could also significantly improve the life chances of those minority language individuals and groups who are presently disadvantaged in their access to, and participation in public services, employment and education, since linguistic consequences cannot be separated from socioeconomic and sociopolitical consequences, and vice versa. Likewise, changing 'the rules of the game' that automatically presume an exclusive relationship between dominant languages and modernity should make the process of maintaining minority languages a little easier.

Even so, it should be clear that achieving a greater recognition and acceptance of minority languages, and their speakers, remains a formidable task. The challenge for European language policies, and their academic analysis, is to dispense with the largely ahistorical, apolitical and synchronic approach that has predominated until now in order to engage critically with the wider social and political conditions – and, crucially, their historical antecedents – that have shaped such policies in the first place. As Jan Blommaert (1999) argues, a synchronic analysis takes no account of human agency, political intervention, power and authority in the formation of particular (national) language ideologies. Nor, by definition, is it able to identify the establishment and maintenance of majority languages as a specific 'form of practice, historically contingent and socially embedded' (Blommaert 1999: 7).

Only when a socio-historical, socio-political and diachronic approach to minority language policy is adopted can we come to a critical understanding of how particular (European) language ideologies have been created in the first place and subsequently legitimated politically (Blommaert 1999). Likewise, only via such an approach can we effectively challenge and contest the idea of cultural and linguistic homogeneity, which has so monopolised the social and political organisation of modern nation-states. Finally, majority language speakers will themselves only 'tolerate' such developments when they are made to realise that the principle of linguistic homogeneity is neither inevitable, nor inviolate, but rather the specific and largely contrived product of the (European) nationalism of the last few centuries.

Notes

1. This chapter is a revised and expanded version of May (2002).
2. Following accepted distinctions within both political theory and international law, national minorities may be regarded as groups which are historically associated with a particular territory (i.e. they have not migrated to the territory from elsewhere) but because of conquest, confederation, or

colonisation are now regarded as minorities within that territory (see Kymlicka 1995; May 2001).

3. The examples where this has occurred as the result of a minority language policy remain extremely rare. The post-Soviet language policies of Latvia and Estonia, however, may be said to fall into this category. This is because the significant majority of Russian-speaking population in these areas have been denied citizenship rights since independence unless they can demonstrate a conversational ability in Latvian or Estonian (see de Varennes 1996; see also Hogan-Brun, this volume).

4. Kloss's distinction between tolerance- and promotion-oriented language rights is also broadly comparable to one drawn by Churchill (1986), in his typology of minority language policy approaches within the OECD, between the maintenance of languages for private use versus the widespread institutional recognition of languages (for an extended discussion, see May 2001: Ch. 5).

5. The equivalence argument, which is usually dressed up in the guise of practicality, invariably goes something like this. If we recognise minority language rights for one linguistic minority, then we would surely have to recognise all other such groups as well. A variation on this theme is that if we recognise a certain level of linguistic entitlement for one minority language group, we must surely provide the same level of entitlement for all others. These arguments are, more often than not of course, simply employed as an all-too-convenient excuse for ongoing state inaction with respect to implementing minority language rights. However, I should reiterate that, in distinguishing between the rights of national and ethnic minorities here, I am still arguing that the latter can and should be accorded far greater linguistic protection than many such groups currently enjoy – that is, active linguistic protection by the state for the unhindered maintenance of their first languages, at the very least in the private domain and, 'where numbers warrant', a principle again drawn from international law, in the public domain as well. In other words, arguing that only national minorities can claim minority language rights, as of right, is not an argument for simply ignoring the claims of other ethnic groups (see May 2001, 2002 for an extended discussion).

References

Anderson, B., 1991, *Imagined Communities: Reflections on the Origin and Spread of Nationalism.* London: Verso.

Artigal, J., 1997, 'The Catalan Immersion Program', in R. Johnson and M. Swain (eds) *Immersion Education: International Perspectives*, Cambridge: Cambridge University Press, 133–50.

Atkinson, D., 1997, 'Attitudes towards Language Use in Catalonia: Politics or Sociolinguistics?' *International Journal of Iberian Studies* 10: 5–14.

Atkinson, D., 1998, 'Normalisation: Integration or Assimilation? A Response to Miquel Strubell', *Current Issues in Language and Society* 5(3): 210–14.

Bauman, Z., 1993, *Postmodern Ethics*. London: Routledge.

Billig, M., 1995, *Banal Nationalism*. London: Sage.

Blommaert, J., 1999, 'The Debate is Open', in J. Blommaert (ed.) *Language Ideological Debates*, Berlin: Mouton de Gruyter, 1–38.

Bullman, U. (ed.), 1994, *Die Politik der dritten Ebene. Regionen im Europa der Union*. Baden-Baden, Germany: Nomos.

Churchill, S., 1986, *The Education of Linguistic and Cultural Minorities in the OECD Countries*. Clevedon, England: Multilingual Matters.

Costa, J. and Wynants, S., 1999, 'Catalan Linguistic Policy Act: External Protection or Internal Restriction?' Paper presented to the *Nationalism, Identity and Minority Rights Conference*. University of Bristol, September 1999.

Coulmas, F., 1998, 'Language Rights: Interests of States, Language Groups and the Individual', *Language Sciences* 20: 63–72.

de Varennes, F., 1996, *Language, Minorities and Human Rights*. The Hague: Kluwer Law International.

DiGiacomo, S., 1999, 'Language Ideological Debates in an Olympic City: Barcelona 1992–1996' in J. Blommaert (ed.) *Language Ideological Debates*, Berlin: Mouton de Gruyter, 105–42.

Dorian, N., 1998, 'Western Language Ideologies and Small-language Prospects', in L. Grenoble and L. Whaley (eds) *Endangered Languages: Language Loss and Community Response*, Cambridge: Cambridge University Press, 3–21.

Edwards, J., 1994, *Multilingualism*. London: Routledge.

Esteve, J., 1992, 'Multicultural Education in Spain: The Autonomous Communities Face the Challenge of European Unity', *Education Review* 44: 255–72.

Fishman, J., 1995, 'On the Limits of Ethnolinguistic Democracy', in T. Skutnabb-Kangas and R. Phillipson (eds) *Linguistic Human Rights: Overcoming Linguistic Discrimination*, Berlin: Mouton de Gruyter, 49–61.

Gellner, E., 1983, *Nations and Nationalism: New Perspectives on the Past*. Oxford: Basil Blackwell.

Grillo, R., 1989, *Dominant Languages: Language and Hierarchy in Britain and France*. Cambridge: Cambridge University Press.

Grin, F., 1995, 'Combining Immigrant and Autochthonous Language Rights: A Territorial Approach to Multilingualism', in T. Skutnabb-Kangas, and R. Phillipson (eds) *Linguistic Human Rights: Overcoming Linguistic Discrimination*, Berlin: Mouton de Gruyter, 31–48.

Hall, S., Held, D. and McGrew, T. (eds) 1992, *Modernity and its Futures*. Cambridge: Polity Press.

Held, D., 1995, *Democracy and the Global Order: From the Modern State to Cosmopolitan Governance*. Cambridge: Polity Press.

Hinsley, F., 1986, *Sovereignty*. Cambridge: Cambridge University Press.

Hoffmann, C., 1999, 'Language Autonomy and National Identity in Catalonia', in D. Smith and S. Wright (eds) *Whose Europe? The Turn towards Democracy*, Oxford: Blackwell/Sociological Review, 82–8.

Hoffmann, C., 2000, 'Balancing Language Planning and Language Rights: Catalonia's Uneasy Juggling Act', *Journal of Multilingual and Multicultural Development* 21(5): 425–41.

Jones, B. and Keating, M. (eds) 1995, *The European Union and the Regions.* Oxford: Clarendon Press.

Keating, M., 1996, *Nations against the State: The New Politics of Nationalism in Québec, Catalonia and Scotland.* London: Macmillan Press.

Keating, 1997, 'Stateless Nation-building: Québec, Catalonia and Scotland in the Changing State System', *Nations and Nationalism* 3: 689–717.

Keating, M. and Hooghe, L., 1996, 'Bypassing the Nation-state? Regions and the EU Policy Process', in J. Richardson (ed.) *European Union: Power and Policy,* London: Routledge, 216–29.

Kloss, H., 1997, *The American Bilingual Tradition.* Rowley, MA: Newbury House.

Kymlicka, W., 1995, *Multicultural Citizenship: A Liberal Theory of Minority Rights.* Oxford: Clarendon Press.

Labrie, N., 1993, *La Construction de la Communauté Européenne.* Paris: Honoré Champion.

May, S., 1999, 'Extending Ethnolinguistic Democracy in Europe: The Case of Wales', in D. Smith, and S. Wright (eds) *Whose Europe? The Turn towards Democracy,* Oxford: Blackwell/Sociological Review, 142–67.

May, S., 2000, 'Accommodating and Resisting Minority Language Policy: The Case of Wales', *International Journal of Bilingual Education and Bilingualism* 3(2): 101–28.

May, S., 2001, *Language and Minority Rights: Ethnicity, Nationalism and the Politics of Language.* London and New York: Longman.

May, S., 2002, 'Developing Greater Ethnolinguistic Democracy in Europe: Minority Language Policies, Nation-states, and the Question of Tolerability.' *Sociolinguistica* 16: 1–13.

McCrone, D., 1992, *Understanding Scotland: The Sociology of a Stateless Nation.* London: Routledge.

Miller, H. and Miller, K., 1996, 'Language Policy and Identity: The Case of Catalonia', *International Studies in Sociology of Education* 6: 113–28.

Milward, A., 1992, *The European Rescue of the Nation-State.* London: Routledge.

Myhill, J., 1999, 'Identity, Territoriality, and Minority Language Survival', *Journal of Multilingual and Multicultural Development* 20: 34–50.

Nelde, P., Strubell, M. and Williams, G., 1996, *Euromosaic: The Production and Reproduction of the Minority Language Groups in the European Union.* Luxembourg: Office for Official Publications of the European Communities.

Petschen, S., 1993, *La Europa de las Regiones.* Barcelona, Catalonia: Generalitat de Catalunya.

Phillipson, R., 1998, 'Globalizing English: Are Linguistic Human Rights an Alternative to Linguistic Imperialism?', *Language Sciences* 20: 101–12.

Phillipson, R., 2003, *English-only Europe? Challenging Language Policy.* London: Routledge.

Robertson, R., 1992, *Globalization: Social Theory and Global Culture.* London: Sage.

Shore, C. and Black, A., 1994, 'Citizen's Europe and the Construction of European Identity', in V. Goddard, J. Llobera, and C. Shore (eds) *The Anthropology of Europe,* Oxford: Berg, 275–98.

Skutnabb-Kangas, T., 2000, *Linguistic Genocide in Education – or Worldwide Diversity and Human Rights?* Mahwah, NJ.: Lawrence Erlbaum.

Smith, A., 1998, *Nationalism and Modernism*. London: Routledge.

Soysal, Y., 1994, *Limits of Citizenship: Migrants and Post-national Membership in Europe*. Chicago, IL.: University of Chicago Press.

Strubell, M., 1998, 'Language, Democracy and Devolution in Catalonia', *Current Issues in Language and Society* 5: 146–80.

Tarrow, N., 1992, 'Language, Interculturalism and Human Rights: Three European Cases', *Prospects* 22: 489–509.

Taylor, B. and Thompson, K. (eds) 1999, *Scotland and Wales: Nations Again?* Cardiff: University of Wales Press.

Tollefson, J., 1991, *Planning Language, Planning Inequality: Language Policy in the Community*. London: Longman.

Woolard, K., 1989, *Double Talk: Bilingualism and the Politics of Ethnicity in Catalonia*. Stanford, CA: Stanford University Press.

Index